Life, Language, and Literature

Linda Robinson Fellag
University of Houston-Downtown
English Language Institute

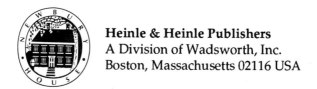

Heinle & Heinle Publishers
A Division of Wadsworth, Inc.
Boston, Massachusetts 02116 USA

Publisher: Stanley J. Galek
Editorial Director: David C. Lee
Assistant Editor: Ken Mattsson
Editorial Production Manager: Elizabeth Holthaus
Production Editor: Kristin M. Thalheimer
Project Manager: Margaret Cleveland
Photo Coordinator: Martha Leibs-Heckly
Photo Research: Susan Doheny
Manufacturing Coordinator: Jerry Christopher
Interior Design: Nancy Lindgren
Cover Illustration: Annie Gusman
Cover Design: Bortman Design Group/Lisa Sheehan
Manufactured in the United States of America

Library of Congress Cataloging-in-Publication Data
Fellag, Linda Robinson
    Life, language, and literature/Linda Robinson Fellag.
      p.   cm.
    ISBN 0-8384-3965-9
    1. English language—Textbooks for foreign speakers.
    2. Literature—Collections.
    3. Readers—1950-
  I. Title.
PE1128.F424 1993
428.2'4—dc20   92-31731
                                        CIP

Contents

Acknowledgments

The author wishes to express her gratitude to Laura Le Dréan and Marsha Abramovich lecturers at the University of Houston-Downtown, for comments and suggestions about this text. In addition, the late Sunda Holmes, former director of the English Language Institute, University of Houston-Downtown, provided continual encouragement, and ESL editorial director David C. Lee of Heinle & Heinle Publishers, unflagging cheer and sensibility. Finally, to Fodil, Nadia, and Nora Fellag, I am grateful for your patience and understanding.

CREDITS

"The Corduroy Pants" by Erskine Caldwell, published in *Scribner's Magazine* of May 1931, published by Charles Scribner's Sons. Copyright 1931 by Erskine Caldwell. Copyright © renewed 1958 by Erskine Caldwell. Reprinted by permission of McIntosh and Otis, Inc.

"The Standard of Living," Copyright © 1941 by Dorothy Parker, renewed © 1969 by Lillian Hellman, from *The Portable Dorothy Parker* by Dorothy Parker, Introduction by Brendan Gill. Used by permission of Viking Penguin, a division of Penguin Books USA Inc.

"Butch Minds the Baby" by Damon Runyon. Copyright renewed 1957 by Mary Runyon McCann and Damon Runyon, Jr. as children of the author. Copyright © 1992 Sheldon Abend. By special arrangement with Sheldon Abend, President, American Play Company, Inc., 19 West 44th Street, Suite 1204, New York, New York 10036.

"Of Missing Persons" by Jack Finney. Published in *Good Housekeeping* published by Hearst Publishing, 1955. Copyright © 1955, renewed 1983 by Jack Finney. Reprinted by permission of Don Congdon Associates, Inc.

"Dream Deferred" from *The Panther and the Lash* by Langston Hughes. Copyright © 1951 by Langston Hughes. Reprinted by permission of Alfred A. Knopf, Inc.

"The Rule of Names" by Ursula K. LeGuin. Copyright © 1964 by Ursula K. LeGuin; first appeared in *Fantastic*; reprinted by permission of the author and the author's agent, Virginia Kidd.

"The Magic Barrel" from *The Magic Barrel* by Bernard Malamud. Copyright © 1954, 1982 by Bernard Malamud. Reprinted by permission of Farrar, Straus and Giroux, Inc.

"I Stand Here Ironing," from *Tell Me a Riddle* by Tillie Olsen. Copyright © 1956, 1957, 1960, 1961 by Tillie Olsen. Used by permission of Delacorte Press/Seymour Lawrence, a division of Bantam Doubleday Dell Publishing Group, Inc.

"Snow" by Ann Beattie from *Where You'll Find Me*. Copyright © 1986 by Ivory & Pity, Inc. Reprinted by permission of Simon & Schuster, Inc.

PHOTO CREDITS

p. 2, Alaska Pictorial Service; p. 24, The Image Works; p. 52, UPI/Bettmann; p. 66, Susan Lapides; p. 82, Archive Photos; p. 110, UPI/Bettmann; p. 124, Robert Brenner/Photo Edit; p. 164, North Wind Picture Archives; p. 184, Culver Pictures, Inc.; p. 196, Culver Pictures, Inc.; p. 230, Tim Barnwell/Stock Boston; p. 242, David Conklin/Photo Edit.

To the Teacher

Life, Language, and Literature is an advanced level, integrated skills reading text for English as a Second Language learners. The title reflects three foci: life (the enrichment of critical analytical skills and cultural knowledge, and the relation of texts to student experience); language (the exploitation of texts for reading skills, vocabulary, writing, speaking and structure fluency) and literature (the development of an understanding of and familiarity with literary texts and concepts).

This text is especially suitable for preacademic students who will encounter requisite literature/literary analysis courses in a university. The texts are also valid for any advanced English learner engaged in language and cultural study.

The 16 texts (12 stories and 4 poems) were selected for their high artistic quality, linguistic accessibility, interest level, and representativeness of diverse settings within the United States. The texts are subjectively graded here on the basis of linguistic difficulty (vocabulary level, syntactic complexity and level of abstraction), with *E* denoting "Easy," *M* "Moderate" and *D* "Difficult": "The White Silence"-M, "The Luck of Roaring Camp"-D, "The Corduroy Pants"-E, "The Standard of Living"-E, "Butch Minds the Baby"-E, "The Cop and the Anthem"-D, "Of Missing Persons"-M, "Acquainted with the Night"-E, "Harlem"-M, "The Rules of Names"-M, "The Story of an Hour"-M, "The Magic Barrel"-D, "A Dream within a Dream"-E, "Snow"-M, "I Stand Here Ironing"-D, and "The Letter"-D.

TEXT ORDER AND TEXT GLOSSARY

The linguistic difficulty of texts varies throughout the book; essentially, as the unit openers explain, stories are ordered in terms of their organizational accessibility to students. Stories with clear narrative plots are presented in Units 1 and 2, and texts with more difficult plots and abstract themes appear in Units 3–5. Text length is purposely varied throughout the book. Each text is glossed for text-specific vocabulary and university-level vocabulary items which advanced students on whom these materials were tested over two years found problematic. While controversy exists regarding the merits of text glossing in general, the author feels that without some glossing the readings would be less accessible, and to adapt literary texts would be to destroy their unique artistic form.

INTRODUCTION

At the beginning of this course, the instructor should spend at least one class period discussing the subject of literature, since for some students, this may be a new subject. Such a starting point is offered in the form of a discussion-reading in the Introduction.

Also, students should be encouraged from the onset to read each text for main ideas, rather than individual vocabulary items. The author recommends that instructors urge students to read each literary text twice: once without a dictionary to get the main ideas, and again, in closer detail, with a dictionary.

TEXT INTERPRETATION

It is also worthwhile to note that students should be allowed to contribute their own interpretations and views of texts. Rather than prescribe one set interpretation of a story, students can be led to become confident proponents of their text analyses skill. It must be stressed that the student must prove his or her inter-pretations by drawing support from the text. This experience will enable readers to independently analyze university-level texts in any field.

TEXT-RELATED ACTIVITIES

Tasks, in general, are designed to integrate skills and encour-age communication. Hopefully, instructors will find that texts are supported by a sufficient number of exercises to allow instruc-tors to select according to their class foci.

Exercises that accompany texts vary according to the demands of the text, and include:

PREREADING EXERCISES

Each fiction work is prefaced by a short introductory quota-tion. On the same page, artwork relating to the story is pre-sented. The author recommends that students be asked to personally reflect on these two items before reading a story, or discuss them briefly in class as part of prereading work.

At First Glance and The Writer's Perspective exercises provide background on topics, themes, historical settings, cultural situations, writing genre, and author background, which students

will find in readings. In texts with more challenging vocabulary, Prereading Vocabulary study introduces key vocabulary items.

Postreading exercises vary according to the demands of each text and include:

Understanding the Text

Activities include text analysis, retelling the story, finding main ideas and details, drawing inferences, scanning, and determining plot.

Looking at Language

Language exercises examine grammatical and rhetorical patterns in the texts, and expand vocabulary by theme, in context, through word-generating tasks and other means.

Literary Concepts

Literary elements such as plot, narrator, setting, theme, characterization, tone, symbolism, and figurative language are presented and practiced through student-oriented tasks. Concepts are also reinforced in unit projects.

Culture Points

Cultural values and behavior that figure importantly in a text are examined in cross-cultural group discussions.

Reading Journal

Students are encouraged to respond to literary texts through regular journal entries as preparation for the writing assignments, which will be assigned in unit projects. It is suggested that instructors respond to reading journal entries in a nonjudgmental way, as in journal writing in writing classes.

PROJECTS

At the end of each unit, two projects are offered to further develop language and literary analysis skills as well as engage interest. These assignments spiral from unit to unit; for example, a written plot summary in Unit One introduces summary skills that are required in written character and theme analyses in Units Two and Five. In addition, oral character analysis in Unit Two leads to written character analysis in Unit Three.

VIDEO/AUDIO

These components are included in chapters whenever possible as an optional source of language study and theme exploration. Public and university libraries, in addition to local video stores and off-air television recording, will supply many film versions of the literary works in this book, as well as films with related themes. Biographical videos of all the writers included in this book are also available through the above sources. In addition, instructors may want to explore libraries and video stores for audiotapings of the stories. The author has developed integrated-skills "chunking" activities to accompany small segments of videos that relate to literary works; to a lesser degree, larger "chunks" or entire film versions of literary works or related stories have been shown to a class (along with accompanying language tasks) to add another dimension to the course.

To the Student

Welcome to the world of literature!

Some of you may come to this book having previously enjoyed the literature of your culture. Others may have no experience in reading literature. If you fall into either of these groups, the reading of literature in English will offer many benefits to you.

By reading literature in English, you will learn about the lives of Americans at different periods in history and in different parts of this vast, multicultural society, and be able to compare this culture to your own. You will also explore rich samples of writing to expand your vocabulary and reinforce your grammatical and rhetorical knowledge of English. And, of course, you will learn to understand the writings of some of the most esteemed literary artists of the United States.

This book is designed to make reading literature in English as accessible to you as possible. You will discuss the main subject of each story, the writer, and other background information before you read. Vocabulary will also be studied before you read some stories. In addition, you will find glossaries within each text to help you with difficult words as you read. However, you should not let the difficult vocabulary hinder you from reading. Try to grasp the main ideas of the text; the vocabulary will be studied in depth after you read. In addition, after you read, you will find tasks that help you comprehend main ideas, find details, and understand underlying ideas. Furthermore, you will explore the cultural meanings of the texts, and be able to respond to what you read in a reading journal.

A major focus of this book—and the real reason that this book is here—is that literature and literary analysis are required courses in nearly all American universities. Many students struggle with how to read and write about literature in these classes, so this book will help you understand literary concepts and guide you through reading and writing assignments. In these ways, you will be much better prepared to handle the work in required literature classes. If you use this book in an academic literature class, it will supply you with suggested plans for organizing essays about literature as well as language help in understanding the texts.

Hopefully, once you enter the worlds of the literary characters who have been gathered here for your benefit, you will also reap enjoyment from the stories and poems. You may find stories that remind you of your own experiences, or teach you life lessons that will assist you in the future.

To all of you, good reading!

Introduction: What Is Literature?

Since this textbook is entitled *Life, Language, and Literature*, you can expect to be exploring aspects of American life, as well as literature. By reading and discussing literature, you can improve your language skills as well as your knowledge of this culture in which you live. If you intend to pursue a college education in the United States, then this course will also prepare you for tasks that lie ahead of you. By the time you finish this class, you will have read and analyzed challenging texts, given and supported your interpretations to texts, and written about literature.

But before we begin, consider some essential questions.

1. What is literature? Is a newspaper literature? Is a magazine literature? Can any type of writing be called literature?

    Before you open a dictionary to define this term, let your own experience guide you. To understand literature, begin by thinking about writers.

2. Do you think that great writers write to kill time? Do they write to make money? Is their goal to gain fame? Or, do you think that they write because they have nothing better to do?

3. Is writing important to a serious writer? Is there something inside that pushes him or her to write? What is it?

4. In fact, what is a writer? Is a person who writes instructions for operating a machine a writer? Is someone who writes a guide for gardening a writer?

At this point, perhaps you have more questions than answers. So pause a moment and return to the notion of literature. Some of you may have defined literature as "writing that lasts a long time." Others may consider literature "good writing" that a large number of people have judged to be "good."

That is a beginning of a definition of literature. But you must look deeper than that, deeper even than the meaning a dictionary might give you to understand what makes writing literature, and how literature can aid you in understanding about American life—or life itself.

For if you are to use American literature in this class to tell you about American culture and life, then you must be certain you are using authentic literature that gives you an honest portrayal of this culture at different historic times and in different regions, and presents a true picture of life experiences, from the eye of the writer.

You must look inward to the writer. The writer is an artist, like other kinds of artists. Think of what qualities or values artists have in common. Of course, they produce art. And through their art, they create beauty.

But great artists such as great writers do not create functional beauty such as a gardening guide or machinery instructions. Instead, the beauty they produce is artistic, or aesthetic. It appeals to your senses and our emotions.

To understand the difference between functional and aesthetic beauty, consider these examples. Close your eyes and imagine you see two draught horses hitched to a wagon. The horses are broad and look heavy. Their stomachs bulge, and their legs and thighs are thick and hairy. When you envision these breeds of horses, you might think of their function as work animals. They may be beautiful, but you may not focus on their aesthetic or artistic beauty. You might think of their strength, their functional beauty.

On the other hand, picture in your mind an intricate oil painting of an old metal garbage can with cats climbing on its side, in search of food. Now, a garbage can is not, in itself, beautiful, but it can be represented as beautiful by the artist. He or she can transform something ugly into something of aesthetic beauty.

So it is with great writers. Each writer you will study in this course gives you his or her unique world view, his or her own perspective of life, and the times in which he or she lives. Each writer has made certain judgments about the world that you can detect, even if the writer purports to be simply describing what is taking place at the time. And so you will use American literature, exploring the judgments of these American writers, to gain insights into this culture, into your own lives, and into the human experience.

Finally, to return to the meaning of literature, you can open various dictionaries and find the word defined in similar terms: excellent writing or higher forms of writing. This course is aimed at presenting excellence in American writing by sharing the views of writers compelled to voice their judgments about the world. Here are writers who will show you America from their unique, heartfelt perspectives.

DISCUSSION:

After you have read the Introduction and discussed it in class, answer these questions in your group.

1. Think of a writer from your country who appeals to you. Why do you like him or her? What subjects do his or her stories deal with? Are his or her stories relevant to life in your country today? Share your ideas with your group.

2. What do you expect to gain from reading American literature?

3. What American writers have you heard of? Have you read any American literature? If so, think of one story you know and explain to your group what that story tells you about American life.

UNIT ONE

Frontiers

Unit One presents two short stories about American frontiers. These tales of adventure are narrated clearly by writers who lived the experiences themselves. With the benefit of strong story lines, or plots, the reader will be able to follow the tales easily, even when the vocabulary is challenging. Both stories focus on action, rather than characters or abstract themes. "The White Silence" will evoke images of the natural perils of life in the Arctic, while "The Luck of Roaring Camp" will bring to life the gold rush of the "wild West."

"Nature has many tricks wherewith she convinces man of his finity . . . but the most tremendous, the most stupefying of all, is the passive phase of the White Silence. All movement ceases, the sky clears, the heavens are as brass; the slightest whisper seems sacrilege, and man becomes timid, affrighted at the sound of his own voice."

CHAPTER ONE

The White Silence

by Jack London

About the Author

Jack London (1876–1916), more than any other American writer, wrote of life on the frontiers of the American West: the Yukon territory of northwest Canada, Alaska, California, and Utah. In 17 years, London wrote nearly 200 short stories and 22 novels, including *The Call of the Wild* and *White Fang*. Heroic figures and heroic deeds were represented in London's tales. Many of his Yukon stories also dealt with the clash of Native American and white cultures, as in "The White Silence."

❋Reading Short Stories

The short story is a brief work of fiction generally centered around a single incident. Because it is unified in action and theme, it is an ideal introduction to the study of literature and language. In this textbook, you will begin first with stories that focus on action, and later read stories that emphasize theme, or main idea, and characters. The two stories in Unit One are appropropriate opening stories not only because they are action-driven, but also because they were written in the 1800s, shortly after the short story form was recognized in the United States.

As you begin the first story, follow the reading pattern that was suggested in the preface: First, answer the prereading questions to familiarize yourself with the subject, author, historical period, vocabulary, and other background information. Read each story straight through without a dictionary the first time. (The stories in this textbook vary in length but should be read at one or two sittings each.) Then, answer the assigned Understanding the Text questions. Next, read the story again, this time consulting a dictionary, and complete the postreading activities on text comprehension, language, literary concepts, and cultural topics.

❋At First Glance

1. Each story in this book will be preceded by a quotation from the story and a related photograph to introduce the story. Read the quotation preceding "The White Silence" and examine the photograph above it. What do they suggest about the story?

2. Read the title of the story. What do you think "The White Silence" will be about?

3. Look at the following words and phrases which London uses to describe this story set in northern Canada:

cruel   miserable
motionless void   primeval
stillness   treacherous
the sudden danger, the quick death   pitiless
frost-encrusted forest   clear and cold
sixty-five degrees below zero

Discuss the words with a partner. Check unfamiliar items in a dictionary. What do they suggest about the story?

4. Have you ever traveled or lived in sub-zero temperatures? If so, what was it like? If not, how do you imagine it would be?

The Writer's Perspective

1. Jack London's personal experiences provided the material for his adventurous stories. What kind of man do you suppose London was to seek out danger as he did?

2. London's stories usually described man's struggle with his environment, often, man being defeated by his environment. How do you feel about stories that depict how man fights nature and often loses?

The White Silence

by Jack London

1   "Carmen won't last more than a couple of days." Mason spat out a chunk of ice and surveyed the poor animal ruefully,[1] then put her foot in his mouth and proceeded to bite out the ice which clustered cruelly between the toes.

2   "I never saw a dog with a highfalutin'[2] name that ever was worth a rap," he said, as he concluded his task and shoved her aside. "They just fade away and die under the responsibility. Did ye ever see one go wrong with a sensible name like Cassiar, Siwash, or Husky? No, sir! Take a look at Shookum here, he's—"

3   Snap! The lean brute flashed up, the white teeth just missing Mason's throat.

4   "Ye will, will ye?" A shrewd clout[3] behind the ear with the butt of the dogwhip stretched the animal in the snow, quivering softly, a yellow slaver[4] dripping from its fangs.[5]

5   "As I was saying, just look at Shookum, here—he's got the spirit. Bet ye he eats Carmen before the week's out."

6   "I'll bank another proposition against that," replied Malemute Kid, reversing the frozen bread placed before the fire to thaw. "We'll eat Shookum before the trip is over. What d' ye say, Ruth?"

7   The Indian woman settled the coffee with a piece of ice, glanced from Malemute Kid to her husband, then at the dogs, but vouchsafed no reply. It was such a palpable[6] truism that none was necessary. Two hundred miles of unbroken trail in prospect, with a scant six days' grub for themselves and none for the dogs, could admit no other alternative. The two men and the woman grouped about the fire and began their meager[7] meal. The dogs lay in their harnesses, for it was midday halt, and watched each mouthful enviously.

8   "No more lunches after today," said Malemute Kid. "And we've got to keep a close eye on the dogs—they're getting vicious. They'd just as soon pull a fellow down as not, if they get a chance."

---

1. *sorrowfully,* 2. *pretending to be high-class,* 3. *blow,* 4. *saliva,* 5. *teeth,*
6. *believable,* 7. *small*

9   "And I was president of an Epworth[8] once, and taught in the Sunday school." Having irrelevantly delivered himself of this, Mason fell into a dreamy contemplation of his steaming moccasins, but was aroused by Ruth filling his cup. "Thank God, we've got slathers of tea! I've seen it growing, down in Tennessee. What wouldn't I give for a hot corn pone[9] just now. Never mind, Ruth; you won't starve much longer, nor wear moccasins[10] either."

10   The woman threw off her gloom at this, and in her eyes welled up a great love for her white lord—the first white man she had ever seen—the first man whom she had known to treat a woman as something better than a mere animal or beast of burden.

11   "Yes, Ruth," continued her husband, having recourse[11] to the macaronic jargon[12] in which it was alone possible for them to understand each other; "wait till we clean up and pull for the Outside. We'll take the White Man's canoe and go to the Salt Water. Yes, bad water, rough water—great mountains dance up and down all the time. And so big, so far, so far away—you travel ten sleep, twenty sleep, forty sleep" (he graphically enumerated the days on his fingers), "all the time water, bad water. Then you come to great village, plenty people, just the same mosquitoes next summer. Wigwams oh, so high—ten, twenty pines. Hi-yu skookum!"

12   He paused impotently,[13] cast an appealing glance at Malemute Kid, then laboriously placed the twenty pines, end on end, by sign language. Malemute Kid smiled with cheery cynicism, but Ruth's eyes were wide with wonder, and with pleasure; for she half believed he was joking, and such condescension pleased her poor woman's heart.

13   "And then you step into a—a box, and pouf! up you go." He tossed his empty cup in the air by way of illustration, and as he deftly caught it, cried: "And biff! down you come. Oh, great medicine-men! You go Fort Yukon, I go Arctic City—twenty-five sleep—big string, all the time—I catch him string—I say, 'Hello, Ruth! How are ye?'—and you say, 'Is that my good husband?'—and I say 'Yes'—and you say, 'No can bake good bread, no more soda'—then I say, 'Look in cache,[14] under flour; good-by.' You look and catch plenty soda. All the time you Fort Yukon, me Arctic City. Hi-yu medicine-man!"

14   Ruth smiled so ingenuously[15] at the fairy story, that both men burst into laughter. A row[16] among the dogs cut short the wonders

---

8. *Methodist church; Methodist is a Christian denomination,* 9. *bread,* 10. *shoes made of animal skin,* 11. *security,* 12. *special bilingual language,* 13. *powerlessly,* 14. *storage place,* 15. *insincerely,* 16. *fight*

of the Outside, and by the time the snarling combatants were separated, she had lashed the sleds and all was ready for the trail.

15   "Mush! Baldy! Hi! Mush on!" Mason worked his whip smartly, and as the dogs whined low in the traces, broke out the sled with the gee-pole. Ruth followed with the second team, leaving Malemute Kid, who had helped her start, to bring up the rear. Strong man, brute that he was, capable of felling an ox at a blow, he could not bear to beat the poor animals, but humored them as a dog-driver rarely does—nay, almost wept with them in their misery.

16   "Come, mush on there, you poor sorefooted brutes!" he murmured, after several ineffectual attempts to start the load. But his patience was at last rewarded, and though whimpering with pain, they hastened to join their fellows.

17   No more conversation; the toil of the trail will not permit such extravagance. And of all deadening labors, that of the Northland trail is the worst. Happy is the man who can weather a day's travel at the price of silence, and that on a beaten track.

18   And of all heart-breaking labors, that of breaking[17] trail is the worst. At every step the great webbed shoe sinks till the snow is level with the knee. Then up, straight up, the deviation of a fraction of an inch being a certain precursor[18] of disaster, the snowshoe must be lifted till the surface is cleared; then forward, down, and the other foot is raised perpendicularly for the matter of half a yard. He who tries this for the first time, if haply[19] he avoids bringing his shoes in dangerous propinquity[20] and measures not his length on the treacherous footing, will give up exhausted at the end of a hundred yards; he who can keep out of the way of the dogs for a whole day may well crawl into his sleeping-bag with a clear conscience and a pride which passeth all understanding; and he who travels twenty sleeps on the Long Trail is a man whom the gods may envy.

19   The afternoon wore on, and with the awe, born of the White Silence, the voiceless travelers bent to[21] their work. Nature has many tricks wherewith[22] she convinces man of his finity[23]—the ceaseless flow of the tides, the fury of the storm, the shock of the earthquake, the long roll of heaven's artillery—but the most tremendous, the most stupefying[24] of all, is the passive phase of the White Silence. All movement ceases, the sky clears, the heavens are as brass; the slightest whisper seems sacrilege,[25] and

---

17. *starting off onto*, 18. *sign*, 19. *accidentally*, 20. *nearness*, 21. *continued with*, 22. *by which*, 23. *mortality*, 24. *amazing*, 25. *misuse of something sacred*

man becomes timid, affrighted at the sound of his own voice. Sole speck of life journeying across the ghostly wastes of a dead world, he trembles at his audacity,[26] realizes that his is a maggot's[27] life, nothing more. Strange throughts arise unsummoned, and the mystery of all things strives for utterance. And the fear of death, of God, of the universe, comes over him—the hope of the Resurrection and the Life, the yearning for immortality, the vain striving of the imprisoned essence—it is then, if ever, man walks alone with God.

20   So wore the day away. The river took a great bend, and Mason headed his team for the cut-off across the narrow neck of land. But the dogs balked[28] at the high bank. Again and again, though Ruth and Malemute Kid were shoving on the sled, they slipped back. Then came the concerted effort. The miserable creatures, weak from hunger, exerted their last strength. Up—up—the sled poised[29] on the top of the bank; but the leader swung the string of dogs behind him to the right, fouling Mason's snowshoes. The result was grievous. Mason was whipped off his feet; one of the dogs fell in the traces[30]; and the sled toppled back, dragging everything to the bottom again.

21   Slash! the whip fell among the dogs savagely, especially upon the one which had fallen.

22   "Don't, Mason," entreated[31] Malemute Kid; "the poor devil's on its last legs.[32] Wait and we'll put my team on."

23   Mason deliberately withheld the whip till the last word had fallen, then out flashed the long lash, completely curling about the offending creature's body. Carmen—for it was Carmen—cowered[33] in the snow, cried piteously, then rolled over on her side.

24   It was a tragic moment, a pitiful incident of the trail—a dying dog, two comrades in anger. Ruth glanced solicitously[34] from man to man. But Malemute Kid restrained himself, though there was a world of reproach in his eyes, and bending over the dog, cut the traces. No word was spoken. The teams were double-spanned and the difficulty overcome; the sleds were under way again, the dying dog dragging herself along in the rear. As long as an animal can travel, it is not shot, and this last chance is accorded it—the crawling into camp, if it can, in the hope of a moose being killed.

---

26. *boldness,* 27. *larva of a fly, usually found in decaying food,* 28. *refused to go,* 29. *positioned,* 30. *straps connecting dogs to sled,* 31. *begged,* 32. *almost dead,* 33. *moved away in fear,* 34. *attentively*

25   Already penitent[35] for his angry action, but too stubborn to make amends, Mason toiled on at the head of the cavalcade,[36] little dreaming that danger hovered in the air. The timber clustered thick in the sheltered bottom, and through this they threaded their way. Fifty feet or more from the trail towered a lofty pine. For generations destiny had had this one end in view—perhaps the same had been decreed[37] of Mason.

26   He stopped to fasten the loosened thong[38] of his moccasin. The sleds came to a halt and the dogs lay down in the snow without a whimper. The stillness was weird; not a breath rustled the frost-encrusted forest; the cold and silence of outer space had chilled the heart and smote[39] the trembling lips of nature. A sigh pulsed through the air—they did not seem to actually hear it, but rather felt it, like the premonition[40] of movement in a motionless void.[41] Then the great tree, burdened with its weight of years and snow, played its last part in the tragedy of life. He heard the warning crash and attempted to spring up, but almost erect, caught the blow squarely on the shoulder.

27   The sudden danger, the quick death—how often had Malemute Kid faced it! The pine needles were still quivering as he gave his commands and sprang into action. Nor did the Indian girl faint or raise her voice in idle wailing, as might many of her white sisters. At his order, she threw her weight on the end of a quickly extemporized handspike,[42] easing the pressure and listening to her husband's groans, while Malemute Kid attacked the tree with his axe. The steel rang merrily as it bit into the frozen trunk, each stroke being accompanied by a forced, audible respiration, the "Huh!" "Huh!" of the woodsman.

28   At last the Kid laid the pitiable thing that was once a man in the snow. But worse than his comrade's pain was the dumb anguish[43] in the woman's face, the blended look of hopeful, hopeless query. Little was said; those of the Northland are early taught the futility[44] of words and the inestimable value of deeds. With the temperature at sixty-five below zero, a man cannot lie many minutes in the snow and live. So the sled lashings were cut, and the sufferer, rolled in furs, laid on a couch of boughs. Before him roared a fire, built of the very wood which wrought the mishap. Behind and partially over him was stretched the primitive fly—a piece of canvas, which caught the radiating heat and threw it back and down upon him—a trick which men may know who study physics at the fount.

---

35. *sorry,* 36. *procession,* 37. *commanded,* 38. *strap,* 39. *killed,* 40. *signal,* 41. *emptiness,* 42. *quickly made bar, or lever,* 43. *pain,* 44. *wastefulness*

29   And men who have shared their bed with death know when the call is sounded. Mason was terribly crushed. The most cursory[45] examination revealed it. His right arm, leg, and back, were broken; his limbs were paralyzed from the hips; and the likelihood of internal injuries was large. An occasional moan was his only sign of life.

30   No hope; nothing to be done. The pitiless night crept slowly by—Ruth's portion, the despairing stoicism of her race, and Malemute Kid adding new lines to his face of bronze. In fact, Mason suffered least of all, for he spent his time in Eastern Tennessee, in the Great Smoky Mountains, living over the scenes of his childhood. And most pathetic was the melody of his long-forgotten Southern vernacular,[46] as he raved of swimming holes and coon hunts and watermelon raids. It was as Greek to Ruth, but the Kid understood and felt—felt as only one can feel who has been out for years from all that civilization means.

31   Morning brought consciousness to the stricken man, and Malemute Kid bent closer to catch his whispers.

32   "You remember when we foregathered[47] on the Tanana,[48] four years come next ice-run? I didn't care so much for her then. It was more like she was pretty, and there was a smack of excitement about it, I think. But d'ye know, I've come to think a heap of her. She's been a good wife to me, always at my shoulder in the pinch.[49] And when it comes to trading, you know there isn't her equal. D'ye recollect[50] the time she shot[51] the Moosehorn Rapids[52] to pull you and me off that rock, the bullets whipping the water like hailstones?—and the time of the famine at Nuklukyeto?—or when she raced the ice-run to bring the news? Yes, she's been a good wife to me, better'n that other one. Didn't know I'd been there? Never told you, eh? Well, I tried it once, down in the States. That's why I'm here. Been raised together, too. I came away to give her a chance for divorce. She got it.

33   "But that's got nothing to do with Ruth. I had thought of cleaning up and pulling[53] for the Outside next year—her and I—but it's too late. Don't send her back to her people, Kid. It's beastly hard for a woman to go back. Think of it!—nearly four years on our bacon and beans and flour and dried fruit, and then to go back to her fish and caribou.[54] It's not good for her to have tried our ways, to come to know they're better'n her

---

45. *quick,* 46. *speech,* 47. *met,* 48. *a river which feeds into the Yukon River,* 49. *in bad times,* 50. *remember,* 51. *rode in a boat,* 52. *swift water,* 53. *leaving,* 54. *deer*

people's, and then return to them. Take care of her, Kid—why don't you—but no, you always fought shy of them—and you never told me why you came to this country. Be kind to her, and send her back to the States as soon as you can. But fix it so as she can come back—liable to get homesick, you know.

34   "And the youngster—it's drawn us closer, Kid. I only hope it is a boy. Think of it!—flesh of my flesh, Kid. He mustn't stop in this country. And if it's a girl, why she can't. Sell my furs; they'll fetch at least five thousand, and I've got as much more with the company. And handle my interests with yours. I think that bench claim[55] will show up. See that he gets a good schooling; and Kid, above all, don't let him come back. This country was not made for white men.

35   "I'm a gone man, Kid. Three or four sleeps at the best. You've got to go on. You must go on! Remember, it's my wife, it's my boy—O God! I hope it's a boy! You can't stay by me—and I charge you, a dying man, to pull on."

36   "Give me three days," pleaded Malemute Kid. "You may change for the better; something may turn up."

37   "No."

38   "Just three days."

39   "You must pull on."

40   "Two days."

41   "It's my wife and my boy, Kid. You would not ask it."

42   "One day."

43   "No, no! I charge"—

44   "Only one day. We can shave it through on the grub, and I might knock over a moose."

45   "No—all right; one day, but not a minute more. And, Kid, don't—don't leave me to face it alone. Just a shot, one pull on the trigger. You understand. Think of it! Think of it! Flesh of my flesh, and I'll never live to see him!

46   "Send Ruth here. I want to say good-by and tell her that she must think of the boy and not wait till I'm dead. She might refuse to go with you if I didn't. Good-by, old man; good-by.

47   "Kid! I say—a—sink a hole above the pup, next to the slide. I panned out forty cents on my shovel there.

48   "And, Kid!" he stooped lower to catch the last faint words, the dying man's surrender of his pride. "I'm sorry—for—you know—Carmen."

49   Leaving the girl crying softly over her man, Malemute Kid slipped into his parka[56] and snowshoes, tucked his rifle under

---

55. *legal claim,* 56. *hooded coat*

his arm, and crept away into the forest. He was no tyro[57] in the stern[58] sorrow of the Northland, but never had he faced so stiff a problem as this. In the abstract, it was a plain, mathematical proposition—three possible lives as against one doomed one. But now he hesitated. For five years, shoulder to shoulder, on the rivers and trails, in the camps and mines, facing death by field and flood and famine, had they knitted the bonds of their comradeship. So close was the tie, that he had often been conscious of a vague jealousy of Ruth, from the first time she had come between. And now it must be severed[59] by his own hand.

50   Though he prayed for a moose, just one moose, all game seemed to have deserted the land, and nightfall found the exhausted man crawling into camp, light-handed, heavy-hearted. An uproar from the dogs and shrill cries from Ruth hastened him.

51   Bursting into the camp, he saw the girl in the midst of the snarling pack, laying about her with an axe. The dogs had broken the iron rule of their masters and were rushing the grub.[60] He joined the issue with his rifle reversed, and the hoary[61] game of natural selection was played out with all the ruthlessness of its primeval environment. Rifle and axe went up and down, hit or missed with monotonous regularity; lithe[62] bodies flashed, with wild eyes and dripping fangs; and man and beast fought for supremacy to the bitterest conclusion. Then the beaten brutes crept to the edge of the firelight, licking their wounds, voicing their misery to the stars.

52   The whole stock of dried salmon had been devoured, and perhaps five pounds of flour remained to tide them over[63] two hundred miles of wilderness. Ruth returned to her husband, while Malemute Kid cut up the warm body of one of the dogs, the skull of which had been crushed by the axe. Every portion was carefully put away, save the hide and offal,[64] which were cast to his fellows of the moment before.

53   Morning brought fresh trouble. The animals were turning on each other. Carmen, who still clung to her slender thread of life, was downed[65] by the pack. The lash fell among them unheeded. They cringed[66] and cried under the blows, but refused to scatter till the last wretched bit had disappeared—bones, hide, hair, everything.

54   Malemute Kid went about his work, listening to Mason, who was back in Tennessee, delivering tangled discourses and wild exhortations to his brethren of other days.

---

57. *beginner*, 58. *severe*, 59. *cut*, 60. *food*, 61. *ancient*, 62. *graceful*,
63. *sustain them*, 64. *waste parts*, 65. *forced to the ground*, 66. *moved away*

55   Taking advantage of neighboring pines, he worked rapidly, and Ruth watched him make a cache similar to those sometimes used by hunters to preserve their meat from the wolverines[67] and dogs. One after the other, he bent the tops of two small pines toward each other and nearly to the ground, making them fast with thongs of moosehide. Then he beat the dogs into submission and harnessed them to two of the sleds, loading the same with everything but the furs which enveloped Mason. These he wrapped and lashed tightly about him, fastening either end of the robes to the bent pines. A single stroke of his hunting knife would release them and send the body high in the air.

56   Ruth had received her husband's last wishes and made no struggle. Poor girl, she had learned the lesson of obedience well. From a child, she had bowed, and seen all women bow, to the lords of creation, and it did not seem in the nature of things for woman to resist. The Kid permitted her one outburst of grief, as she kissed her husband—her own people had no such custom— then led her to the foremost sled and helped her into her snowshoes. Blindly, instinctively, she took the gee-pole and whip, and "mushed" the dogs out on the trail. Then he returned to Mason, who had fallen into a coma; and long after she was out of sight, crouched by the fire, waiting, hoping, praying for his comrade to die.

57   It is not pleasant to be alone with painful thoughts in the White Silence. The silence of gloom is merciful, shrouding one as with protection and breathing a thousand intangible sympathies; but the bright White Silence, clear and cold, under steely[68] skies, is pitiless.

58   An hour passed—two hours—but the man would not die. At high noon, the sun, without raising its rim above the southern horizon, threw a suggestion of fire athwart[69] the heavens, then quickly drew it back. Malemute Kid roused and dragged himself to his comrade's side. He cast one glance about him. The White Silence seemed to sneer, and a great fear came upon him. There was a sharp report[70]; Mason swung into his aerial sepulchre[71]; and Malemute Kid lashed the dogs into a wild gallop[72] as he fled across the snow.

---

67. *small bushy-tailed animal,* 68. *gray,* 69. *toward,* 70. *noise,* 71. *grave in the air,* 72. *run*

Understanding the Text: *Main Ideas*

After you have read "The White Silence" once quickly, check your comprehension of the most important events and ideas by answering the questions below, which trace the chronological events of the story. Check your answers with a partner or in a group.

1. Where does this story take place? What is the situation?

2. Who are the main characters?

3. Who is the leader of this group?

4. What is happening to Carmen, one of the dogs, at the beginning of the story? What happens to her at the end of the story?

5. Who has an accident on the trip? What happens?

6. What is the reaction of his friend? his wife?

7. What does the friend do to the injured man in the end?

8. How can you describe life in this area?

Literary Concept: *Plot*

The series of related events presented by a writer in his or her story is called the plot. Here, London introduces his three main characters on a trail in the Yukon region of northwest Canada. In "The White Silence," like other stories, the events build to the point of highest interest, or climax, and end in the resolution of the conflict or problem.

To piece together the plot of "The White Silence," put the following list of events into correct order. Afterward, identify which event is the climax, and which is the resolution of the conflict or problem.

EVENTS:

a. A tree falls on Mason's shoulders and crushes him.
b. Ruth obeys her husband's last wishes and agrees to leave with Malemute Kid.
c. The three characters break trail for lunch.

d. Mason whips the sick dog after the dog falls over and causes his sled to capsize.

e. Malemute Kid ends Mason's life by cutting a rope that sends him flying into the air.

f. Malemute Kid searches for a moose to kill in hopes of saving his friend.

g. Ruth and Malemute Kid fight the dogs for the food.

h. Malemute Kid cuts down the tree that has fallen on Mason.

i. Mason talks about Tennessee and his unborn son.

j. Malemute Kid and Ruth continue the journey.

k. The other dogs kill and eat Carmen.

CORRECT ORDER:

1. ____

2. ____

3. ____

4. ____

5. ____

6. ____

7. ____

8. ____

9. ____

10. ____

11. ____

Climax Event: _____

_____

Resolution: _____

_____

✿Understanding the Text: *Analysis*

After you have read the text, answer the questions below in groups or on your own. These questions focus on the main ideas of small sections of the story and are especially helpful in clarifying difficult segments of the text.

1. In the first paragraph, Mason puts a dog's foot in his mouth to bite out the ice between the dog's toes. What is your reaction to this? Why would a man care for a dog in this way?

2. In paragraph 3 (and later in the story), a dog "flashed up, the white teeth just missing Mason's throat." What is happening here? Explain why you think this is happening.

3. In paragraph 6, the two men bet about which of two dogs will be eaten before their journey is finished. Then, in paragraph 7, London explains: "Two hundred miles of unbroken trail in prospect, with a scant six days' grub for themselves and none for the dogs, could admit no other alternative." How do you feel about the men's conversation? What does London's explanation in paragraph 7 tell you about life in the Yukon?

4. In paragraph 10, we learn that Mason's wife Ruth loves "her white lord" husband because he treated her well. How do you feel about Ruth thinking of her husband as a "lord"?

5. When Mason tells Ruth of his plans for a future journey, he describes in "Indian English" a trip to "the Salt Water" (paragraph 11) to a village with houses "so high—ten, twenty pines" (paragraph 11) where "you step into a—a box, and pouf! up you go." (paragraph 13). What place could Mason be describing? What could the "box" be?

6. In paragraph 14, London writes that a fight "among the dogs cut short the wonders of the Outside . . ." and Mason stopped telling his story. What could "the Outside" signify?

7. Reread paragraph 15. What kind of man is Malemute Kid?

8. In paragraph 17, what are the chief dangers involved in "breaking trail"?

9. As the group continues to travel, London describes in paragraph 18, "the White Silence" as being so "tremendous" and "stupefying" that a person "realizes that his is a maggot's life, nothing more." How does a man who travels here feel?

10. In paragraph 20, when one of the dogs falls as they move up a high bank, what happens to Mason, the sled, and the other dogs? What does Mason do in reaction to the accident?

11. How does Malemute Kid react to Mason's deed, in paragraph 24?

12. Unfortunately, Mason stops on the trail and suffers an accident. What causes his injury? How badly is he hurt, as described in paragraphs 28-29?

13. What is his wife's reaction, in paragraph 27?

14. What does Malemute Kid do immediately to help his friend, in paragraphs 27 and 28?

15. Beginning in paragraph 32, what does Mason talk about in his sick state?

16. In paragraph 34, Mason tells his friend: "And the youngster— it's drawn us closer. Think of it!—flesh of my flesh, Kid." What does he mean?

17. Reread paragraph 55, in which Malemute Kid constructs a device by which he will end his friend's life. Explain simply how he makes the device and its purpose.

Looking at Language: *Vocabulary Parts*

Jack London uses a wealth of descriptive words—adjectives and adverbs—to convey a picture of life in the Northland. Many of his descriptive words can be more easily understood through a review of word parts. As an experienced reader of English, you use prefixes and affixes to assist you in comprehending challenging vocabulary.

For example, look at these words taken from "The White Silence":

piteously (paragraph 23)
pitiable (paragraph 28)
pitiless (paragraph 57)

As you have learned, these words stem from the root, "pity," and knowing the meanings of the suffixes enables you to understand the words. London's story is rich in words whose suffixes will be familiar to you.

As a review, and to prepare you for future texts, define the words below taken from the text with a partner. Be aware of the suffixes and identify the words as adjectives or adverbs. Use a dictionary to find the meanings of unfamiliar words.

1. palpable (par. 7)

2. irrelevantly (par. 9)

3. impotently (par. 12)

4. ineffectual (par. 16)

5. savagely (par. 21)

6. merciful (par. 57)

7. intangible (par. 57)

Now, with your partner, complete the sentences below with words from the list above.

a. The efforts of Malemute Kid to ease Mason's pain were

_____. Mason was already too badly hurt to be helped.

b. The two men were talking about the trail, and Mason

_____ started discussing how he had once been a church leader.

c. The Northland is never _____. It does not help the weak; instead, the weak die and the strong survive.

d. Ruth did not find her husband's story about traveling to the

ocean _____. She thought it was too good to be true.

e. The Northland makes man conscious of _____ things such as fear, love, and loneliness.

f. The dogs _____ killed Carmen, the sick dog, in order to survive.

g. Mason lay _____ on the bed of furs after he had been crushed by the great tree. His case was hopeless.

✻Understanding the Text: *Drawing Inferences*

One aspect of reading skill is the ability to read a text and draw conclusions, or inferences, based on what you have read. In "The White Silence," for example, Jack London never writes directly that Mason and the Malemute Kid are friends. However, you can infer, or conclude, this by their behavior toward each other.

Consider the information given in the text and draw inferences about the following statements. Mark each one *True*, *False*, or *Don't Know*. Then discuss your answers with a partner.

1. Malemute Kid was more experienced in living in the Northland than Mason.

2. Mason was a white man.

3. Malemute Kid was a cruel person.

4. Ruth was jealous of Malemute Kid's friendship with Mason.

5. Malemute Kid was jealous of Ruth's relationship with Mason.

6. Mason and Malemute Kid had been friends for a long time.

7. Ruth and Malemute Kid survived to reach the next town.

✻Looking at Language: *Narration and Verb Tenses*

From your studies, you know that English uses several verb tenses to convey past time. In London's story, which deals with the events of one Arctic journey, simple past verbs predominate as the tense used to tell the story. However, interspersed in the narration of the story, you will also find other verb tenses.

With a partner, examine the sentences below and discuss why particular verb tenses are present. If you wish, return to the text to read the sentence in the larger context of a paragraph. Label the sentences according to the time they represent: *During The Journey*, *Before the Journey*, and *General Facts*.

After you have discussed the examples, find two additional sentences from the story that represent each of the above three time categories. Be prepared to discuss which verb tenses are used and why.

1. "The two men and the woman grouped about the fire and began their meager meal." (paragraph 7)

2. "Ruth followed with the second team, leaving Malemute Kid, who had helped her start, to bring up the rear." (paragraph 15)

3. "No more conversation; the toil of the trail will not permit such extravagance." (paragraph 17)

4. "And of all heart-breaking labors, that of breaking trail is the worst. At every step the great webbed shoe sinks till the snow is level with the knee." (paragraph 18)

5. "Again and again, though Ruth and Malemute Kid were shoving on the sled, they slipped back." (paragraph 20)

6. "The sudden danger, the quick death—how often had Malemute Kid faced it!" (paragraph 27)

7. "And men who have shared their bed with death know when the call is sounded." (paragraph 29)

8. "For five years, shoulder to shoulder, on the rivers and trails, in the camps and mines, facing death by field and flood and famine, had they knitted the bonds of their comradeship." (paragraph 49)

Culture Point: *White–Native American Relations*

London's stories of the Yukon and Alaska depict in detail the lives of Native Americans. In "The White Silence," Ruth, the Indian wife of Mason, is traveling with her husband and his friend. Perhaps the picture London gives us here of "white"-Indian relations is a different one than you have gotten from viewing films or television programs. From this story, what differences can you find between the "white" and Native American cultures? What impression does London give us of how whites and Native Americans related to one another? Discuss these questions with a partner by analyzing the lines below taken from the story.

1. ". . . in her [Ruth's] eyes welled up a great love for her white lord—the first white man she had ever seen—the first man whom she had known to treat a woman as something better than a mere animal or beast of burden." (par. 10)

2. "It was a tragic moment, a pitiful incident of the trail—a dying dog, two comrades in anger. Ruth glanced solicitously from man to man." (par. 24)

3. "You remember when we foregathered on the Tanana, four years come next ice-run? I didn't care so much for her then . . . But d'ye know, I've come to think a heap of her. She's been a good wife to me, always at my shoulder in the pinch. And when it comes to trading, you know there isn't her equal. D'ye recollect the time she shot the Moosehorn Rapids to pull you and me off that rock . . . " (par. 32)

4. "Don't send her back to her people, Kid. It's beastly hard for a woman to go back. Think of it!—nearly four years on our bacon and beans and flour and dried fruit, and then to go back to her fish and caribou. It's not good for her to have tried our ways, to come to know they're better'n her people's, and then return to them . . . " (par. 33)

Literary Concept: *Conflict*

As mentioned earlier, Jack London's tales of adventure thrive on conflict, partly because they are set in the wilds of Canada, Alaska, California, rural Mexico, and other frontiers. London's heroes face storms, famine, cold, injustice, and self-criticism as they attempt to overcome the challenges.

In "The White Silence," there are several kinds of conflicts. In literary texts, conflicts usually involve one person against another; one person against society, or a group; one person against nature; or one person against himself or herself.

Examine the list of events in the story that you placed in chronological order in the previous Literary Concept exercise to identify Plot. In each of these events, which type of conflict, if any, is involved: one person against another person, one person against society, one person against nature, or one person against himself or herself. Also, who is the winner in each conflict? Discuss your responses with a partner.

Literary Concept: *Setting*

Setting refers to the time and place in which a text occurs. "Time" can be identified as a specific year, or a decade, or even

by a part of a century. "Place" can be expressed as a particular town or city, state, region, or country. Often exact dates and places for stories are supplied. Other times the writer gives such vague indications of the setting so that you can only guess a story takes place in "present day" or in "a city," for example.

Answer the questions below that relate to setting:

1. What information in a story do you think would help you guess the time of a story, if it was not stated precisely?

2. How could you guess the place in which a story was set?

3. Guess the time of "The White Silence" based on information from the story.

4. What is the place? How can you know this from the story itself (not information supplied by your instructor or this book)?

READING JOURNAL

In this class, you will be asked to keep a Reading Journal so that you can respond to each literary text with your unique ideas. The journal will also prepare you to write about literature. Keep your journal entries in a separate notebook.

Write in response to one of the questions below about "The White Silence" in your journal.

1. Did you like this story?

2. Was it too gruesome?

3. Does this story make you think about your own death? How does that make you feel?

VIDEO

To get a graphic picture of life in the Northland, view all or parts of the following commercial films, which are adapted from other stories of the same titles by Jack London: *The Call of the Wild* (novel), *White Fang* (novel) and "The Unexpected" (short story). Documentaries available at local video stores or through the public library will give you more insight into life in the Yukon region of Canada and Alaska, as well as information about Native American cultures.

"Gamblers and adventurers are generally superstitious, and Oakhurst one day declared that the baby had brought 'the luck' to Roaring Camp. It was certain that of late they had been successful. 'Luck' was the name agreed upon . . . "

CHAPTER TWO

The Luck of Roaring Camp

by Bret Harte

About the Author

Francis Bret Harte, (1836–1902), was born in Albany, New York, of English, Dutch, and Hebrew descent, and moved to California in 1854. He worked as a drugstore clerk, teacher, expressman, miner, typesetter, and government clerk, all the time practicing his writing. By 1868, he was recognized as San Francisco's leading author. Many of his stories about life in California mining camps were published in magazines. "The Luck of Roaring Camp" and "The Outcasts of Poker Flat," two such stories, made Harte famous, although some

people found the "colorful" characters he wrote about improper and indecent. Later in his life, Harte lived in England and France, where he continued to write about the California West.

At First Glance

1. Read the quotation that precedes "The Luck of Roaring Camp" and examine the photograph above it. What do they suggest this story will be about?

2. Next, read the first paragraph of the story. What does this passage tell you about life in "Roaring Camp"? What does the word "roaring" mean? Why do you think the camp is called by this name?

3. With a partner, discuss the words below, which are used in the story to describe the inhabitants of the mining camp. Look up unfamiliar words in the dictionary. What do the words suggest about what kind of people live in Roaring Camp?

coarse	dissolute	scamp
reckless	courageous	philosophical
rough	fugitives	

The Writer's Perspective

1. Bret Harte is a nineteenth century U.S. writer who depicted life on the Western frontiers. In particular, Harte is noted for his stories about life in California gold mining camps in the middle to late 1800s. How do you imagine life would be in such a camp?

2. Are you familiar with other stories or films that have given you impressions of how life was in the American West in this time period?

3. What is a "gold rush"? What do you know about the California Gold Rush?

The Luck of Roaring Camp

by Bret Harte

1   *T*here was commotion[1] in Roaring Camp. It could not have been a fight, for in 1850 that was not novel[2] enough to have called together the entire settlement. The ditches and claims were not only deserted, but "Tuttle's grocery" had contributed its gamblers, who, it will be remembered, calmly continued their game the day that French Pete and Kanaka Joe shot each other to death over the bar in the front room. The whole camp was collected before a rude[3] cabin on the outer edge of the clearing. Conversation was carried on in a low tone, but the name of a woman was frequently repeated. It was a name familiar enough in the camp, —"Cherokee Sal."

2   Perhaps the less said of her the better. She was a coarse and, it is to be feared, a very sinful woman. But at that time she was the only woman in Roaring Camp, and was just then lying in sore[4] extremity, when she most needed the ministration[5] of her own sex. Dissolute,[6] abandoned, and irreclaimable, she was yet suffering a martyrdom[7] hard enough to bear even when veiled[8] by sympathizing womanhood, but now terrible in her loneliness. The primal[9] curse had come to her in that original isolation which must have made the punishment of the first transgression[10] so dreadful. It was, perhaps, part of the expiation[11] of her sin that, at a moment when she most lacked her sex's intuitive tenderness and care, she met only the half-contemptuous[12] faces of her masculine associates. Yet a few of the spectators were, I think, touched by her sufferings. Sandy Tipton thought it was "rough on Sal," and, in the contemplation[13] of her condition, for a moment superior to the fact that he had an ace and two bowers[14] in his sleeve.

---

1. *noise,* 2. *unusual,* 3. *humble,* 4. *sorrowful,* 5. *aid,* 6. *immoral,*
7. *suffering,* 8. *protected,* 9. *basic,* 10. *sin,* 11. *atonement,* 12. *half-scornful,* 13. *consideration,* 14. *hidden playing cards*

3   It will be seen also that the situation was novel. Deaths were by no means uncommon in Roaring Camp, but a birth was a new thing. People had been dismissed from the camp effectively, finally, and with no possibility of return; but this was the first time that anybody had been introduced ab initio.[15] Hence the excitement.

4   "You go in there, Stumpy," said a prominent citizen known as "Kentuck," addressing one of the loungers. "Go in there, and see what you kin[16] do. You've had experience in them things."

5   Perhaps there was a fitness in the selection. Stumpy, in other climes, had been the putative[17] head of two families; in fact, it was owing to some legal informality in these proceedings that Roaring Camp—a city of refuge—was indebted to his company. The crowd approved the choice, and Stumpy was wise enough to bow[18] to the majority. The door closed on the extempore[19] surgeon and midwife,[20] and Roaring Camp sat down outside, smoked its pipe, and awaited the issue.

6   The assemblage[21] numbered about a hundred men. One or two of these were actual fugitives[22] from justice, some were criminal, and all were reckless. Physically they exhibited no indication of their past lives and character. The greatest scamp[23] had a Raphael[24] face, with a profusion[25] of blonde hair; Oakhurst, a gambler, had the melancholy air and intellectual abstraction of a Hamlet[26]; the coolest and most courageous man was scarcely over five feet in height, with a soft voice and an embarrassed, timid manner. The term "roughs" applied to them was a distinction rather than a definition. Perhaps in the minor details of fingers, toes, ears, etc., the camp may have been deficient, but these slight omissions did not detract from their aggregate[27] force. The strongest man had but three fingers on his right hand; the best shot had but one eye.

7   Such was the physical aspect of the men that were dispersed[28] around the cabin. The camp lay in a triangular valley between two hills and a river. The only outlet was a steep trail over the summit of a hill that faced the cabin, now illuminated by the rising moon. The suffering woman might have seen it from the rude bunk whereon she lay,—seen it winding like a silver thread until it was lost in the stars above.

---

15. *without a beginning, Latin,* 16. *can, slang,* 17. *supposed,* 18. *give in,* 19. *unprepared, Latin; extemporaneous in English,* 20. *usually, a woman who delivers a baby in place of a doctor,* 21. *gathering,* 22. *one who flees,* 23. *mischievous character,* 24. *15th century Italian painter,* 25. *mass,* 26. *prince in Shakespeare play,* 27. *collective,* 28. *spread*

8   A fire of withered pine boughs added sociability to the gathering. By degrees the natural levity[29] of Roaring Camp returned. Bets were freely offered and taken regarding the result. Three to five that "Sal would get through with it"; even that the child would survive; side bets as to the sex and complexion of the coming stranger. In the midst of an excited discussion an exclamation came from those nearest the door, and the camp stopped to listen. Above the swaying and moaning of the pines, the swift rush of the river, and the crackling of the fire rose a sharp, querulous[30] cry,—a cry unlike anything heard before in the camp. The pines stopped moaning, the river ceased to rush, and the fire to crackle. It seemed as if Nature had stopped to listen too.

9   The camp rose to its feet as one man! It was proposed to explode a barrel of gunpowder; but in consideration of the situation of the mother, better counsels prevailed, and only a few revolvers were discharged; for whether owing to the rude surgery of the camp, or some other reason, Cherokee Sal was sinking fast.[31] Within an hour she had climbed, as it were, that rugged road that led to the stars, and so passed out of Roaring Camp, its sin and shame, forever. I do not think that the announcement disturbed them much, except in speculation[32] as to the fate of the child. "Can he live now?" was asked of Stumpy. The answer was doubtful. The only other being of Cherokee's sex and maternal condition in the settlement was an ass.[33] There was some conjecture[34] as to fitness, but the experiment was tried. It was less problematical than the ancient treatment of Romulus and Remus,[35] and apparently as successful.

10   When these details were completed, which exhausted another hour, the door was opened, and the anxious crowd of men, who had already formed themselves into a queue,[36] entered in single file. Beside the low bunk or shelf, on which the figure of the mother was starkly[37] outlined below the blankets, stood a pine table. On this a candle-box was placed, and within it, swathed[38] in staring red flannel, lay the last arrival at Roaring Camp. Beside the candle-box was placed a hat. Its use was soon indicated. "Gentlemen," said Stumpy, with a singular mixture of authority and ex officio[39] complacency,[40]—"gentlemen will please pass in at the front door, round the table, and out at the back door.

---

29. *light manner*, 30. *complaining*, 31. *dying, slang*, 32. *deep thinking*,
33. *donkey*, 34. *theorizing*, 35. *the founders of Rome, raised as infants by wolves, according to legend*, 36. *line*, 37. *clearly*, 38. *wrapped*,
39. *unofficial, Latin*, 40. *self-satisfaction*

Them as wishes to contribute anything toward the orphan will find a hat handy." The first man entered with his hat on; he uncovered, however, as he looked about him, and so unconsciously set an example to the next. In such communities good and bad actions are catching.[41] As the procession filed in comments were audible,—criticisms addressed perhaps rather to Stumpy in the character of showman: "Is that him?" "Mighty small specimen;" "Hasn't more'n got the color;" "Ain't bigger nor[42] a derringer."[43] The contributions were as characteristic: A silver tobacco box; a doubloon[44]; a navy revolver, silver mounted; a gold specimen; a very beautiful embroidered lady's handkerchief (from Oakhurst the gambler); a diamond breastpin; a diamond ring (suggested by the pin, with the remark from the giver that he "saw that pin and went two diamonds better"[45]); a slung-shot[46]; a Bible (contributor not detected); a golden spur; a silver teaspoon (the initials, I regret to say, were not the giver's); a pair of surgeon's shears; a lancet[47]; a Bank of England note for £5; and about $200 in loose gold and silver coin. During these proceedings Stumpy maintained a silence as impassive[48] as the dead on his left, a gravity[49] as inscrutable[50] as that of the newly born on his right. Only one incident occurred to break the monotony of the curious procession. As Kentuck bent over the candle-box half curiously, the child turned, and, in a spasm of pain, caught at his groping finger, and held it fast for a moment. Kentuck looked foolish and embarrassed. Something like a blush tried to assert itself in his weather-beaten cheek. "The d—d little cuss!" he said, as he extricated[51] his finger, with perhaps more tenderness and care than he might have been deemed capable of showing. He held that finger a little apart from its fellows as he went out, and examined it curiously. The examination provoked the same original remark in regard to the child. In fact, he seemed to enjoy repeating it. "He rastled[52] with my finger," he remarked to Tipton, holding up the member, "the d—d little cuss!"

11   It was four o'clock before the camp sought repose.[53] A light burnt in the cabin where the watchers sat, for Stumpy did not go to bed that night. Nor did Kentuck. He drank quite freely, and related with great gusto[54] his experience, invariably ending with

---

41. *contagious, slang,* 42. *than, slang,* 43. *small handgun,* 44. *old Spanish gold coin,* 45. *in card-playing, an expression used in betting, slang,* 46. *a Y-shaped stick with an elastic strap used for flinging stones,* 47. *knife,* 48. *motionless,* 49. *seriousness,* 50. *difficult to understand,* 51. *removed,* 52. *fought,* 53. *rest,* 54. *spirit*

his characteristic condemnation of the newcomer. It seemed to relieve him of any unjust implication of sentiment, and Kentuck had the weaknesses of the nobler sex.[55] When everybody else had gone to bed he walked down to the river and whistled reflectingly. Then he walked up the gulch[56] past the cabin, still whistling with demonstrative unconcern. At a large redwood-tree he paused and retraced his steps, and again passed the cabin. Halfway down to the river's bank he again paused, and then returned and knocked at the door. It was opened by Stumpy. "How goes it?" said Kentuck, looking past Stumpy toward the candle-box. "All serene!" replied Stumpy. "Anything up?" "Nothing." There was a pause—an embarrassing one—Stumpy still holding the door. Then Kentuck had recourse to his finger, which he held up to Stumpy. "Rastled with it,—the d—d little cuss," he said, and retired.

12   The next day Cherokee Sal had such rude sepulture[57] as Roaring Camp afforded. After her body had been committed to the hillside, there was a formal meeting of the camp to discuss what should be done with her infant. A resolution to adopt it was unanimous and enthusiastic. But an animated discussion in regard to the manner and feasibility of providing for its wants at once sprang up. It was remarkable that the argument partook of[58] none of those fierce personalities with which discussions were usually conducted at Roaring Camp. Tipton proposed that they should send the child to Red Dog,—a distance of forty miles,—where female attention could be procured.[59] But the unlucky suggestion met with fierce and unanimous opposition. It was evident that no plan which entailed[60] parting from their new acquisition would for a moment be entertained. "Besides," said Tom Ryder, "them fellows at Red Dog would swap[61] it, and ring in somebody else on us."[62] A disbelief in the honesty of other camps prevailed at Roaring Camp, as in other places.

13   The introduction of a female nurse in the camp also met with objection. It was argued that no decent woman could be prevailed to accept Roaring Camp as her home, and the speaker urged that "they didn't want any more of the other kind." This unkind allusion to the defunct[63] mother, harsh as it may seem, was the first spasm of propriety,[64]—the first symptom of the camp's regeneration.[65] Stumpy advanced[66] nothing. Perhaps he felt a certain delicacy in interfering with the selection of a

---

55. *females,* 56. *small canyon,* 57. *burial, archaic,* 58. *involved,* 59. *gotten,* 60. *required,* 61. *exchange, slang,* 62. *replace it with a substitute, slang,* 63. *dead,* 64. *ownership,* 65. *rebirth,* 66. *proposed*

possible successor in office. But when questioned, he averred[67] stoutly that he and "Jinny"—the mammal before alluded to—could manage to rear the child. There was something original, independent, and heroic about the plan that pleased the camp. Stumpy was retained. Certain articles were sent for to Sacramento. "Mind," said the treasurer, as he pressed a bag of gold-dust into the expressman's[68] hand, "the best that can get got,—lace, you know, and filigree-work and frills,—d—n the cost!"

14   Strange to say, the child thrived. Perhaps the invigorating climate of the mountain camp was compensation for material deficiencies. Nature took the foundling[69] to her broader breast. In that rare atmosphere of the Sierra foothills,—that air pungent[70] with balsamic odor, that ethereal[71] cordial[72] at once bracing and exhilarating,—he may have found food and nourishment, or a subtle chemistry that transmuted[73] ass's milk to lime and phosphorus. Stumpy inclined to the belief that it was the latter and good nursing. "Me and that ass," he would say, "has been father and mother to him! Don't you," he would add, apostrophizing[74] the helpless bundle before him, "never go back on us."

15   By the time he was a month old the necessity of giving him a name became apparent. He had generally been known as "The Kid," "Stumpy's Boy," "The Coyote" (an allusion to his vocal powers), and even by Kentuck's endearing[75] diminutive[76] of "The d—d little cuss." But these were felt to be vague and unsatisfactory, and were at last dismissed under another influence. Gamblers and adventurers are generally superstitious, and Oakhurst one day declared that the baby had brought "the luck" to Roaring Camp. It was certain that of late they had been successful. "Luck" was the name agreed upon, with the prefix of Tommy for greater convenience. No allusion was made to the mother, and the father was unknown. "It's better," said the philosophical Oakhurst, "to take a fresh deal all round.[77] Call him Luck, and start him fair." A day was accordingly set apart for the christening.[78] What was meant by this ceremony the reader may imagine who has already gathered some idea of the reckless irreverence of Roaring Camp. The master of ceremonies was one "Boston," a noted wag,[79] and the occasion seemed to promise

---

67. *declared*, 68. *transport company worker*, 69. *orphan*, 70. *sharp*, 71. *delicate*, 72. *liqueur*, 73. *transformed*, 74. *addressing*, 75. *inspiring affection*, 76. *shortened name*, 77. *reference to dealing playing cards, slang*, 78. *baptism, or initiation of infant into a Christian church*, 79. *mischievous person*

the greatest facetiousness.[80] This ingenious satirist[81] had spent two days in preparing a burlesque[82] of the Church service, with pointed local allusions. The choir was properly trained, and Sandy Tipton was the stand godfather. But after the procession had marched to the grove with music and banners, and the child had been deposited before a mock altar, Stumpy stepped before the expectant crowd. "It ain't my style to spoil fun, boys," said the little man, stoutly eying the faces around him, "but it strikes me that this thing ain't exactly on the squar.[83] It's playing it pretty low down[84] on this yer[85] baby to ring in fun on him that he ain't goin' to understand. And ef there's goin' to be any godfathers round, I'd like to see who's got any better rights than me." A silence followed Stumpy's speech. To the credit of all humorists be it said that the first man to acknowledge its justice was the satirist thus stopped of his fun. "But," said Stumpy, quickly following up his advantage, "we're here for a christening, and we'll have it. I proclaim you Thomas Luck, according to the laws of the United States and the State of California, so help me God." It was the first time that the name of the Deity had been otherwise uttered than profanely[86] in the camp. The form of christening was perhaps even more ludicrous[87] than the satirist had conceived; but strangely enough, nobody saw it and nobody laughed. "Tommy" was christened as seriously as he would have been under a Christian roof, and cried and was comforted in as orthodox[88] fashion.

16 And so the work of regeneration began in Roaring Camp. Almost imperceptibly[89] a change came over the settlement. The cabin assigned to "Tommy Luck"—or "The Luck," as he was more frequently called—first showed signs of improvement. It was kept scrupulously clean and whitewashed. Then it was boarded, clothed, and papered. The rosewood cradle, packed eighty miles by mule, had, in Stumpy's way of putting it, "sorter killed the rest of the furniture." So the rehabilitation of the cabin became a necessity. The men who were in the habit of lounging in at Stumpy's to see "how 'The Luck' got on" seemed to appreciate the change, and in self-defense the rival establishment of "Tuttle's grocery" bestirred itself and imported a carpet and mirrors. The reflections of the latter on the appearance of Roaring Camp tended to produce stricter habits of personal cleanliness. Again Stumpy imposed a kind of quarantine[90] upon

---

80. *humor,* 81. *writer of humor,* 82. *literary work that makes fun,* 83. *fair, slang,* 84. *unfair, slang,* 85. *here, slang,* 86. *in cursing,* 87. *ridiculous,* 88. *traditional,* 89. *hard to see,* 90. *restriction*

those who aspired to the honor and privilege of holding The Luck. It was a cruel mortification to Kentuck—who, in the carelessness of a large nature and the habits of frontier life, had begun to regard all garments as a second cuticle,[91] which, like a snake's, only sloughed off[92] through decay—to be debarred[93] this privilege from certain prudential[94] reasons. Yet such was the subtle influence of innovation that he thereafter appeared regularly every afternoon in a clean shirt and face still shining from his ablutions.[95] Nor were moral and social sanitary laws neglected. "Tommy," who was supposed to spend his whole existence in a persistent attempt to repose, must not be disturbed by noise. The shouting and yelling, which had gained the camp its infelicitous[96] title, were not permitted within hearing distance of Stumpy's. The men conversed in whispers or smoked with Indian gravity. Profanity was tacitly[97] given up in these sacred precincts, and throughout the camp a popular form of expletive,[98] known as "D—n the luck!" and "Curse the luck!" was abandoned, as having a new personal bearing. Vocal music was not interdicted,[99] being supposed to have a soothing, tranquilizing quality; and one song, sung by "Man-o'-War Jack," an English sailor from Her Majesty's Australian colonies, was quite popular as a lullaby. It was a lugubrious[100] recital of the exploits of "The Arethusa, Seventy-four," in a muffled minor,[101] ending with a prolonged dying fall at the burden of each verse, "On b-oo-o-ard of the Arethusa." It was a fine sight to see Jack holding The Luck, rocking from side to side as if with the motion of a ship, and crooning forth this naval ditty.[102] Either through the peculiar rocking of Jack or the length of his song,— it contained ninety stanzas, and was continued with conscientious deliberation to the bitter end,—the lullaby generally had the desired effect. At such times the men would lie at full length under the trees in the soft summer twilight, smoking their pipes and drinking in the melodious utterances. An indistinct idea that this was pastoral happiness pervaded the camp. "This 'ere kind o' think," said the Cockney Simmons, meditatively reclining on his elbow, "is 'evingly." It reminded him of Greenwich.

---

91. *skin,* 92. *came off,* 93. *refused,* 94. *cautious,* 95. *washing,*
96. *unhappy,* 97. *silently,* 98. *curse word,* 99. *prohibited,* 100. *mournful,*
101. *a musical scale that sometimes invokes sadness,* 102. *song*

17 On the long summer days The Luck was usually carried to the gulch from whence the golden store of Roaring Camp was taken. There, on a blanket spread over pine boughs,[103] he would lie while the men were working in the ditches below. Latterly there was a rude attempt to decorate this bower[104] with flowers and sweet-smelling shrubs, and generally some one would bring him a cluster of wild honeysuckles, azaleas, or the painted blossoms of Las Mariposas. The men had suddenly awakened to the fact that there were beauty and significance in these trifles,[105] which they had so long trodden[106] carelessly beneath their feet. A flake of glittering mica,[107] a fragment of variegated quartz,[108] a bright pebble[109] from the bed of the creek, became beautiful to eyes thus cleared and strengthened, and were invariably put aside for The Luck. It was wonderful how many treasures the woods and hillsides yielded that "would do for Tommy." Surrounded by playthings such as never child out of fairyland had before, it is to be hoped that Tommy was content. He appeared to be serenely happy, albeit there was an infantine gravity about him, a contemplative light in his round gray eyes, that sometimes worried Stumpy. He was always tractable and quiet, and it is recorded that once, having crept beyond his "corral,"—a hedge of tesellated[110] pine boughs, which surrounded his bed,—he dropped over the bank on his head in the soft earth, and remained with his mottled[111] legs in the air in that position for at least five minutes with unflinching[112] gravity. He was extricated without a murmur. I hesitate to record the many other instances of his sagacity,[113] which rest, unfortunately, upon the statements of prejudiced friends. Some of them were not without a tinge[114] of superstition. "I crep' up on the bank just now," said Kentuck one day, in a breathless state of excitement, "and dern my skin if he wasn't a-talking to a jaybird as was a-sittin' on his lap. There they was, just as free and sociable as anything you please, a-jawin' at each other just like two cherrybums." Howbeit,[115] whether creeping over the pine boughs or lying lazily on his back blinking at the leaves above him, to him the birds sang, the squirrels chattered, and the flowers bloomed. Nature was his nurse and playfellow. For him she would let slip between the leaves golden shafts[116] of sunlight that fell just within his grasp; she would send wandering breezes to visit him with the balm[117]

---

103. *branches,* 104. *hiding place,* 105. *unimportant things,* 106. *walked on,*
107. *rock,* 108. *rock,* 109. *small rock,* 110. *patterned,* 111. *spotted,*
112. *continuous,* 113. *wisdom,* 114. *touch,* 115. *although, archaic,*
116. *columns,* 117. *pleasant smell*

of bay[118] and resinous gum[119]; to him the tall redwoods nodded familiarly and sleepily, the bumblebees buzzed, and the rooks[120] cawed a slumbrous accompaniment.

18   Such was the golden summer of Roaring Camp. They were "flush times," and the luck was with them. The claims had yielded enormously. The camp was jealous of its privileges and looked suspiciously on strangers. No encouragement was given to immigration, and, to make their seclusion more perfect, the land on either side of the mountain wall that surrounded the camp they duly preempted.[121] This, and a reputation for singular proficiency[122] with the revolver, kept the reserve of Roaring Camp inviolate.[123] The expressman—their only connecting link with the surrounding world—sometimes told wonderful stories of the camp. He would say, "They've a street up there in 'Roaring' that would lay over any street in Red Dog. They've got vines and flowers round their houses, and they wash themselves twice a day. But they're mighty rough on strangers, and they worship an Ingin[124] baby."

19   With the prosperity of the camp came a desire for further improvement. It was proposed to build a hotel in the following spring, and to invite one or two decent families to reside there for the sake of The Luck, who might perhaps profit by female companionship. The sacrifice that this concession to the sex cost these men, who were fiercely skeptical[125] in regard to its general virtue and usefulness, can only be accounted for by their affection for Tommy. A few still held out. But the resolve could not be carried into effect for three months, and the minority meekly yielded in the hope that something might turn up to prevent it. And it did.

20   The winter of 1851 will long be remembered in the foothills. The snow lay deep on the Sierras,[126] and every mountain creek became a river, and every river a lake. Each gorge and gulch was transformed into a tumultuous[127] watercourse that descended the hillsides, tearing down giant trees and scattering its drift and debris along the plain. Red Dog had been twice under water, and Roaring Camp had been forewarned. "Water put the gold into them gulches," said Stumpy. "It's been here once and will be here again!" And that night the North Fork suddenly leaped over its banks and swept up the triangular valley of Roaring Camp.

---

118. *a spice,* 119. *a liquid that comes out of some plants and trees,* 120. *a type of bird,* 121. *seized,* 122. *skill,* 123. *not violated,* 124. *Indian, slang,* 125. *doubting,* 126. *Sierra Nevada Mountains in eastern California,* 127. *violent*

21   In the confusion of rushing water, crashing trees, and crackling timber, and the darkness which seemed to flow with the water and blot out the fair valley, but little could be done to collect the scattered camp. When the morning broke, the cabin of Stumpy, nearest the river-bank, was gone. Higher up the gulch they found the body of its unlucky owner; but the pride, the hope, the joy, The Luck, of Roaring Camp had disappeared. They were returning with sad hearts when a shout from the bank recalled them.

22   It was a relief-boat from down the river. They had picked up, they said, a man and an infant, nearly exhausted, about two miles below. Did anybody know them, and did they belong here?

23   It needed but a glance to show them Kentuck lying there, cruelly crushed and bruised, but still holding The Luck of Roaring Camp in his arms. As they bent over the strangely assorted pair, they saw that the child was cold and pulseless. "He is dead," said one. Kentuck opened his eyes. "Dead?" he repeated feebly. "Yes, my man, and you are dying too." A smile lit the eyes of the expiring Kentuck. "Dying!" he repeated; "he's a-taking me with him. Tell the boys I've got The Luck with me now"; and the strong man, clinging to the frail babe as a drowning man is said to cling to a straw, drifted away into the shadowy river that flows forever to the unknown sea.

Understanding the Text: *Main Ideas*

With a partner, answer these questions, which will test your comprehension of the main events in "The Luck of Roaring Camp."

1. What interesting thing happened in Roaring Camp in the beginning of the story?

2. What happened to the baby's mother?

3. What did the citizens of Roaring Camp decide to do with the baby?

4. Who was declared chief caretaker for the infant?

5. How did the baby fare in the camp?

6. How did the town change as a result of the baby?

7. What happened to the baby in the end?

Understanding the Text: *Analysis*

With a partner, reread the paragraphs indicated below to ensure that you understand the important ideas in each section of the story.

1. In paragraph 1, the writer says that a fight, or even "the day that French Pete and Kanaka Joe shot each other to death over the bar," did not catch the attention of the inhabitants of Roaring Camp. What does that say about the camp?
2. Also in paragraph 1, what is the origin of "Cherokee Sal"?
3. The facts that Sal "was the only woman in Roaring Camp" (par. 2) and "deaths were by no means uncommon in Roaring Camp, but a birth was a new thing" (par. 3) gives us information about the inhabitants there. Why do you think there were no women? Why were deaths common and births uncommon?
4. In paragraph 5, "the door [is] closed on the extempore surgeon and midwife," Stumpy, who was chosen by the group. What is Stumpy about to do?
5. Also, in paragraphs 5 and 9, why does Harte write that "Roaring Camp sat down outside, smoked its pipe, and awaited the issue" and later "rose to its feet as one man"? How can a camp sit, smoke and wait, and then stand up?
6. In paragraph 6, what kind of men lived in the camp?
7. In paragraph 6, why do you suppose that some of the men had missing fingers and eyes?
8. In paragraph 8, what is your reaction to the townsfolk placing bets on whether Sal would survive?
9. In paragraph 9, how does the camp celebrate the birth of the baby?
10. Paragraph 9 states about Cherokee Sal: "Within an hour she had climbed, as it were, that rugged road that led to the stars, and so passed out of Roaring Camp, its sin and shame, forever." What does this mean?
11. After Sal dies, the men discuss how the baby can survive. In paragraph 9, Harte writes: "The only other being of Cherokee Sal's sex and maternal condition in the settlement was an ass." What does this mean?

12. The passage continues: "There was some conjecture as to fitness, but the experiment was tried . . . and apparently . . . successful." What event does this passage relate?

13. In paragraph 10, why do the men put money and items of value into a hat?

14. What happens to Kentuck when he examines the newborn child?

15. In paragraphs 12 and 13, what proposals are made to deal with the infant? Which one is finally agreed on?

16. In paragraph 15, what name do the townsfolk give the baby? Why is this name selected?

17. In paragraph 15, what happens to the infant?

18. What examples of "regeneration" of the camp and its citizens can be found in paragraph 16?

19. How is the baby's emotional condition described in paragraph 17?

20. What clever action does Kentuck say he witnessed the baby performing, in paragraph 17?

21. In paragraph 18, this period is described as "the golden summer of Roaring Camp." What is "golden" about this period?

22. What do the citizens of Roaring Camp do to secure their town, in paragraph 18?

23. What plans do they make for the future of the camp, in paragraph 19? Do these plans come true?

24. Finally, what occurs in paragraphs 20 through the end of the story?

Looking at Language: *Vocabulary by Theme/Word Parts*

One feature of Harte's writing is that he frequently uses nouns that end in "tion" and "ion," which may make his writing seem complicated. However, if you examine these nouns with "ion" affixes carefully, you may be able to detect the roots, or the verb forms, to help you determine the meanings.

For instance, Harte uses the word "transgression" in paragraph 2, which means "sin." The verb form is "transgress," which means "to sin."

Examples of these types of nouns are listed below. All of the words listed deal with the behavior of the inhabitants of Roaring Camp; many of the words particularly relate to the men's collective decision-making.

With a partner, define these words. Then, use a dictionary to find the verb form of each noun. Next, use the nouns to complete the sentences which follow. (Two words in the list have almost the same meaning.)

1. contemplation (par. 2)

   definition: _____

   verb: _____

2. speculation (par. 9)

   definition: _____

   verb: _____

3. condemnation (par. 20)

   definition: _____

   verb: _____

4. resolution (par. 21)

   definition: _____

   verb: _____

5. deliberation (par. 25)

   definition: _____

   verb: _____

6. rehabilitation (par. 25)

   definition: _____

   verb: _____

7. concession (par. 28)

definition: _____

verb: _____

1. Before the baby was born, there was much _____ in Roaring Camp about the color of his eyes and his complexion.

2. After much _____, the group decided to take care of the infant themselves.

3. The citizens made a _____ to keep the baby.

4. With the presence of the baby in Roaring Camp, there was now a _____ of shouting and using profanity.

5. The men also had to make a _____ by bathing regularly if they wished to hold the baby.

6. In general, the infant produced a _____ of the citizens of Roaring Camp.

Understanding the Text: *Drawing Inferences*

The activity in Roaring Camp centers around mining, gambling, and the new infant. With a partner, read the statements below which ask you to draw inferences, or conclusions, about these activities in the story. Based on your knowledge of the story, discuss with your partner whether the statements are true or false. You may want to reread the paragraphs listed beside the statement to gain more background information.

1. Most of the men of Roaring Camp accepted responsibility for the infant's upbringing. (par. 10)

2. Roaring Camp's citizens were poor. (par. 16)

3. Stumpy was a leader in the camp. (par. 16)

4. The baby did not receive much attention from the men. (par. 17)

5. To the men, the infant was the reason for their "flush times," or good luck. (par. 18)

6. Prosperity also meant the town would have to change from a sinful place to a decent community. (par. 19)

Looking at Language: *Vocabulary by Theme/Guessing Meaning from Context*

In "The Luck of Roaring Camp," Harte describes in detail the natural landscape of the camp. In paragraph 26, he writes, the men work in the mine, while "the golden store," the baby, sits on pine branches. With a partner, reread the parts of paragraph 26 given below. Then, guess the meanings of the descriptive words listed after each passage.

1. ". . . whether creeping over the pine boughs or lying lazily on his back blinking at the leaves above him, to him the birds sang, the squirrels chattered, and the flowers bloomed."

   pine boughs: _____

   squirrels chattered: _____

2. "Nature was his nurse and playfellow. For him she would let slip between the leaves golden shafts of sunlight that fell just within his grasp; she would send wandering breezes to visit him with the balm[1] of bay[2] and resinous gum[3] ; . . . "

   shafts of sunlight: _____

   wandering breezes: _____

3. "to him the tall redwoods nodded familiarly and sleepily, the bumblebees buzzed, and the rooks[4] cawed a slumbrous accompaniment."

   the tall redwoods nodded: _____

   cawed: _____

   slumbrous: _____

---

1. *pleasant smell,* 2. *a spice,* 3. *a liquid that comes out of some plants and trees,* 4. *a type of bird*

Looking at Language: *Related Meanings in Vocabulary*

"The Luck of Roaring Camp" provides us with examples of words that have more than one meaning. With a partner, look up the vocabulary items below in the text. Then, use a dictionary to find the various meanings of each word. Make up sentences together that show the different meanings of the words.

camp (par. 1)
novel (par. 1)
rude (par. 1)
coarse (par. 2)
sore (par. 2)
gravity (par. 20)

Looking at Language: *Regional Dialect/Slang*

In the speech of the adventurous citizens of Roaring Camp, we find many dialectal or slang expressions. For example, the speech of Stumpy and Kentuck contains ungrammatical expressions such as "them things" instead of "those things." Also, slang and idiomatic expressions that are still in use today can be found in narrative passages in the story. With a partner, examine the following words or phrases from the story and be prepared to explain their meanings, or "translate" them into grammatically correct English.

1. "Go in there, and see what you kin do. You've had experience in them things." (par. 4)

2. Cherokee Sal was sinking fast. (par. 18)

3. In such communities good and bad actions are catching. (par. 19)

4. (In commenting on the newborn's appearance:) "Hasn't more'n got the color" . . . "Ain't bigger nor a derringer." (par. 19)

5. (Stumpy's speech in objection to the fake christening:) ". . . it strikes me that this thing ain't exactly on the squar. It's playing it pretty low down on this yer baby . . . " (par. 24)

✺Literary Concept: *Plot*

As with "The White Silence," Bret Harte's story has a well-defined plot. With a partner, review the major events in the story by completing the sentences below.

"The Luck of Roaring Camp" by Bret Harte begins when _____

_____.

After the baby is born, _____.

The men decide to take care of the baby in the camp. Stumpy

_____

_____.

They buy _____.

In consideration of the baby, the men of Roaring Camp are

now prohibited from _____.

While the men work, _____

_____.

The men bring the baby _____

_____. One night the snow

from the mountains _____

_____.

Stumpy's house _____

_____ and Stumpy _____

_____.

In the end, the baby _____

_____.

✿Literary Concept: *Setting*

Setting refers to the time and place in which a story takes place. The time can be expressed by a year or a period in a century, and the place can be identified by location and description. Fill in the sentences that follow to describe the setting of "The Luck of Roaring Camp."

This story takes places in a _____

(name of type of town) in _____

(name of state) in _____

(country.) The year is _____.

✿Culture Point: *The Western Community*

Roaring Camp is a rough mining camp, not unlike communities that are typically portrayed in films about the "wild West" of nineteenth-century United States. However, throughout the story the inhabitants act as one community. For example, they wait as a group for the birth of the infant, and they make decisions collectively about what will be done with the child. On the other hand, the inhabitants of Roaring Camp include "fugitives," "gamblers and adventurers." Discuss with your group how this community operated, beginning with the questions below.

1. Do you think this would have been a nice place to live?

2. How do you think the townsfolk treated each other?

3. Would you have felt safe in Roaring Camp?

4. How would you describe the form of government used in this community?

5. Do communities in your culture operate the way Roaring Camp did?

Culture Point: *Luck*

As Harte writes, "gamblers and adventurers are superstitious," which is why they named the infant "Luck." Think about the conditions in which the inhabitants of this camp lived, their daily activities, and the historical time. Then, with your group, answer the questions below, which deal with the subject of luck.

1. Why do you think the citizens of Roaring Camp were super-stitious?

2. What parts of their daily lives required luck?

3. Are Americans today superstitious?

4. Are people of your culture superstitious? Are there particular groups who are more superstitious than others? Do these groups have anything in common with the men of Roaring Camp?

READING JOURNAL

For your reading journal, answer one of the following questions.

1. Did you like this story?

2. Was the ending sad?

3. Did you like the men of Roaring Camp?

VIDEO

To see the lives of men in mining camps like Roaring Camp, you may want to view one of two commercial films based on Harte stories. One, *The Luck of Roaring Camp*, starring Craig Sheffer, relates the story we have just read, and *California Gold Rush* (1985), starring Robert Hays, is a compilation of this story and Harte's "The Outcasts of Poker Flat." Also, a recent musical, *Paint Your Wagon* (1969), starring Lee Marvin and Clint Eastwood, presents a colorful view of the inhabitants of a rough mining settlement like Roaring Camp during the California Gold Rush.

Projects: UNIT ONE

Project I: Written Plot Summary

In literature classes, which are required in virtually all American universi-ties, the main class activity is to write about what you have read. In this course, you will practice different types of writing about literature, including describing characters and writing about meaning, which requires you at the same time to summarize the plot.

Your first writing project will aid you in completing later writing projects both in this course and in university literature courses. Your assignment will be to do a plot summary, that is, to retell a story briefly. A summary is defined as a condensation of the substance of a larger work. The "sub-stance" in a literary text is the plot, or series of main events.

For this assignment, choose one of the two stories you have covered in this unit. Write a plot summary in short essay form (three paragraphs) for one of them. Here is a suggested plan for organizing the summary:

I. Introduction

Give the title and author of story.

Tell briefly what the story is about and where it takes place.

II. Body

In chronological order, tell in paragraph form the main events of the story. Do not include all events in the story, only the most important ones. Remember to include transitional time words to link one event to the next.

III. Conclusion

Tell what happens in the end of the story.

Give your opinion of the story.

GRAMMAR NOTE:

When you write about a book or other literary text, you may describe the events in the story in simple present/present continuous tenses to make the action seem more alive and real to the reader. Or, if you choose, you may use simple past/past continuous/past perfect tenses to tell the story. Decide which verb tense you will use, present or past, and be consistent through-out your summary.

Project II: Class Questionnaire

When you began your study of literature, you discussed the meaning of literature and writers that you are familiar with. You will explore the previous knowledge and interest in literature of your class in the second project in this unit.

For this project, you will conduct an informal survey of your classmates to find out their feelings about literature. You and your group members will complete a questionnaire relating to literature in which each of you will contribute your feelings about literature. Then, the questionnaires will be assembled to get a picture of the class feelings about this subject.

In your group, ask each other the following questions aloud. Solicit additional comments from each group member and write those on the bottom of the questionnaire. Then, compile the questionnaires for each group member and average the responses to each question. Be prepared to report your group average response to each question. Summarize your group's response to the comment questions.

CLASS QUESTIONNAIRE

Please answer each question by rating your response on the scale of 1 (strongly agree) to 5 (strongly disagree).

___ 1 ___	___ 2 ___	___ 3 ___	___ 4 ___	___ 5 ___
strongly agree	agree somewhat	undecided	disagree somewhat	strongly disagree

1. ____ Literature is boring.

2. ____ I look forward to studying literature in the university.

3. ____ I enjoy reading literature in my language.

4. ____ I am having trouble right now understanding these stories.

5. ____ I don't like to talk about the stories I read because I'm afraid my ideas may be wrong.

6. ____ One reason I don't like reading literature is because the texts are often too long.

7. ____ Reading poems appeals to me.

8. ____ I would enjoy writing my own story or poem.

COMMENT QUESTIONS:

Have you ever written an original story or poem? When? What was it about?

Do you have any additional comments about literature in general or about the study of literature?

UNIT TWO

Wit and Wisdom

Unit Two offers three simple stories that provide
insights into human life. Here, readers will find stories
that progress in clear, chronological order but also
hold deeper meanings. Representative of the serious
messages one often finds behind humor are "The
Corduroy Pants," "The Standard of Living," and
"Butch Minds the Baby." Through these stories,
readers will not only explore plot but also detect
themes. As such, the stories have been selected for
their ease of reading so that students may focus on
themes, and thus develop a valuable academic skill.

"Abe started the engine and turned around in the road toward Skowhegan. Bert sat beside him sucking his pipe. Neither of them had anything to say to each other all the time they were riding. Abe drove as fast as his old car would go, because he was in a hurry to get Bert arrested."

CHAPTER THREE

The Corduroy Pants

by Erskine Caldwell

About the Author

Erskine Caldwell (1903–1987) is better known as a novelist, his two most famous novels, *God's Little Acre* and *Tobacco Road*, having been made into films. However, Caldwell has written many short stories which often portray life in small towns in the South. Caldwell struggled as a writer, so he worked at many jobs, including plowboy, football player, stock clerk, soda jerk and stonemason's helper. In some stories,

Caldwell writes of the ill treatment of African Americans, and violence. However, his writing is often humorous, as exemplified by "The Corduroy Pants."

At First Glance

1. What are "corduroy" pants? In what situation can you imagine that pants would be so important that one would make them the title of a story?

2. Read the first paragraph of the story. What is the situation? What do you think will happen?

The Writer's Perspective

1. Erskine Caldwell grew up in a small town in Georgia, in the southern United States. Imagine that you lived in a small town where most people had known each other since they were children. What would happen if you sold a house to your friend but forgot to remove a small item like a pair of pants?

2. Why do you think Erskine Caldwell wrote a story about such a simple subject: two men and a pair of pants?

The Corduroy Pants

by Erskine Caldwell

1   *T*wo weeks after he had sold his farm on the back road for twelve hundred dollars and the Mitchells had moved in and taken possession, Bert Fellows discovered that he had left his other pair of corduroy pants up attic.[1] When he had finished hauling his furniture and clothes to his other place on the Skowhegan road, he was sure he had left nothing behind, but the morning that he went to put on his best pair of pants he could not find them anywhere. Bert thought the matter over two or three days and decided to go around on the back road and ask Abe Mitchell to let him go up attic and get the corduroys. He had known Abe all his life and he felt certain Abe would let him go into the house and look around for them.

2   Abe was putting a new board on the doorstep when Bert came up the road and turned into the yard. Abe glanced around but kept right on working.

3   Bert waited until Abe had finished planing[2] the board before he said anything.

4   "How be you, Abe?" he inquired cautiously.

5   "Hell, I'm always well," Abe said, without looking up from the step.

6   Bert was getting ready to ask permission to go into the house. He waited until Abe hammered the twenty-penny[3] into the board.

7   "I left a pair of corduroys in there, Abe," he stated preliminarily. "You wouldn't mind if I went up attic and got them, would you?"

8   Abe let the hammer drop out of his hands and fall on the step. He wiped his mouth with his handkerchief and turned around facing Bert.

9   "You go in my house and I'll have the law on you. I don't give a cuss if you've left fifty pair of corduroys up attic. I bought and paid for this place and the buildings on it and I don't want nobody tracking around here. When I want you to come on my land, I'll invite you."

---

1. *up in the attic, informal,* 2. *smoothing the surface of,* 3. *a size of nail*

10   Bert scratched his head and looked up at the attic window. He began to wish he had not been so forgetful when he was moving his belongings down to his other house on the Skowhegan road.

11   "They won't do you no good, Abe," he said. "They are about ten sizes too big for you to wear. And they belong to me, anyway."

12   "I've already told you what I'm going to do with them corduroys," Abe replied, going back to work. "I've made my plans for them corduroys. I'm going to keep them, that's what I'm going to do."

13   Bert turned around and walked toward the road, glancing over his shoulder at the attic window where his pants were hanging on a rafter.[4] He stopped and looked at Abe several minutes, but Abe was busy hammering twenty-penny nails into the new step he was making and he paid no attention to Bert's sour looks. Bert went back down the road, wondering how he was going to get along without his other pair of pants.

14   By the time Bert reached his house he was good and mad.[5] In the first place, he did not like the way Abe Mitchell had ordered him away from his old farm, but most of all he missed his other pair of corduroys. And by bedtime he could not sit still. He walked around the kitchen mumbling to himself and trying to think of some way by which he could get his trousers away from Abe.

15   "Crusty-faced Democrats never were no good," he mumbled to himself.

16   Half an hour later he was walking up the back road toward his old farm. He had waited until he knew Abe was asleep, and now he was going to get into the house and go up attic and bring out the corduroys.

17   Bert felt in the dark for the loose window in the barn and discovered it could be opened just as he had expected. He had had good intentions of nailing it down, for the past two or three years, and now he was glad he had left it as it was. He went through the barn and the woodshed and into the house.

18   Abe had gone to bed about nine o'clock, and he was asleep and snoring when Bert listened at the door. Abe's wife had been stone-deaf[6] for the past twenty years or more.

19   Bert found the corduroy pants, with no trouble at all. He struck only one match up attic, and the pants were hanging on the first nail he went to. He had taken off his shoes when he climbed through the barn window and he knew his way through

---

4. *roof board,* 5. *very mad, slang,* 6. *completely unable to hear*

the house with his eyes shut. Getting into the house and out again was just as easy as he had thought it would be. And as long as Abe snored, he was safe.

20   In another minute he was out in the barn again, putting on his shoes and holding his pants under his arm. He had put over a good joke on Abe Mitchell, all right. He went home and got into bed.

21   The next morning Abe Mitchell drove his car up to the front of Bert's house and got out. Bert saw him from his window and went to meet Abe at the door. He was wearing the other pair of corduroys, the pair that Abe had said he was going to keep for himself.

22   "I'll have you arrested for stealing my pants," Abe announced as soon as Bert opened the door, "but if you want to give them back to me now I might consider calling off[7] the charges. It's up to you what you want to do about it."

23   "That's all right by me," Bert said. "When we get to court I'll show you that I'm just as big a man as you think you are. I'm not afraid of what you'll do. Go ahead and have me arrested, but if they lock you up in place of me, don't come begging me to go your bail[8] for you."

24   "Well, if that's the way you think about it," Abe said, getting red in the face, "I'll go ahead with the charges. I'll swear out a warrant right now and they'll put you in county jail before bedtime tonight."

25   "They'll know where to find me," Bert said, closing the door. "I generally stay pretty close to home."

26   Abe went out to his automobile and got inside. He started the engine, and promptly shut it off again.

27   "Come out here a minute, Bert," he called.

28   Bert studied him for several minutes through the crack in the door and then went out into the yard.

29   "Why don't you go swear out the warrant? What you waiting for now?"

30   "Well, I thought I'd tell you something, Bert. It will save you and me both a lot of time and money if you'd go to court right now and save the cost of having a man come out here to serve the warrant on you. If you'll go to court right now and let me have you arrested there, the cost won't be as much."

31   "You must take me for a cussed fool, Abe Mitchell," Bert said. "Do I look like a fool to pay ten dollars for a hired car to take me to county jail?"

---

7. *stopping,*   8. *money paid to get a person released from jail before his trial*

32   Abe thought to himself several minutes, glancing sideways at Bert.

33   "I'll tell you what I'll do, Bert," he proposed. "You get in my car and I'll take you there and you won't have to pay ten dollars for a hired car."

34   Bert took out his pipe and tobacco. Abe waited while he thought the proposition over thoroughly. Bert could not find a match, so Abe handed him one.

35   "You'll do that, won't you, Bert?" he asked.

36   "Don't hurry me—I need plenty of time to think this over in my mind."

37   Abe waited, bending nervously toward Bert. The match-head crumbled off and Abe promptly gave Bert another one.

38   "I guess I can accommodate you that little bit, this time," he said at length. "Wait until I lock up my house."

39   When Bert came back to the automobile Abe started the engine and turned around in the road toward Skowhegan. Bert sat beside him sucking his pipe. Neither of them had anything to say to each other all the time they were riding. Abe drove as fast as his old car would go, because he was in a hurry to get Bert arrested and the trial started.

40   When they reached the courthouse, they went inside and Abe swore out the warrant and had it served on Bert. The sheriff took them into the courtroom and told Bert to wait in a seat on the first row of benches. The sheriff said they could push the case ahead and get a hearing some time that same afternoon. Abe sat still, waiting until he was called to give his testimony.

41   Bert stood up while the charge was read to him. When it was over, the judge asked him if he wanted to plead guilty or not guilty.

42   "Not guilty," Bert said.

43   Abe jumped off his seat and waved his arms.

44   "He's lying!" he shouted at the top of his voice. "He's lying—he did steal my pants!"

45   "Who is that man?" the judge asked somebody.

46   "That's the man who swore out the warrant," the clerk said. "He's the one who claims the pants were stolen from him."

47   "Well, if he yells out like that again," the judge said, "I'll swear out a warrant against him for giving me a headache. And I guess somebody had better tell him there's such a thing as contempt of court. He looks like a Democrat, so I suppose he never heard of anything like that before."

48   The judge rapped for order and bent over towards Bert.

49   "Did you steal a pair of corduroy pants from this man?" he asked.

50   "They were *my* pants," Bert explained. "I left them in my house when I sold it to Abe Mitchell and when I asked him for them he wouldn't turn them over to me. I didn't steal them. They belonged to me all the time."

51   "He's lying!" Abe shouted again, jumping up and down. "He stole my pants—he's lying!"

52   "Ten dollars for contempt of court, whatever your name is," the judge said, aiming his gavel at Abe, "and case dismissed for lack of evidence."

53   Abe's face sunk into his head. He looked first at the judge and then around the courtroom at the strange people.

54   "You're not going to make me pay ten dollars, are you?" he demanded angrily.

55   "No," the judge said, standing up again. "I made a mistake. I forgot that you are a Democrat. I meant to say *twenty-five dollars.*"

56   Bert went outside and waited at the automobile until Abe paid his fine. In a quarter of an hour Abe came out of the courtroom.

57   "Well, I guess I'll have to give you a ride back home," he said, getting under the steering wheel and starting the engine. "But what I ought to do is leave you here and let you ride home in a hired car."

58   Bert said nothing at all. He sat down beside Abe and they drove out of town toward home.

59   It was almost dark when Abe stopped the car in front of Bert's house. Bert got out and slammed shut the door.

60   "I'm mighty much obliged for the ride," he said. "I been wanting to take a trip over Skowhegan way for a year or more. I'm glad you asked me to go along with you, Abe, but I don't see how the trip was worth twenty-five dollars to you."

61   Abe shoved his automobile into gear and jerked down the road toward his place. He left Bert standing beside the mailbox rubbing his hands over the legs of his corduroy pants.

62   "Abe Mitchell ought to have better sense than to be a Democrat," Bert said, going into his house.

✺Understanding the Text: *Main Ideas*

Answer these questions with a partner to check your comprehension of the main ideas of the story.

1. In paragraph 1, what do we learn is Bert's problem?

2. Who is Abe Mitchell?

3. How does Abe react when Bert asks for his pants?

4. What does Bert do after his first meeting with Abe?

5. Later, when Abe visits Bert's house, what does Abe threaten to do? Why?

6. Why do the two men go to town together?

7. In court, how does Bert plead?

8. What is Abe's reaction to this?

9. In the end, what is the final decision in the case?

10. How do the two men act toward each other in the end?

✺Understanding the Text: *Drawing Inferences*

With a partner, evaluate the statements below by drawing inferences, or conclusions, based on the information given in the story. Mark the statements True or False, or if there is insufficient information to judge them, Don't Know.

1. Abe and Bert are good friends.

2. Abe and Bert are relatively rich.

3. Bert owns many pairs of pants.

4. Abe really loves the corduroy pants, which is the reason he wants to take Bert to court to get them back.

5. Abe gives Bert a ride to and from the court because Bert is his friend.

6. Abe and Bert will remain friends after this incident.

Looking at Language: *Vocabulary by Theme*

Because "The Corduroy Pants" deals with a legal dispute, we find here many terms and phrases that relate to the court system in the United States. Discuss the items below with a partner. Define the known terms and use a dictionary or the text glossary to define the others. Then, use the items to complete the sentences that follow.

"go your bail" (par. 23)
"swear out a warrant" (par. 24)
"serve the warrant" (par. 30)
"case" (par. 40)
"testimony" (par. 40)
"plead guilty or not guilty" (par. 41)
"order" (par. 48)
"contempt of court" (par. 52)
"case dismissed" (par. 52)
"fine" (par. 56)

1. The court _____ in this story involves a pair of corduroy pants.

2. Abe tells Bert that he will _____ against him because Bert has taken the pants from Abe's home.

3. Bert does not get upset. He says that the police can _____ easily; they will always find him at home.

4. Abe warns Bert: "I will not _____ if you are arrested."

5. In the courtroom, the judge asks Bert if he will _____ . Bert replies that he is not guilty.

6. This makes Abe mad, and because he starts yelling, the judge raps his gavel and demands _____ in the court.

7. Finally, the judge finds Abe in _____ and gives him a $25 _____ .

8. The judge also declares the _____ because of lack of evidence, and Bert keeps the corduroy pants.

✿Looking at Language: *Past Tense Verbs*

Now that you know the order of events in "The Corduroy Pants," test your use of verb tenses to express past events by completing the sentences below, taken from the story. Complete the paragraphs with the correct form of the verbs in parentheses. Compare your answers with a partner. Then, check your verb choices against paragraphs 1 through 3 in the story. Discuss Caldwell's use of verb tenses.

"Two weeks after he _____ (sold) his farm on the back road

for twelve hundred dollars and the Mitchells _____ (moved) in

and _____ (take) possession, Bert Fellows _____ (discover)

that he _____ (leave) his other pair of corduroy pants up attic.

When he _____ (finish) hauling his furniture and clothes to his

other place on the Skowhegan road, he _____ (be) sure he

_____ (leave) nothing behind, but the morning that he _____

(go) to put on his best pair of pants he _____ (can, not, find)

them anywhere. Bert _____ (think) the matter over two or

three days and _____ (decide) to go around on the back road

and ask Abe Mitchell to let him go up attic and get the corduroys.

He _____ (know) Abe all his life and he _____ (feel) certain Abe

would let him go into the house and look around for them.

"Abe _____ (put) a new board on the doorstep when Bert

_____ (come) up the road and _____ (turn) into the yard. Abe

_____ (glance) around but _____ (keep) right on working.

"Bert _____ (wait) until Abe _____ (finish) planing the

board before he _____ (say) anything."

Literary Concepts: *Theme*

In literary works like Caldwell's "The Corduroy Pants," the reader can usually find more than one theme, or central idea. That is because literature is writing that is rich in meaning, not one-dimensional, like a newspaper report. The theme of a literary work can be an account of one person's experiences, a commentary about life at a certain historical time or in a certain social group, or an observation about human behavior in general.

Look at the diagram below, which illustrates the themes a reader can find as one looks at various levels of meaning of a literary work:

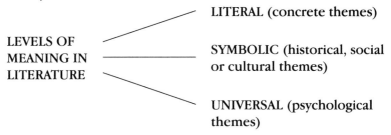

LEVELS OF
MEANING IN
LITERATURE

LITERAL (concrete themes)

SYMBOLIC (historical, social or cultural themes)

UNIVERSAL (psychological themes)

By considering the meaning of a piece of literature in terms of "levels of meaning"—from the surface to the deepest level—a reader finds central themes that relate only to those characters in the story, to a larger social group, or to all people.

For example, in "The Corduroy Pants," one could say that on the literal, or concrete, level this is a story about Abe and Bert and their dispute over a pair of pants.

But you can guess that the writer meant more of the story than simply that. On the symbolic level, people, events, and things in literary works may represent more than simply the literal story. They can be symbols or representations of larger ideas. Likewise, the story of Abe and Bert could represent the lives of similar people who lived in small southern American towns in that period, or poor people in general.

On an even larger level, "The Corduroy Pants" could represent universal values and conditions, such as emotions and desires that everyone shares. Universal emotions like love, hate, envy, or curiosity may be found in characters and events in literature. Even though you may not realize that a story contains these universal, deeper themes, it is in this way that literature becomes an important source of information about humankind. That is one reason literature appeals to so many people—the reader relates to stories that reflect her or his life dreams and experiences.

In your group, discuss the possible universal themes in "The Corduroy Pants," and answer these questions.

1. Do Abe or Bert have qualities that remind you of yourself or someone you know well?

2. What emotions do Abe and Bert exhibit?

3. What universal needs or desires do they pursue?

4. What human emotions, needs, or desires do you think this story relates to us?

Culture Point: *Friendship and Money*

1. "The Corduroy Pants" deals with the friendship between two men who have known each other all their lives. However, their friendship is unusual, because although they appear to be friends in some ways, when it comes to ownership of a piece of property they act like enemies. Discuss the kind of friendship Abe and Bert have by answering these questions in a group.

   a. What actions do Bert and/or Abe do that shows they are friends?
   b. What actions do they do that shows they are not friends?
   c. Do these two seem like typical friends?

2. Like Abe and Bert, one characteristic that Americans have been accused of having is the tendency to settle disputes in court, rather than through discussion. Many Americans can tell you firsthand stories of friends, relatives, or neighbors who have sued each other over disputes involving property or money. Discuss these questions, which deal with this method of settling arguments.

   a. In your country, how do friends, relatives, or neighbors generally settle disputes involving property?
   b. What is your reaction to the American way of taking your friend, relative, or neighbor to court?
   c. How would two people in your country have settled a dispute like the one described in "The Corduroy Pants"?

✵Culture Point: *Political Parties*

In this story, the fact that Abe Mitchell is a Democrat figures importantly in the final outcome. His affiliation with the Democratic party makes his fellow townsfolk treat him as an outsider. This indicates that most of the people in this small town are probably members of the other major political party, the Republican party. With your group, read quickly the descriptions of both the Democratic and Republican parties in an encyclopedia, and then discuss the following questions.

1. What do you think is one major difference between the Democratic and Republican parties? (If your encyclopedia does not help you answer this question, ask your instructor.)

2. Why do you think the townspeople didn't like Abe being a Democrat?

3. Are political party affiliations important in your country?

4. Are there certain regions of your country that have supported certain political parties for a long period of time?

READING JOURNAL

Respond in your reading journal to the Caldwell story by answering one or more of the questions below.

1. Do you like this story?

2. What do you think is the main point of the story?

3. Do you agree with the judge's decision in the case?

4. Will Abe and Bert remain friends?

VIDEO

Characters like Bert Fellows and Abe Mitchell can be found in two films based on Erskine Caldwell novels, both set in small Southern towns. *God's Little Acre* (1958), starring Robert Ryan and Aldo Ray, is a story of poor dirt farmers who search for gold. *Tobacco Road* (1941), starring Dana Andrews and Gene Tierney, is the story of poor whites in Georgia who are turned off their land.

"*Always the girls went to walk on Fifth Avenue on their free afternoons, for it was the ideal ground for their favorite game. The game could be played anywhere, and, indeed, was, but the great shop windows stimulated the two players to their best form.*"

CHAPTER FOUR

The Standard of Living

by Dorothy Parker

About the Author

Dorothy Parker, (1893–1967), has been called America's
wittiest woman. Widely quoted for her satirical remarks
about love and American life, Parker wrote humorous
poems and stories that epitomized life in the Jazz Age
of the 1920s. Her books of poetry, including *Death
and Taxes* (1931) and *Not So Deep as a Well* (1936),
were best sellers. Born in West End, N.J., she grew up
in New York City, and began her writing career as a
play and book reviewer for magazines such as *Vanity
Fair* and *The New Yorker*. Her short story "Big

Blonde" won the O. Henry Award in 1929. Parker considered "The Standard of Living" her "nicest and most workmanlike bit of writing."

At First Glance

1. Since you know that Parker is renowned for her wit, can you imagine how a story entitled "The Standard of Living" could be humorous?

2. Read the first few lines of the story. What can you infer about the lives of the two characters, Annabel and Midge?

The Writer's Perspective

1. Parker's story deals with the lives of two young women office workers in New York City in the 1920s. What work do you imagine women typically did in an office at that time? How does that compare with women's work in offices today?

2. A central part of the story involves the two girls' fantasies about becoming extremely rich. How would you spend an incredibly large amount of money if it suddenly came to you? Would you spend it on yourself or on others?

The Standard of Living

by Dorothy Parker

1   Annabel and Midge came out of the tea room with the arrogant slow gait[1] of the leisured, for their Saturday afternoon stretched ahead of them. They had lunched, as was their wont, on sugar, starches, oils and butter-fats. Usually they ate sandwiches of spongy new white bread greased with butter and mayonnaise; they ate thick wedges of cake lying wet beneath ice cream and whipped cream and melted chocolate gritty with nuts. As alternates, they ate patties, sweating beads of inferior oil, containing bits of bland meat bogged in pale, stiffening sauce; they ate pastries, limber[2] with rigid icing, filled with an indeterminate yellow sweet stuff, not still solid, not yet liquid, like salve[3] that has been left in the sun. They chose no other sort of food, nor did they consider it. And their skin was like the petals of wood anemones, and their bellies were as flat and their flanks as lean as those of young Indian braves.

2   Annabel and Midge had been best friends almost from the day that Midge had found a job as stenographer with the firm that employed Annabel. By now, Annabel, two years longer in the stenographic department, had worked up to the wages of eighteen dollars and fifty cents a week; Midge was still at sixteen dollars. Each girl lived at home with her family and paid half her salary to its support.

3   The girls sat side by side at their desks, they lunched together every noon, together they set out for home at the end of the day's work. Many of their evenings and most of their Sundays were passed in each other's company. Often they were joined by two young men, but there was no steadiness to any such quartet; the two young men would give place, unlamented, to two other young men, and lament would have been inappropriate, really, since the newcomers were scarcely distinguishable from their predecessors. Invariably the girls spent the fine idle hours of their hot-weather Saturday afternoons together. Constant use had not worn ragged the fabric of their friendship.

---

1. *walk,* 2. *flexible,* 3. *ointment*

4 They looked alike, though the resemblance did not lie in their features. It was in the shape of their bodies, their movements, their style, and their adornments. Annabel and Midge did, and completely, all that young office workers are besought[4] not to do. They painted their lips and their nails, they darkened their lashes and lightened their hair, and scent seemed to shimmer from them. They wore thin, bright dresses, tight over their breasts and high on their legs, and tilted slippers, fancifully strapped. They looked conspicuous and cheap and charming.

5 Now, as they walked across to Fifth Avenue with their skirts swirled by the hot wind, they received audible admiration. Young men grouped lethargically[5] about newsstands awarded them murmurs, exclamations, even—the ultimate tribute—whistles. Annabel and Midge passed without the condescension of hurrying their pace; they held their heads higher and set their feet with exquisite precision, as if they stepped over the necks of peasants.

6 Always the girls went to walk on Fifth Avenue on their free afternoons, for it was the ideal ground for their favorite game. The game could be played anywhere, and, indeed, was, but the great shop windows stimulated the two players to their best form.

7 Annabel had invented the game; or rather she had evolved it from an old one. Basically, it was no more than the ancient sport of what-would-you-do-if-you-had-a-million dollars? But Annabel had drawn a new set of rules for it, had narrowed it, pointed it, made it stricter. Like all games, it was the more absorbing for being more difficult.

8 Annabel's version went like this: You must suppose that somebody dies and leaves you a million dollars, cool. But there is a condition to the bequest.[6] It is stated in the will that you must spend every nickel of the money on yourself.

9 There lay the hazard of the game. If, when playing it, you forgot, and listed among your expenditures the rental of a new apartment for your family, for example, you lost your turn to the other player. It was astonishing how many—and some of them among the experts, too—would forfeit all their innings[7] by such slips.

10 It was essential, of course, that it be played in passionate seriousness. Each purchase must be carefully considered and, if

---

4. *begged,* 5. *sluggishly,* 6. *legacy,* 7. *turns*

necessary, supported by argument. There was no zest to playing wildly. Once Annabel had introduced the game to Sylvia, another girl who worked in the office. She explained the rules to Sylvia and then offered her the gambit[8] "What would be the first thing you'd do?" Sylvia had not shown the decency of even a second of hesitation. "Well," she said, "the first thing I'd do, I'd go out and hire somebody to shoot Mrs. Gary Cooper, and then . . . " So it is to be seen that she was no fun.

11   But Annabel and Midge were surely born to be comrades, for Midge played the game like a master from the moment she learned it. It was she who added the touches that made the whole thing cozier. According to Midge's innovations, the eccentric who died and left you the money was not anybody you loved, or, for the matter of that, anybody you even knew. It was somebody who had seen you somewhere and had thought, "That girl ought to have lots of nice things. I'm going to leave her a million dollars when I die." And the death was to be neither untimely nor painful. Your benefactor, full of years and comfortably ready to depart, was to slip softly away during sleep and go right to heaven. These embroideries[9] permitted Annabel and Midge to play their game in the luxury of peaceful consciences.

12   Midge played with a seriousness that was not only proper but extreme. The single strain on the girls' friendship had followed an announcement once made by Annabel that the first thing she would buy with her million dollars would be a silver-fox coat. It was as if she had struck Midge across the mouth. When Midge recovered her breath, she cried that she couldn't imagine how Annabel could do such a thing—silver-fox coats were common! Annabel defended her taste with the retort that they were not common, either. Midge then said that they were so. She added that everybody had a silver-fox coat. She went on, with perhaps a slight loss of head, to declare that she herself wouldn't be caught dead in silver fox.

13   For the next few days, though the girls saw each other as constantly, their conversation was careful and infrequent, and they did not once play their game. Then one morning, as soon as Annabel entered the office, she came to Midge and said that she had changed her mind. She would not buy a silver-fox coat with any part of her million dollars. Immediately on receiving the legacy, she would select a coat of mink.

8. *opening remark,* 9. *here, decorative touches*

14   Midge smiled and her eyes shone. "I think," she said, "you're doing absolutely the right thing."

15   Now, as they walked along Fifth Avenue, they played the game anew. It was one of those days with which September is repeatedly cursed; hot and glaring, with slivers of dust in the wind. People drooped and shambled, but the girls carried themselves tall and walked a straight line, as befitted young heiresses on their afternoon promenade. There was no longer need for them to start the game at its formal opening. Annabel went direct to the heart of it.

16   "All right," she said. "So you've got this million dollars. So what would be the first thing you'd do?"

17   "Well, the first thing I'd do," Midge said, "I'd get a mink coat." But she said it mechanically, as if she were giving the memorized answer to an expected question.

18   "Yes," Annabel said, "I think you ought to. The terribly dark kind of mink." But she, too, spoke as if by rote.[10] It was too hot; fur, no matter how dark and sleek and supple, was horrid to the thoughts.

19   They stepped along in silence for a while. Then Midge's eye was caught by a shop window. Cool, lovely gleamings were there set off by chaste[11] and elegant darkness.

20   "No," Midge said, "I take it back. I wouldn't get a mink coat the first thing. Know what I'd do? I'd get a string of pearls. Real pearls."

21   Annabel's eyes turned to follow Midge's.

22   "Yes," she said, slowly. "I think that's a kind of a good idea. And it would make sense, too. Because you can wear pearls with anything."

23   Together they went over to the shop window and stood pressed against it. It contained but one object—a double row of great, even pearls clasped by a deep emerald around a little pink velvet throat.

24   "What do you suppose they cost?" Annabel said.

25   "Gee, I don't know," Midge said. "Plenty, I guess."

26   "Like a thousand dollars?" Annabel said.

27   "Oh, I guess like more," Midge said. "On account of the emerald."

28   "Well, like ten thousand dollars?" Annabel said.

29   "Gee, I wouldn't even know," Midge said.

30   The devil nudged Annabel in the ribs. "Dare you to go in and price them," she said.

10. *mechanical memorization,*   11. *pure*

31   "Like fun!" Midge said.

32   "Dare you," Annabel said.

33   "Why, a store like this wouldn't even be open this afternoon," Midge said.

34   "Yes, it is so, too," Annabel said. "People just came out. And there's a doorman on. Dare you."

35   "Well," Midge said. "But you've got to come too."

36   They tendered thanks, icily, to the doorman for ushering them into the shop. It was cool and quiet, a broad, gracious room with paneled walls and soft carpet. But the girls wore expressions of bitter disdain,¹² as if they stood in a sty.

37   A slim, immaculate clerk came to them and bowed. His neat face showed no astonishment at their appearance.

38   "Good afternoon," he said. He implied that he would never forget it if they would grant him the favor of accepting his soft-spoken greeting.

39   "Good afternoon," Annabel and Midge said together, and in like freezing accents.

40   "Is there something—?" the clerk said.

41   "Oh, we're just looking," Annabel said. It was as if she flung the words down from a dais.¹³

42   The clerk bowed.

43   "My friend and myself merely happened to be passing," Midge said, and stopped, seeming to listen to the phrase. "My friend here and myself," she went on, "merely happened to be wondering how much are those pearls you've got in your window."

44   "Ah, yes," the clerk said. "The double rope. That is two hundred and fifty thousand dollars, Madam."

45   "I see," Midge said.

46   The clerk bowed. "An exceptionally beautiful necklace," he said. "Would you care to look at it?"

47   "No, thank you," Annabel said.

48   "My friend and myself merely happened to be passing," Midge said.

49   They turned to go; to go, from their manner, where the tumbrel¹⁴ awaited them. The clerk sprang ahead and opened the door. He bowed as they swept by him.

50   The girls went on along the Avenue and disdain was still on their faces.

51   "Honestly!" Annabel said. "Can you imagine a thing like that?"

---

12. *contempt,* 13. *raised platform,* 14. *cart used to carry prisoners to execution*

52   "Two hundred and fifty thousand dollars!" Midge said. "That's a quarter of a million dollars right there!"

53   "He's got his nerve!" Annabel said.

54   They walked on. Slowly the disdain went, slowly and completely as if drained from them, and with it went the regal carriage and tread. Their shoulders dropped and they dragged their feet; they bumped against each other, without notice or apology, and caromed[15] away again. They were silent and their eyes were cloudy.

55   Suddenly Midge straightened her back, flung her head high, and spoke, clear and strong.

56   "Listen, Annabel," she said. "Look. Suppose there was this terribly rich person, see? You don't know this person, but this person has seen you somewhere and wants to do something for you. Well, it's a terribly old person, see? And so this person dies, just like going to sleep, and leaves you ten million dollars. Now, what would be the first thing you'd do?"

---

15. *collided*

Understanding the Text: *Analysis*

Answer the questions below with a partner or in a small group.

1. What impression do you get of the girls from reading about what they eat in paragraph 1?

2. If, in paragraph 1, you learn that the girls eat what they like and yet have flat bellies and "flanks as lean as . . . young Indian braves," how old would you guess they are?

3. What work do the girls do?

4. What do you learn about their love lives, in paragraph 3?

5. Paragraph 4 depicts the two girls as "conspicuous and cheap and charming." What is your opinion of the way the girls "adorn" themselves? Is this still typical today?

6. In paragraph 5, the author describes the girls walking to Fifth Avenue, where "with their skirts swirled by the hot wind, they received audible admiration." What does this mean? What is your reaction to this behavior?

7. As Parker states in paragraph 7, the game of "what-would-you-do-if-you-had-a-million dollars" is an "ancient sport." But Annabel and Midge have stipulated that all the imaginary money must be spent on oneself. What does that make you feel the two girls are like?

8. On the other hand, in paragraph 9, the girls do not approve when a coworker suggests that with the money she would pay someone to murder actor Gary Cooper's wife. What does this say about the "morals" of Annabel and Midge?

9. In paragraph 12, why do you think Midge so strongly opposes her friend's suggestion that she buy a silver-fox coat with the million dollars?

10. In paragraphs 13–14, when Annabel decides instead to purchase a mink coat, Midge replies that "you're doing absolutely the right thing." Why does Midge use the present continuous verb tense?

11. Why do you think Annabel and Midge walk along Fifth Avenue as proudly as "young heiresses" in paragraph 15, and

wear "expressions of bitter disdain" when they enter the expensive jewelry store, in paragraph 36?

12. In paragraph 43, Midge tells the jewelry clerk that she and Annabel are only passing by. Note the grammar of the sentence she utters. Is Midge speaking correctly?

13. After the girls learn the price of the necklace, their disdain changes. Parker describes the girls in paragraph 54 as they walk. Why does their attitude change?

14. In reading the last paragraph of the story, what do you suppose happens to Annabel and Midge afterward?

Looking at Language: *Conditional*

1. In "The Standard of Living," Annabel's and Midge's game of "what-would-you-do-if-you-had-a-million dollars" is an imaginative way for the two girls to escape the ordinariness of their everyday lives.

This game requires Parker to utilize conditional verbs and expressions extensively, as in the example below. Discuss the example with the class, and then answer the questions with a partner.

Example:

"If, when playing it, you forgot, and listed among your expenditures the rental of a new apartment for your family, for example, you lost your turn to the other player. It was astonishing how many—and some of them among the experts, too—would forfeit all their innings[1] by such slips." (paragraph 9)

a. Which type of conditional situation (real or unreal, present or past tense) is reflected in the example above?
b. Find at least three other sentences in the story which use these conditional patterns. Identify them by paragraph number.

2. The two girls also have an imaginary view of their status in relation to other people they meet. Throughout the story, one finds another type of conditional expression—"as if"—used because the two girls walk and act "as if" they are wealthy

---

1. *turns*

young women, rather than office workers. "As if" is a way to compare the girls' real status with their perception of their status. Recall the words the author uses to describe the way the girls walk down Fifth Avenue in the example below. Examine the example by answering the first question and related questions below with your partner.

Example:

". . . they held their heads higher and set their feet with exquisite precision, as if they stepped over the necks of peasants." (paragraph 5)

a. In the example sentence above, do the two girls really "step over the necks of peasants" when they walk? What does this mean? How do the girls feel about themselves as compared with the people they passed on Fifth Avenue?

b. Look at the verb tenses in the example above. Why is the time of the verb "held" the same as "stepped"?

c. Now, read over the next passage, which contains another example of "as if."

"The single strain on the girls' friendship had followed an announcement once made by Annabel that the first thing she would buy with her million dollars would be a silver-fox coat. It was as if she had struck Midge across the mouth." (paragraph 12)

Why are the verbs "was" and "had struck" different in time? What can you deduce about the tense of verbs in expressions with "as if"?

d. Find the "as if" sentences in paragraphs 36 and 41. Discuss the verb tenses used before and after the "as if" and determine why they are the same or different in time.

e. With your partner, write two original sentences that describe how Annabel and Midge behaved, using "as if."

f. "As if" can also be used with a present tense verb, as in the slang expression, "You look as if you saw a ghost." What do you think this saying means? Why do you think the verbs "look" and "saw" differ in time?

With a partner, complete the tasks below to reinforce your vocabulary by studying words that have related meanings.

arrogant (par. 1)   regal (par. 54)

1. Look at the two descriptive words above. What do they mean? How are they related in meaning?

    Reexamine their contexts. In paragraph 1:
    "Annabel and Midge came out of the tea room with the arrogant slow gait (walk) of the leisured, for their Saturday afternoon stretched ahead of them."

    How does the word "arrogant" describe how the two girls behave? Find the paragraph in which "regal" appears and discuss how the word characterizes Annabel and Midge.

2. Next, to expand your vocabulary further, generate other adjectives with your partner that describe how self-important people act.

    To help you generate related vocabulary items, imagine a very wealthy woman interacting with her servant, or a famous actor talking with a fan. Write down adjectives that would describe the woman's or the actor's behavior. Write the definitions of these descriptive words, and check your guesses in a dictionary. Then, exchange lists with other classmates and discuss them.

Word _____

Guessed Definition _____

Real Definition _____

Word _____

Guessed Definition _____

Real Definition _____

Word _____

Guessed Definition _____

Real Definition _____

Word _____

Guessed Definition _____

Real Definition _____

Word _____

Guessed Definition _____

Real Definition _____

Word _____

Guessed Definition _____

Real Definition _____

Word _____

Guessed Definition _____

Real Definition _____

Word _____

Guessed Definition _____

Real Definition _____

Literary Concepts: *Narrator and Theme*

1. As we have found with previous readings, the narrator or
   storyteller brings to a story his or her subjective viewpoint as
   well as his or her knowledge of the events and characters. A
   story may be written from the perspective of a major or minor
   character, for example, or it may be told by an omniscient
   person who may or may not participate in the story events.
   The role of the narrator in the story, of course, determines
   whether the story is told with the first person "I" or "we," the
   second person "you," or the third person "he/she" or "they."
   With a partner, consider these questions below, which deal
   with the narrator of "The Standard of Living."

a. Who is the narrator of the story?

b. Is the story told in first, second, or third person?

c. What effect do you think the type of narration used has on the story? Would the story be different if Annabel or Midge had told it? How?

2. In Chapter Three, you examined themes in "The Corduroy Pants" by Erskine Caldwell by discovering levels of meaning in the story. You can see that "The Standard of Living," on the literal, or concrete, level is a story of two young working girls, Annabel and Midge, who amuse themselves by playing a wishing game. But, as with Caldwell's story, you can assume that Dorothy Parker meant her story to have another level or levels of meaning than merely a tale of two girls. On the symbolic level, Annabel and Midge could represent other similar people, or their game could represent other wishes or desires by people of a certain group or of a certain time period. Universal themes you might derive from the story would be those ideas, characteristics, or emotions that apply to all people.

Discuss the questions below with a partner and decide which symbolic themes may exist in "The Standard of Living."

a. Do Annabel and Midge act like young girls in your country or are they characteristically American? Why?

b. Why do the two girls play their game?

c. What symbolic (historical, social, etc.) themes can you identify in this story? In other words, what other groups, perhaps in the 1920s, or in the United States, or in the same social group, might Annabel and Midge symbolize? What do the girls have in common with these groups?

d. What universal themes can you find, that is, what universal emotions or needs does the girls' behavior illustrate?

Culture Point: *The American Dream*

The title of this story, "The Standard of Living," focuses the reader's attention from the onset on money. The daydream that fills Annabel and Midge's thoughts is that they might one day become rich through a lucky inheritance. Many Americans believe in "the American dream" that with hard work, opportunity, and a little luck, they will attain a comfortable "standard of living," and, perhaps, even become rich. Many immigrants to this country expect to find a land of opportunity where their dreams

will be realized. This "dream" has different meanings; some believe it will come true, while others doubt.

Discuss "the American dream" with your group mates:

1. Do you believe in "the American dream"?

2. What did you hear about the standard of living in this country that you found to be true/untrue after you arrived here?

3. Is it healthy to dream about improving your living standard? Why or why not?

4. How do the opportunities here compare with the opportunities in your country?

5. Is standard of living the most important measure of a successful life? If not, what is?

READING JOURNAL

In your reading journal, respond to the story by answering one or more of these questions.

1. Do you like the characters in this story? Why or why not?

2. Do you enjoy daydreaming? Are your daydreams similar to the girls'?

VIDEO

Dorothy Parker's story of two working girls with active imaginations is similar in theme to other films in which the characters create imaginary worlds to escape the ordinariness of their real lives. On your own, or with your class, you may wish to view scenes from the following video and compare the daydreams of the character with Annabel and Midge's. In *The Secret Life of Walter Mitty* (1968), based on a story by American author James Thurber, a husband daydreams to avoid his overbearing wife.

"Well, it seems that Harry the Horse and Little Isadore and Spanish John wish to get the money out of the safe, but none of them knows anything about opening safes, and while they are standing around over in Brooklyn talking over what is to be done in this emergency Harry suddenly remembers that Big Butch is once in the business of opening safes for a living."

CHAPTER FIVE

Butch Minds the Baby

by Damon Runyon

About the Author

Damon Runyon (1880–1946) wrote about the adventures of gamblers and gangsters in New York City with a comic, slang style. His short story collections include *Guys and Dolls* (1932), *Blue Plate Special* (1934), and *Money from Home* (1935). Born in Manhattan, Kansas, Runyon wrote for various newspapers before coming to New York in 1911 as a sports writer for the *New York American.*

At First Glance

1. Read the title of the story. What does it mean to "mind" a baby? What do you think the story will be about, based on the title?

2. Read the first paragraph. Where is Brooklyn? What do the names Harry the Horse, Little Isadore, and Spanish John suggest to you? Who could the narrator, the "I" in the first paragraph, be?

The Writer's Perspective

1. Runyon described New York City gamblers and gangsters in a comic way. If a story were written about such people today, how would these criminals be portrayed? As you read Runyon's story, think about how he viewed the gangsters of the 1920s and 1930s.

2. Also, as you read the story, notice that when the criminals speak, they use formal language and no verb contractions. If these characters supposedly do disrespectable work, why do you suppose they talk in such a formal way?

Butch Minds the Baby

by Damon Runyon

1   *O*ne evening along about seven o'clock I am sitting in Mindy's restaurant putting on the gefillte fish,[1] which is a dish I am very fond of, when in comes three parties[2] from Brooklyn wearing caps[3] as follows: Harry the Horse, Little Isadore and Spanish John.

2   Now these parties are not such parties as I will care to have much truck[4] with, because I often hear rumors about them that are very discreditable, even if the rumors are not true. In fact, I hear that many citizens of Brooklyn will be very glad indeed to see Harry the Horse, Little Isadore and Spanish John move away from there, as they are always doing something that is considered a knock to the community, such as robbing people, or maybe shooting or stabbing them, and throwing pineapples,[5] and carrying on generally.

3   I am really much surprised to see these parties on Broadway, as it is well known that the Broadway coppers just naturally love to shove such parties around, but here they are in Mindy's, and there I am, so of course I give them a very large hello, as I never wish to seem inhospitable, even to Brooklyn parties. Right away they come over to my table and sit down, and Little Isadore reaches out and spears himself a big hunk of my gefillte fish with his fingers, but I overlook this, as I am using the only knife on the table.

4   Then they all sit there looking at me without saying anything, and the way they look at me makes me very nervous indeed. Finally I figure that maybe they are a little embarrassed being in a high-class spot such as Mindy's, with legitimate people around and about, so I say to them, very polite: "It is a nice night."

5   "What is nice about it?" asks Harry the Horse, who is a thin man with a sharp face and sharp eyes.

6   Well, now that it is put up to me in this way, I can see there

---

1. *chopped fish,* 2. *persons,* 3. *names,* 4. *dealings, slang,* 5. *hand grenades, slang*

is nothing so nice about the night, at that, so I try to think of something else jolly to say, while Little Isadore keeps spearing at my gefillte fish with his fingers, and Spanish John nabs one of my potatoes.

7   "Where does Big Butch live?" Harry the Horse asks.

8   "Big Butch?" I say, as if I never hear the name before in my life, because in this man's town it is never a good idea to answer any question without thinking it over, as some time you may give the right answer to the wrong guy, or the wrong answer to the right guy. "Where does Big Butch live?" I ask them again.

9   "Yes, where does he live?" Harry the Horse says, very impatient. "We wish you to take us to him."

10   "Now wait a minute, Harry," I say. I am now more nervous than somewhat. "I am not sure I remember the exact house Big Butch lives in, and furthermore I am not sure Big Butch will care to have me bringing people to see him, especially three at a time, and especially from Brooklyn. You know Big Butch has a very bad disposition, and there is no telling what he may say to me if he does not like the idea of me taking you to him."

11   "Everything is very kosher,"[6] Harry the Horse says. "You need not be afraid of anything whatever. We have a business proposition for Big Butch. It means a nice score for him, so you take us to him at once, or the chances are I will have to put the arm on[7] somebody around here."

12   Well, as the only one around there for him to put the arm on at this time seems to be me, I can see where it will be good policy for me to take these parties to Big Butch, especially as the last of my gefillte fish is just going down Little Isadore's gullet,[8] and Spanish John is finishing up my potatoes, and is dunking a piece of rye bread in my coffee, so there is nothing more for me to eat.

13   So I lead them over into West Forty-ninth Street, near Tenth Avenue, where Big Butch lives on the ground floor of an old brownstone-front house, and who is sitting out on the stoop[9] but Big Butch himself. In fact, everybody in the neighborhood is sitting out on the front stoops over there, including women and children, because sitting out on the front stoops is quite a custom in this section.

14   Big Butch is peeled down to his undershirt and pants, and he has no shoes on his feet, as Big Butch is a guy who likes his comfort. Furthermore, he is smoking a cigar, and laid out on the stoop beside him on a blanket is a little baby with not much

---

6. *proper, slang,* 7. *physically harm,* 8. *throat,* 9. *front steps*

clothes on. This baby seems to be asleep, and every now and then Big Butch fans it with a folded newspaper to shoo away the mosquitoes that wish to nibble on the baby. These mosquitoes come across the river from the Jersey side on hot nights and they seem to be very fond of babies.

15   "Hello, Butch," I say, as we stop in front of the stoop.

16   "Sh-h-h-h!" Butch says, pointing at the baby, and making more noise with his shush than an engine blowing off steam. Then he gets up and tiptoes down to the sidewalk where we are standing, and I am hoping that Butch feels all right, because when Butch does not feel so good he is apt to be very short[10] with one and all. He is a guy of maybe six foot two and a couple of feet wide, and he has big hairy hands and a mean look.

17   In fact, Big Butch is known all over this man's town as a guy you must not monkey with[11] in any respect, so it takes plenty of weight off of me when I see that he seems to know the parties from Brooklyn, and nods at them very friendly, especially Harry the Horse. And right away Harry states a most surprising proposition to Big Butch.

18   It seems that there is a big coal company which has an office in an old building down in West Eighteenth Street, and in this office is a safe, and in this safe is the company pay roll of twenty thousand dollars cash money. Harry the Horse knows the money is there because a personal friend of his who is the paymaster for the company puts it there late this very afternoon.

19   It seems that the paymaster enters into a dicker[12] with Harry the Horse and Little Isadore and Spanish John for them to slug[13] him while he is carrying the pay roll from the bank to the office in the afternoon, but something happens that they miss connections on the exact spot, so the paymaster has to carry the sugar[14] on to the office without being slugged, and there it is now in two fat bundles.

20   Personally it seems to me as I listen to Harry's story that the paymaster must be a very dishonest character to be making deals to hold still while he is being slugged and the company's sugar taken away from him, but of course it is none of my business, so I take no part in the conversation.

21   Well, it seems that Harry the Horse and Little Isadore and Spanish John wish to get the money out of the safe, but none of them knows anything about opening safes, and while they are

---

10. *rude, slang*, 11. *play with idly, slang*, 12. *argument*, 13. *hit*, 14. *money*

standing around over in Brooklyn talking over what is to be done in this emergency Harry suddenly remembers that Big Butch is once in the business of opening safes for a living.

22   In fact, I hear afterwards that Big Butch is considered the best safe opener east of the Mississippi River in his day, but the law finally takes to sending him to Sing Sing[15] for opening these safes, and after he is in and out of Sing Sing three different times for opening safes Butch gets sick and tired of the place, especially as they pass what is called the Baumes Law in New York, which is a law that says if a guy is sent to Sing Sing four times hand running,[16] he must stay there the rest of his life, without any argument about it.

23   So Big Butch gives up opening safes for a living, and goes into business in a small way, such as running[17] beer, and handling a little Scotch now and then, and becomes an honest citizen. Furthermore, he marries one of the neighbor's children over on the West Side by the name of Mary Murphy, and I judge the baby on this stoop comes of this marriage between Big Butch and Mary because I can see that it is a very homely baby, indeed. Still, I never see many babies that I consider rose geraniums for looks, anyway.

24   Well, it finally comes out that the idea of Harry the Horse and Little Isadore and Spanish John is to get Big Butch to open the coal company's safe and take the payroll money out, and they are willing to give him fifty per cent of the money for his bother, taking fifty per cent for themselves for finding the plant, and paying all the overhead,[18] such as the paymaster, out of their bit, which strikes me as a pretty fair sort of deal for Big Butch. But Butch only shakes his head.

25   "It is old-fashioned stuff," Butch says. "Nobody opens pete boxes[19] for a living any more. They make the boxes too good, and they are all wired up with alarms and are a lot of trouble generally. I am in a legitimate business now and going along. You boys know I cannot stand another fall, what with being away three times already, and in addition to this I must mind the baby. My old lady[20] goes to Mrs. Clancy's wake[21] tonight up in the Bronx, and the chances are she will be there all night, as she is very fond of wakes, so I must mind little John Ignatius Junior."

26   "Listen, Butch," Harry the Horse says, "this is a very soft pete. It is old-fashioned, and you can open it with a toothpick. There

15. *slang name for a state prison in Ossining, N.Y.,* 16. *in a row,*
17. *transporting, slang,* 18. *operating expenses,* 19. *safes,* 20. *wife, slang,*
21. *festivity for a dead person*

are no wires on it, because they never put more than a dime in it before in years. It just happens they have to put the twenty G's[22] in it tonight because my pal the paymaster makes it a point not to get back from the jug[23] with the scratch[24] in time to pay off today, especially after he sees we miss out on him. It is the softest touch[25] you will ever know, and where can a guy pick up ten G's like this?"

27   I can see that Big Butch is thinking the ten G's over very seriously, at that, because in these times nobody can afford to pass up ten G's, especially a guy in the beer business, which is very, very tough just now. But finally he shakes his head again and says like this:

28   "No," he says, "I must let it go, because I must mind the baby. My old lady is very, very particular about this, and I dast not[26] leave little John Ignatius Junior for a minute. If Mary comes home and finds I am not minding the baby she will put the blast on me[27] plenty. I like to turn a few honest bobs[28] now and then as well as anybody, but," Butch says, "John Ignatius Junior comes first with me."

29   Then he turns away and goes back to the stoop as much as to say he is through arguing, and sits down beside John Ignatius Junior again just in time to keep a mosquito from carrying off one of John's legs. Anybody can see that Big Butch is very fond of this baby, though personally, I will not give you a dime a dozen for babies, male and female.

30   Well, Harry the Horse and Little Isadore and Spanish John are very much disappointed, and stand around talking among themselves, and paying no attention to me, when all of a sudden Spanish John, who never has much to say up to this time, seems to have a bright idea. He talks to Harry and Isadore, and they get all pleasured up over what he has to say, and finally Harry goes to Big Butch.

31   "Sh-h-h-h!" Big Butch says, pointing to the baby as Harry opens his mouth.

32   "Listen, Butch," Harry says in a whisper, "we can take the baby with us, and you can mind it and work, too."

33   "Why," Big Butch whispers back, "this is quite an idea indeed. Let us go into the house and talk things over."

34   So he picks up the baby and leads us into his joint and gets out some pretty fair beer, though it is needled a little,[29] at that,

---

22. *thousand dollars, slang; abbreviation for "grand,"* 23. *jail, slang,* 24. *money,* 25. *making a loan, slang,* 26. *dare not, old,* 27. *get angry with me, slang,* 28. *make money, slang,* 29. *strengthened with alcohol, slang*

and we sit around the kitchen chewing the fat[30] in whispers. There is a crib in the kitchen, and Butch puts the baby in his crib, and it keeps on snoozing away first rate while we are talking. In fact, it is sleeping so sound that I am commencing to figure that Butch must give it some of the needled beer he is feeding us, because I am feeling a little dopey myself.

35   Finally Butch says that as long as he can take John Ignatius Junior with him he sees no reason why he shall not go and open the safe for them, only he says he must have five per cent more to put in the baby's bank when he gets back, so as to round himself up with his ever-loving wife in case of a beef[31] from her over keeping the baby out in the night air. Harry the Horse says he considers this extra five per cent a little strong, but Spanish John, who seems to be a very square guy, says that after all it is only fair to cut the baby in if it is to be with them when they are making the score, and Little Isadore seems to think this is all right, too. So Harry the Horse gives in, and says five per cent it is.

36   Well, as they do not wish to start out until after midnight, and as there is plenty of time, Big Butch gets out some more needled beer, and then he goes looking for the tools with which he opens safes, and which he says he does not see since the day John Ignatius Junior is born, and he gets them out to build the crib.

37   Now this is a good time for me to bid one and all farewell, and what keeps me there is something I cannot tell you to this day, because personally I never before have any idea of taking part in a safe opening, especially with a baby, as I consider such actions very dishonorable. When I come to think things over afterwards, the only thing I can figure is the needled beer, but I wish to say I am really very much surprised at myself when I find myself in a taxicab along about one o'clock in the morning with these Brooklyn parties and Big Butch and the baby.

38   Butch has John Ignatius Junior rolled up in a blanket, and John is still pounding his ear. Butch has a satchel of tools, and what looks to me like a big flat book, and just before we leave the house Butch hands me a package and tells me to be very careful with it. He gives Little Isadore a smaller package, which Isadore shoves into his pistol pocket, and when Isadore sits down in the taxi something goes wa-wa, like a sheep, and Big

---

30. *talking, slang,* 31. *argument, slang*

Butch becomes very indignant[32] because it seems Isadore is sitting on John Ignatius Junior's doll, which says "Mamma" when you squeeze it.

39   It seems Big Butch figures that John Ignatius Junior may wish something to play with in case he wakes up, and it is a good thing for Little Isadore that the mamma doll is not squashed so it cannot say "Mamma" any more, or the chances are Little Isadore will get a good bust in the snoot.[33]

40   We let the taxicab go a block away from the spot we are headed for in West Eighteenth Street, between Seventh and Eighth Avenues, and walk the rest of the way two by two. I walk with Big Butch, carrying my package, and Butch is lugging the baby and his satchel and the flat thing that looks like a book. It is so quiet down in West Eighteenth Street at such an hour that you can hear yourself think, and in fact I hear myself thinking very plain that I am a big sap[34] to be on a job like this, especially with a baby, but I keep going just the same, which shows you what a very big sap I am, indeed.

41   It is agreed before we leave Big Butch's house that Harry the Horse and Spanish John are to stay outside the place as look-outs, while Big Butch is inside opening the safe, and that Little Isadore is to go with Butch. Nothing whatever is said by anybody about where I am to be at any time, and I can see that, no matter where I am, I will still be an outsider, but, as Butch gives me the package to carry, I figure he wishes me to remain with him.

42   It is no bother at all getting into the office of the coal company, which is on the ground floor, because it seems the watchman leaves the front door open, this watchman being a most obliging guy, indeed. In fact he is so obliging that by and by he comes back and lets Harry the Horse and Spanish John tie him up good and tight, and stick a handkerchief in his mouth and chuck[35] him in an areaway next to the office, so nobody will think he has anything to do with opening the safe in case anybody comes around asking.

43   The office looks out on the street, and the safe that Harry the Horse and Little Isadore and Spanish John wish Big Butch to open is standing up against the rear wall of the office facing the street windows. There is one little electric light burning very dim over the safe so that when anybody walks past the place outside, such as a watchman, they can look in through the window and see the safe at all times, unless they are blind. It is not a tall safe,

---

32. *angry,* 33. *nose, slang,* 34. *stupid person, slang,* 35. *throw, slang*

and it is not a big safe, and I can see Big Butch grin when he sees it, so I figure this safe is not much of a safe, just as Harry the Horse claims.

44   Well, as soon as Big Butch and the baby and Little Isadore and me get into the office, Big Butch steps over to the safe and unfolds what I think is the big flat book, and what is it but a sort of screen painted on one side to look exactly like the front of a safe. Big Butch stands this screen up on the floor in front of the real safe, leaving plenty of space in between, the idea being that the screen will keep anyone passing in the street outside from seeing Butch while he is opening the safe, because when a man is opening a safe he needs all the privacy he can get.

45   Big Butch lays John Ignatius Junior down on the floor on the blanket behind the phony safe front and takes his tools out of the satchel and starts to work opening the safe, while Little Isadore and me get back in a corner where it is dark, because there is not room for all of us back of the screen. However, we can see what Big Butch is doing, and I wish to say while I never before see a professional safe opener at work, and never wish to see another, this Butch handles himself like a real artist.

46   He starts drilling into the safe around the combination lock, working very fast and very quiet, when all of a sudden what happens but John Ignatius Junior sits up on the blanket and lets out a squall. Naturally, this is most disquieting to me, and personally I am in favor of beaning[36] John Ignatius Junior with something to make him keep still, because I am nervous enough as it is. But the squalling does not seem to bother Big Butch. He lays down his tools and picks up John Ignatius Junior and starts whispering, "There, there, there, my itty oddleums. Da-dad is here."

47   Well, this sounds very nonsensical to me in such a situation, and it makes no impression whatever on John Ignatius Junior. He keeps on squalling, and I judge he is squalling pretty loud because I see Harry the Horse and Spanish John both walk past the window and look in very anxious. Big Butch jiggles John Ignatius Junior up and down and keeps whispering baby talk to him, which sounds very undignified coming from a high-class safe opener, and finally Butch whispers to me to hand him the package I am carrying.

48   He opens the package, and what is in it but a baby's nursing bottle full of milk. Moreover, there is a little tin stew pan, and Butch hands the pan to me and whispers to me to find a water

---

36. *hitting, slang*

tap somewhere in the joint and fill the pan with water. So I go stumbling around in the dark in a room behind the office and bark[37] my shins several times before I find a tap and fill the pan. I take it back to Big Butch, and he squats there with the baby on one arm, and gets a tin of what is called canned heat out of the package, and lights this canned heat with his cigar lighter, and starts heating the pan of water with the nursing bottle in it.

49   Big Butch keeps sticking his finger in the pan of water while it is heating, and by and by he puts the rubber nipple of the nursing bottle in his mouth and takes a pull at it to see if the milk is warm enough, just like I see dolls who have babies do. Apparently the milk is okay, as Butch hands the bottle to John Ignatius Junior, who grabs hold of it with both hands and starts sucking on the business end. Naturally he has to stop squalling, and Big Butch goes to work on the safe again, with John Ignatius Junior sitting on the blanket, pulling on the bottle and looking wiser than a treeful of owls.

50   It seems the safe is either a tougher job than anybody figures, or Big Butch's tools are not so good, what with being old and rusty and used for building baby cribs, because he breaks a couple of drills and works himself up into quite a sweat without getting anywhere. Butch afterwards explains to me that he is one of the first guys in this country to open safes without explosives, but he says to do this work properly you have to know the safes so as to drill to the tumblers of the lock just right, and it seems that this particular safe is a new type to him, even if it is old, and he is out of practice.

51   Well, in the meantime John Ignatius Junior finishes his bottle and starts mumbling again, and Big Butch gives him a tool to play with, and finally Butch needs this tool and tries to take it away from John Ignatius Junior, and the baby lets out such a squawk that Butch has to let him keep it until he can sneak it away from him, and this causes more delay.

52   Finally, Big Butch gives up trying to drill the safe open, and he whispers to us that he will have to put a little shot in it to loosen up the lock, which is all right with us, because we are getting tired of hanging around and listening to John Ignatius Junior's glug-glugging. As far as I am personally concerned, I am wishing I am home in bed.

53   Well, Butch starts pawing[38] through his satchel looking for something and it seems that what he is looking for is a little bottle of some kind of explosive with which to shake the lock on

---

37. *bump,* 38. *moving his hands, slang*

the safe up some, and at first he cannot find this bottle, but finally he discovers that John Ignatius Junior has it and is gnawing at the cork, and Butch has quite a battle making John Ignatius Junior give it up.

54   Anyway, he fixes the explosive in one of the holes he drills near the combination lock on the safe, and then he puts in a fuse, and just before he touches off the fuse Butch picks up John Ignatius Junior and hands him to Little Isadore, and tells us to go into the room behind the office. John Ignatius Junior does not seem to care for little Isadore, and I do not blame him, at that, because he starts to squirm around quite some in Isadore's arms and lets out a squall, but all of a sudden be comes very quiet indeed, and, while I am not able to prove it, something tells me that Little Isadore has his hand over John Ignatius Junior's mouth.

55   Well, Big Butch joins us right away in the back room, and sound comes out of John Ignatius Junior again as Butch takes him from Little Isadore, and I am thinking that it is a good thing for Isadore that the baby cannot tell Big Butch what Isadore does to him.

56   "I put in just a little bit of a shot," Big Butch says, "and it will not make any more noise than snapping your fingers."

57   But a second later there is a big whoom from the office, and the whole joint shakes, and John Ignatius Junior laughs right out loud. The chances are he thinks it is the Fourth of July.

58   "I guess maybe I put in too big a charge," Big Butch says, and then he rushes into the office with Little Isadore and me after him, and John Ignatius Junior still laughing very heartily for a small baby. The door of the safe is swinging loose, and the whole joint[39] looks somewhat wrecked, but Big Butch loses no time in getting his dukes[40] into the safe and grabbing out two big bundles of cash money, which he sticks inside his shirt.

59   As we go into the street Harry the Horse and Spanish John come running up much excited, and Harry says to Big Butch like this:

60   "What are you trying to do," he says, "wake up the whole town?"

61   "Well," Butch says, "I guess maybe the charge is too strong, at that, but nobody seems to be coming, so you and Spanish John walk over to Eighth Avenue, and the rest of us will walk to Seventh, and if you go along quiet, like people minding their own business, it will be all right."

62   But I judge Little Isadore is tired of John Ignatius Junior's company by this time, because he says he will go with Harry the

---

39. *place, slang,* 40. *hands*

Horse and Spanish John, and this leaves Big Butch and John Ignatius Junior and me to go the other way. So we start moving, and all of a sudden two cops come tearing[41] around the corner toward which Harry and Isadore and Spanish John are going. The chances are the cops hear the earthquake Big Butch lets off and are coming to investigate.

63 But the chances are, too, that if Harry the Horse and the other two keep on walking along very quietly like Butch tells them to, the coppers will pass them up entirely, because it is not likely that coppers will figure anybody to be opening safes with explosives in this neighborhood. But the minute Harry the Horse sees the coppers he loses his nut, and he outs with[42] the old equalizer[43] and starts blasting away, and what does Spanish John do but get his out, too, and open up.

64 The next thing anybody knows, the two coppers are down on the ground with slugs[44] in them, but other coppers are coming from every which direction, blowing whistles and doing a little blasting themselves, and there is plenty of excitement, especially when the coppers who are not chasing Harry the Horse and Little Isadore and Spanish John start poking around the neighborhood and find Harry's pal, the watchman, all tied up nice and tight where Harry leaves him, and the watchman explains that some scoundrels blow open the safe he is watching.

65 All this time Big Butch and me are walking in the other direction toward Seventh Avenue, and Big Butch has John Ignatius in his arms, and John Ignatius is now squalling very loud, indeed. The chances are he is still thinking of the big whoom back there which tickles him so and is wishing to hear some more whooms. Anyway, he is beating his own best record for squalling, and as we go walking along Big Butch says to me like this:

66 "I dast not run," he says, "because if any coppers see me running they will start popping at me and maybe hit John Ignatius Junior, and besides running will joggle the milk up in him and make him sick. My old lady always warns me never to joggle John Ignatius Junior when he is full of milk."

67 "Well, Butch," I say, "there is no milk in me, and I do not care if I am joggled up, so if you do not mind, I will start doing a piece of running at the next corner."

68 But just then around the corner of Seventh Avenue toward which we are headed comes two or three coppers with a big fat

---

41. *running, slang,* 42. *gets out, slang,* 43. *gun, slang,* 44. *bullet wounds, slang*

sergeant with them, and one of the coppers, who is half out of breath as if he has been doing plenty of sprinting,[45] is explaining to the sergeant that somebody blows a safe down the street and shoots a couple of coppers in the getaway.

69 And there is Big Butch, with John Ignatius Junior in his arms and twenty G's in his shirt front and a tough record behind him, walking right up to them.

70 I am feeling very sorry, indeed, for Big Butch, and very sorry for myself, too, and I am saying to myself that if I get out of this I will never associate with anyone but ministers of the gospel as long as I live. I can remember thinking that I am getting a better break than Butch, at that, because I will not have to go to Sing Sing for the rest of my life, like him, and I also remember wondering what they will give John Ignatius Junior, who is still tearing off these squalls, with Big Butch saying: "There, there, there, Daddy's itty woogleums." Then I hear one of the coppers say to the fat sergeant: "We better nail these guys. They may be in on this."

71 Well, I can see it is good-by to Butch and John Ignatius Junior and me, as the fat sergeant steps up to Big Butch, but instead of putting the arm on Butch, the fat sergeant only points at John Ignatius Junior and asks very sympathetic: "Teeth?"

72 "No," Big Butch says. "Not teeth. Colic.[46] I just get the doctor here out of bed to do something for him, and we are going to a drug store to get some medicine."

73 Well, naturally I am very much surprised at this statement, because of course I am not a doctor, and if John Ignatius Junior has colic it serves him right, but I am only hoping that they do not ask for my degree, when the fat sergeant says: "Too bad. I know what it is. I got three of them at home. But," he says, "it acts more like it is teeth than colic."

74 Then as Big Butch and John Ignatius Junior and me go on about our business I hear the fat sergeant say to the copper, very sarcastic: "Yea, of course a guy is out blowing safes with a baby in his arms! You will make a great detective, you will!"

75 I do not see Big Butch for several days after I learn that Harry the Horse and Little Isadore and Spanish John get back to Brooklyn all right, except they are a little nicked up[47] here and there from the slugs the coppers toss at them, while the coppers they clip are not damaged so very much. Furthermore, the

---

45. *running,* 46. *stomach pain in infants,* 47. *hurt, slang*

chances are I will not see Big Butch for several years, if it is left to me, but he comes looking for me one night, and he seems to be all pleasured up about something.

76   "Say," Big Butch says to me, "you know I never give a copper credit for knowing any too much about anything, but I wish to say that this fat sergeant we run into the other night is a very, very smart duck. He is right about it being teeth that is ailing John Ignatius Junior, for what happens yesterday but John cuts in his first tooth."

❋Understanding the Text: *Main Ideas/Plot*

Read the statements below which relate to the main ideas in "Butch Minds the Baby." To check your understanding of the main ideas, mark the statements True, False, or Don't Know. Compare and discuss your responses with a partner. "Correct" any false statements by adding/removing facts. Then order the sentences in the correct chronological order as they occur in the story.

1. Big Butch is a safe opener who is temporarily "retired" from his work.

2. Harry the Horse, Little Isadore, and Spanish John are criminals who ask the narrator of the story to help them locate Big Butch.

3. The three criminals ask Big Butch to rob a bank with them.

4. Big Butch accepts the job immediately.

5. Big Butch decides to take his baby John Ignatius on the job with him.

6. The narrator of the story, a criminal, is eating lunch in a cafe.

7. The police catch the criminals in the end.

8. The three criminals exchange gunfire with the police.

9. Big Butch opens the safe with his tools.

10. The baby, John Ignatius, is very well-behaved while his father is trying to open the safe.

Correct Order:

1. _____   6. _____

2. _____   7. _____

3. _____   8. _____

4. _____   9. _____

5. _____   10. _____

Understanding the Text: *Analysis*

After you have read the story, answer the questions below to help you better understand what you have read.

1. In paragraphs 2 and 3, Runyon introduces the three "parties" from Brooklyn. Reread these paragraphs and explain what kind of characters these three are.

2. The three men ask the narrator to take them to Big Butch's house. What is the narrator's response in paragraphs 8–11? Why do you think the narrator reacts this way?

3. How is Big Butch characterized in paragraph 17?

4. What job do the three men propose?

5. Briefly explain Big Butch's job/personal history as described in paragraphs 22 and 23.

6. What does Big Butch say at first when the three men ask him to take part in the job? Why does he give this answer?

7. What suggestion does Little Isadore make to convince Big Butch to change his mind?

8. Starting in paragraph 33, what do the men do while they are talking over the job?

9. In paragraph 37, the narrator explains his reasons for remaining with the group. Why does he go on the job with them?

10. How does the narrator describe himself in paragraph 40?

11. Scan paragraphs 45 to 54 to find details about what the baby does as his father works on the safe.

12. In paragraph 52, how does Big Butch finally decide to open the safe?

13. In paragraphs 58–59, what do Big Butch and the others do after the explosion?

14. What happens to the three men from Brooklyn in paragraphs 63–64?

15. What do Big Butch, the baby, and the narrator do?

16. In paragraph 74, why doesn't the police sergeant arrest Big Butch and the narrator?

17. In paragraph 75, does the narrator wish to see Big Butch again?

18. What is the cause of the baby's crying, as explained in paragraph 76?

Literary Concept: *Narrator*

The narrator of a story is important because he or she tells the story from his or her viewpoint and with his or her knowledge. The narrator can be a participant in the action of the story, or an outsider who reports the actions.

In some stories, the narration is done in the first person, "I," and the narrator is a main or minor character. Other stories use third-person narration—"he," "she," or "they"—often when the narrator describes the action as an outsider. Furthermore, in longer texts, the narration can change from one person's viewpoint to another.

Answer these questions about "Butch Minds the Baby," which relate to the narrator.

The narrator of "Butch Minds the Baby" is _____,

who lives in _____.

The main characters in the story are _____

_____.

In the story, the narrator is a _____ (major or

minor) character. His relation to the major characters _____

_____.

The profession of the narrator is _____.

Literary Concept: *Characterization*

One element that makes Damon Runyon's stories about life in New York City in the 1930s and 1940s popular today is his skill in characterization. As we read his stories, we want to find out more about the characters he has created from his interesting experiences. Runyon uses many methods to reveal the character and personality of the people in his stories. He explains the character directly in some cases; he also reveals his characters by describing their behavior or others' reactions to them.

Here are the most common methods a writer uses to reveal the personality of a character:

a. direct description of the character
b. description of the character's speech, thoughts, or actions
c. reactions by other characters to the character

With a partner, fill in the sentences below to describe the characters in "Butch Minds the Baby." Afterward, discuss which method has been used to reveal the character's personality.

1. Big Butch is a _____ father. He shows this when

   he _____ and also when he _____.

2. He is _____ his wife. The reader finds this out in

   paragraph _____, which tells us that _____.

3. Butch feels that policemen are _____. Butch shows

   this at the end of the story when _____.

4. Butch is a _____ person because _____. For

   example, when _____, Butch _____.

✽Looking at Language: *Slang*

Runyon's story is filled with colorful slang expressions, most of which are still used today. With a partner, review the following list of words, and identify them as noun, verb, adjective, or adverb. Then use each word or phrase once to complete the sentences below.

monkey with	kosher	joint
sap	old lady	chewing the fat
put the arm on	beef	

1. The narrator took the three "tough guys" to Big Butch's

   house after they threatened to _____ him if he did not cooperate.

2. The three men reassure the narrator that everything is

   _____, meaning that they do not want to hurt Big Butch, only talk to him.

3. Big Butch is described as a big, mean man that a person

   should not _____.

4. On the other hand, Butch is afraid that he will have a

   _____ with his wife if she finds out he has taken the baby out at night.

5. Butch has to mind the baby because his _____ is attending a wake in the Bronx.

6. Butch invites the men to his _____ to drink some beer.

7. As they are _____ in the kitchen, the narrator of the story begins to feel a little drunk, or "dopey."

8. The narrator thinks of himself as a _____ because he is so stupid as to accompany the men to the scene of a crime.

✻Looking at Language: *Verb Tenses*

Damon Runyon's style of telling a story is distinguishable from most other writers by his use of verb tenses.

Read the first sentence of the story:

"One evening along about seven o'clock I am sitting in Mindy's restaurant putting on the gefillte fish[1], which is a dish I am very fond of, when in comes three parties[2] from Brooklyn wearing caps[3] as follows: Harry the Horse, Little Isadore and Spanish John."

What verb tenses does Runyon use?
What is the time of the story?
What verb tenses do you think he should have used?

In this story, as well as in all of Runyon's writing, he tells his stories entirely in the present tense, only rarely using the future tense.

Why do you think he does this? What is the effect? Is his writing formal or informal? What verb tenses do most writers use to tell a story? (Think of the stories was have read thus far in the class.) Is Runyon's style incorrect, or can a writer change grammar "traditions" if he wants to?

With your partner, change the verb tenses in these five sentences taken from the text to traditional narrative style. When you finish, read the altered sentences and discuss how changing the verbs affects the writing.

1. "... personally I never before have any idea of taking part in a safe opening, especially with a baby ..." (par. 37)

2. "... sound comes out of John Ignatius Junior again as Butch takes him from Little Isadore, and I am thinking that it is a good thing for Isadore that the baby cannot tell Big Butch what Isadore does to him." (par. 55)

3. "The chances are the cops hear the earthquake Big Butch lets off and are coming to investigate." (par. 62)

4. "All this time Big Butch and me are walking in the other direction toward Seventh Avenue, and Big Butch has John Ignatius in his arms, and John Ignatius is now squalling very loud, indeed." (par. 65)

---

1. *chopped fish,* 2. *persons,* 3. *names*

Looking at Language: *Verb Forms*

Consider one other feature of Runyon's writing. He uses a great deal of informal language and slang—from "G's" for "thousands of dollars" to "coppers" for "police"—but he does not use contractions, even in dialogue.

For example, in the passage below taken from the story, the narrator and Harry the Horse, a criminal, speak very formally.

With your partner, identify the places in the dialogue where most people would naturally use contractions in their verbs. Also, identify the slang words that exist in contrast to the formal verbs. Discuss why Runyon's characters speak in this unnaturally formal way. What effect do you suppose they are trying to achieve?

The Narrator:
"I am not sure I remember the exact house Big Butch lives in, and furthermore I am not sure Big Butch will care to have me bringing people to see him, especially three at a time, and especially from Brooklyn. You know Big Butch has a very bad disposition, and there is no telling what he may say to me if he does not like the idea of me taking you to him." (par. 10)

Harry the Horse:
"Everything is very kosher," Harry the Horse says. "You need not be afraid of anything whatever. We have a business proposition for Big Butch. It means a nice score for him, so you take us to him at once, or the chances are I will have to put the arm on somebody around here." (par. 11)

Culture Point: *Mobsters in the Media*

Americans have been accused of treating mobsters, rather than police or other "good guys" as heroes in popular media such as stories and films. "Tough guys," like the characters in Damon Runyon's stories have continued to be the stars of popular American movies like *The Godfather* series and *Oscar* (1990).

In small groups, discuss how mobsters are characterized in the popular media. List two or three popular movies, television shows, books, or songs that feature criminals.

1. _____

2. _____

3. _____

Why do you think Americans like mobsters so much? Is this a bad sign of American culture? Do you agree that criminals should be so featured in films, books, etc.? What effect does this have on society, if any?

READING JOURNAL

In your reading journal, respond to "Butch Minds the Baby" by answering one or more of the questions below.

1. Do you like this story?

2. Do you think the criminals should have gotten away with the crime or been caught by the police?

3. Are the main characters in the story good guys or bad guys?

VIDEO

To see and hear the characters who inhabited Damon Runyon's stories about big city "tough guys," view the 1955 musical, *Guys and Dolls*, which starred Marlon Brando, Frank Sinatra, and Jean Simmons. Pay attention to the speech and actions of the main characters and compare them to Harry the Horse, Big Butch, and the others in "Butch Minds the Baby." The film version, *Guys and Dolls*, was inspired by a long-running Broadway musical which was based on Runyon's short stories. In 1991, a theatrical revival of Runyon's stories entitled *Damon Runyon's Tales of Broadway* was presented in New York, and in 1992 *Guys and Dolls* was revived.

Projects: UNIT TWO

Project I: Oral Character Analysis

In the previous unit, you discussed characterization, the methods writers use to reveal the personality and qualities of a character in a story. As mentioned in Chapter Five, the writer reveals the character by direct description; the character's own actions, speech, etc.; and the reactions to the character by other characters.

For this project, you will choose one character from the stories that you have read thus far and speak briefly about one quality or aspect of his or her personality. For example, you may choose Midge from Dorothy Parker's "The Standard of Living." Then, you may wish to discuss Midge's feeling of superiority. This quality is revealed by Midge's own actions: the way she walks down Fifth Avenue, or the way she talks to the jewelry store clerk, for example. In other stories, a character's personality may be revealed by the reactions of other people to the character. For instance, we can recognize the leadership quality of Stumpy, the miner who cares for the baby in Bret Harte's "The Luck of Roaring Camp," by the way he is respected and followed by the other miners. Your assignment will be to choose a character and **one** quality that he or she has. Then, you will need to find specific examples that reveal this quality in the text of the story. In your speech, you will need to read exact quotes from the story, as well as tell parts of the story in your words.

Your speech will be brief, probably two to four minutes. As in all formal speaking assignments, you need to be organized and prepared. First, organize your speech as you do an essay. Second, prepare by practicing the speech at home so that you do not read from your written notes.

Suggested plan for organizing your speech:

I. Introduction

Introduce the character, the story, the author, and the character's role in the story. (You may want to begin by addressing the audience, and introducing the topic with a statement like, "Good morning. Today I would like to discuss Midge, one of the working girls in Dorothy Parker's "The Standard of Living."")

Present the Main Idea: State **one** quality that you think the character displays.

II. Body

Choose **two** or **more** specific examples from the text of the story that show that the character has this quality. (Examples can be stated in your own words, or quoted directly. When you quote directly in your speech, begin the quote by stating "quote" and indicate the end of the quote by stating "end quote.")

III. Conclusion

Restate the main idea. Then, conclude with a comment on the character, i.e., your opinion of the character, or of the story.

Project II: Literary Party

For your second project, you will learn about literature from different cultures, practice English, and have fun.

Think back on your experiences in reading literature. Do you have a favorite writer or character from a story? What appeals to you about this person?

You will have an opportunity to share your literary reading experiences at a Literary Party in which each of you (students and teacher) will assume the identity of a favorite literary figure, that is, a writer, poet, or playwright, or a character from a literary work such as a short story, poem, novel, or play.

At the Literary Party, everyone will try to guess each other's literary identity.

PREPARATIONS:

1. Decide which literary personality you will be. You may choose a writer or character from an American story you have discussed in class or that you have read before, or you may choose a favorite writer or character from the literature of your culture.
2. Research his or her life, or the literature that he or she was or is associated with. (You may choose a literary personality whom you know well; then you will need to do no research. Or you may have to consult textbooks or other sources.)
3. On a piece of paper, write clearly **five simple facts** about your literary personality. You will pin these facts to your clothing and wear them to the party to help everyone guess who you are.
4. If you wish, dress in clothes appropriate for your character.

5. On the day of the party, remember that you are no longer **you**. You **are** the literary character you have chosen. You must act like him or her. You must have the same ideas and values as him or her. When classmates or teachers ask you questions, you must answer as if you were that person.

6. Make sure everyone in your class has the opportunity to read your list of facts and ask you questions to guess your identity.

UNIT THREE

On the Edge

In Unit Three, readers continue to explore themes in two stories that probe the behavior of characters "on the edge" of life, "The Cop and the Anthem" and "Of Missing Persons." Students will find not only engaging action here but also strong themes and an added emphasis on characterization, the development of characters. In addition, poetry is introduced in this unit to expose readers to another literary dimension. Two poems, "Acquainted with the Night" and "Dream Deferred," echo themes about life "on the edge." Finally, the unit culminates in a writing project that builds on analytical skills developed thus far in the text.

"He would be somebody in the world. He would—
Soapy felt a hand laid on his arm. He looked quickly
around into the broad face of a policeman."

CHAPTER SIX

The Cop and the Anthem

by O. Henry

About the Author

O. Henry (1862–1910) was the pen name of William
Sydney Porter. Henry was famous for stories with
sharp, unexpected endings. His own colorful life was
reflected in more than 250 stories. He worked as a
bank teller and a newspaper columnist, among other
trades. Henry spent three years in prison for stealing
bank funds, and wrote many stories in prison. His
stories are often about victims of coincidence or fate,
such as the main character in "The Cop and the

Anthem." His writing is characterized by flowery language and high-level vocabulary.

At First Glance

Read the title of the story. How formal is the word *cop*? What does *anthem* mean? Do these two words go together? How might they tie together into a story?

The Writer's Perspective

1. O. Henry (1862–1910) wrote his story about life in New York City at the turn of the twentieth century. How do you imagine life in New York differed at that time with life there today? How do you imagine relations between people were different?

2. Have you ever gone hungry or spent a night outdoors because you had no money? How would you feel if you had to spend a cold winter's night on the streets? Where would you go if you had no money or friends?

3. Are Americans religious? How would you guess their religious beliefs have changed since around the year 1900?

4. What is the feeling you get from entering a religious building—a church, a mosque, a temple, or a synagogue, for example—if you are religious?

Prereading Vocabulary

With a partner, examine the words and phrases below, which describe the story of "The Cop and the Anthem." Discuss the meanings of the words and look up unfamiliar words in the dictionary. Discuss what the words and phrases suggest about the story.

a dead leaf	park bench
Madison Square	chilling wind
thin coat	Soapy's proud spirit
frayed trousers	charity
a rosy dream	winter quarters

The Cop and the Anthem

by O. Henry

1   On this bench in Madison Square Soapy moved uneasily. When wild geese honk[1] high of nights, and when women without sealskin coats grow kind to their husbands, and when Soapy moves uneasily on his bench in the park, you may know that winter is near at hand.

2   A dead leaf fell in Soapy's lap. That was Jack Frost's[2] card. Jack is kind to the regular denizens[3] of Madison Square, and gives fair warning of his annual call. At the corners of four streets he hands his pasteboard[4] to the North Wind, footman[5] of the mansion of All Outdoors, so that the inhabitants thereof may make ready.

3   Soapy's mind became cognisant[6] of the fact that the time had come for him to resolve himself into a singular Committee of Ways and Means[7] to provide against the coming rigour.[8] And therefore he moved uneasily on his bench.

4   The hibernatorial[9] ambitions of Soapy were not of the highest. In them there were no considerations of Mediterranean cruises, of soporific[10] Southern skies or drifting in the Vesuvian Bay. Three months of the Island was what his soul craved. Three months of assured board and bed and congenial[11] company, safe from Boreas[12] and bluecoats,[13] seemed to Soapy the essence of things desirable.

5   For years the hospitable Blackwell's had been his winter quarters. Just as his more fortunate fellow New Yorkers had bought their tickets to Palm Beach and the Riviera each winter, so Soapy had made his humbler arrangements for his annual

---

1. *call*, 2. *a mythical character who symbolizes cold weather*, 3. *inhabitants*,
4. *sign*, 5. *servant*, 6. *aware; British spelling of cognizant*, 7. *legislative panel*, 8. *hard times; British spelling of rigor*, 9. *relating to hibernation, the annual sleeping period of animals like bears*, 10. *sleep-inducing*,
11. *pleasant*, 12. *the north wind*, 13. *police, slang*

hegira[14] to the Island. And now the time was come. On the previous night three Sabbath newspapers, distributed beneath his coat, about his ankles and over his lap, had failed to repulse the cold as he slept on his bench near the spurting fountain in the ancient square. So the Island loomed big and timely in Soapy's mind. He scorned the provisions made in the name of charity for the city's dependents. In Soapy's opinion the Law was more benign[15] than Philanthropy.[16] There was an endless round of institutions, municipal and eleemosynary,[17] on which he might set out and receive lodging and food accordant with the simple life. But to one of Soapy's proud spirit the gifts of charity are encumbered.[18] If not in coin you must pay in humiliation of spirit for every benefit received at the hands of philanthropy. As Caesar[19] had his Brutus,[20] every bed of charity must have its toll[21] of a bath, every loaf of bread its compensation of a private and personal inquisition.[22] Wherefore it is better to be a guest of the law, which though conducted by rules, does not meddle[23] unduly[24] with a gentleman's private affairs.

6   Soapy, having decided to go to the Island, at once set about accomplishing his desire. There were many easy ways of doing this. The pleasantest was to dine luxuriously at some expensive restaurant; and then, after declaring insolvency,[25] be handed over quietly and without uproar to a policeman. An accommodating magistrate[26] would do the rest.

7   Soapy left his bench and strolled out of the square and across the level sea of asphalt, where Broadway and Fifth Avenue flow together. Up Broadway he turned, and halted at a glittering cafe, where gathered together nightly the choicest products of the grape, the silkworm and the protoplasm.[27]

8   Soapy had confidence in himself from the lowest button of his vest upward. He was shaven, and his coat was decent and his neat black, ready-tied four-in-hand[28] had been presented to him by a lady missionary on Thanksgiving Day. If he could reach a table in the restaurant unsuspected success would be his. The portion of him that would show above the table would raise no doubt in the waiter's mind. A roasted mallard duck, thought Soapy, would be about the thing—with a bottle of Chablis, and then Camembert, a demitasse and a cigar. One dollar for the cigar would be enough. The total would not be so high as to call

---

14. *flight*, 15. *beneficial*, 16. *charity*, 17. *charity*, 18. *burdened*, 19. *Roman emporer*, 20. *general who plotted to murder Caesar*, 21. *price*, 22. *questioning*, 23. *bother*, 24. *unfairly*, 25. *bankruptcy*, 26. *judge*, 27. *living matter*, 28. *tie*

forth any supreme manifestation[29] of revenge from the cafe management; and yet the meal would leave him filled and happy for the journey to his winter refuge.

9   But as Soapy set foot inside the restaurant the head waiter's eye fell upon his frayed[30] trousers and decadent[31] shoes. Strong and ready hands turned him about and conveyed him in silence and haste[32] to the sidewalk and averted[33] the ignoble[34] fate of the menaced[35] mallard.

10   Soapy turned off Broadway. It seemed that his route to the coveted[36] island was not to be an epicurean[37] one. Some other way of entering limbo[38] must be thought.

11   At a corner of Sixth Avenue electric lights and cunningly[39] displayed wares behind plate-glass made a shop window conspicuous.[40] Soapy took a cobble-stone and dashed it through the glass. People came running around the corner, a policeman in the lead. Soapy stood still, with his hands in his pockets, and smiled at the sight of brass buttons.

12   "Where's the man that done that?" inquired the officer excitedly.

13   "Don't you figure out that I might have had something to do with it?" said Soapy, not without sarcasm, but friendly, as one greets good fortune.

14   The policeman's mind refused to accept Soapy even as a clue. Men who smash windows do not remain to parley[41] with the law's minions.[42] They take to their heels.[43] The policeman saw a man half way down the block running to catch a car. With drawn club he joined in pursuit. Soapy, with disgust in his heart, loafed[44] along, twice unsuccessful.

15   On the opposite side of the street was a restaurant of no great pretensions.[45] It catered to large appetites and modest purses. Its crockery[46] and atmosphere were thick; its soup and napery thin. Into this place Soapy took his accusive shoes and telltale trousers without challenge. At a table he sat and consumed beefsteak, flapjacks, doughnuts and pie. And then to the waiter he betrayed the fact that the minutest[47] coin and himself were strangers.

16   "Now, get busy and call a cop," said Soapy. "And don't keep a gentleman waiting."

17   "No cop for youse," said the waiter, with a voice like butter cakes and an eye like the cherry in a Manhattan cocktail. "Hey, Con!"

---

29. *show*, 30. *worn*, 31. *old*, 32. *speed*, 33. *prevented*, 34. *dishonorable*,
35. *threatened*, 36. *desired*, 37. *food-related*, 38. *a place of confinement*,
39. *cleverly*, 40. *attractive*, 41. *talk*, 42. *officials*, 43. *run away, slang*,
44. *walked idly, slang*, 45. *show of extravagance*, 46. *dishes*, 47. *smallest*

18   Next, upon his left ear on the callous[48] pavement two waiters pitched Soapy. He arose, joint by joint, as a carpenter's rule opens, and beat the dust from his clothes. Arrest seemed but a rosy dream. The Island seemed very far away. A policeman who stood before a drug store two doors away laughed and walked down the street.

19   Five blocks Soapy travelled before his courage permitted him to woo[49] capture again. This time the opportunity presented what he fatuously[50] termed to himself a "cinch."[51] A young woman of a modest and pleasing guise[52] was standing before a shop window gazing with sprightly[53] interest at its display of shaving mugs and inkstands, and two yards from the window a large policeman of severe[54] demeanour[55] leaned against a water plug.

20   It was Soapy's design to assume the role of the despicable and execrated[56] "masher." The refined and elegant appearance of his victim and the contiguity[57] of the conscientious[58] cop encouraged him to believe that he would soon feel the pleasant official clutch upon his arm that would insure his winter quarters on the right little, tight little isle.

21   Soapy straightened the lady missionary's ready-made tie, dragged his shrinking cuffs into the open, set his hat at a killing cant[59] and sidled[60] toward the young woman. He made eyes at her, was taken with sudden coughs and "hems," smiled, smirked and went brazenly[61] through the impudent and contemptible[62] litany[63] of the "masher." With half an eye Soapy saw that the policeman was watching him fixedly. The young woman moved away a few steps, and again bestowed[64] her absorbed attention upon the shaving mugs. Soapy followed, boldly stepping to her side, raised his hat and said:

22   "Ah there, Bedelia! Don't you want to come and play in my yard?"

23   The policeman was still looking. The persecuted young woman had but to beckon a finger and Soapy would be practically en route for his insular[65] haven. Already he imagined he could feel the cozy warmth of the station-house. The young woman faced him and, stretching out a hand, caught Soapy's coat sleeve.

24   "Sure, Mike," she said joyfully, "if you'll blow me to a pail of suds.[66] I'd have spoke to you sooner, but the cop was watching."

---

48. *hard*, 49. *seek*, 50. *foolishly*, 51. *easy task, slang*, 52. *appearance*, 53. *lively*, 54. *strict*, 55. *look*, 56. *hateful*, 57. *continuousness*, 58. *dedicated*, 59. *angle*, 60. *moved*, 61. *boldly*, 62. *hateful*, 63. *speech*, 64. *gave*, 65. *protective*, 66. *buy me a beer, slang*

25   With the young woman playing the clinging ivy to his oak[67] Soapy walked past the policeman overcome with gloom. He seemed doomed to liberty.

26   At the next corner he shook off his companion and ran. He halted in the district where by night are found the lightest streets, hearts, vows and librettos.[68] Women in furs and men in greatcoats moved gaily in the wintry air. A sudden fear seized Soapy that some dreadful enchantment had rendered[69] him immune to arrest. The thought brought a little of panic upon him, and when he came upon another policeman lounging grandly in front of a transplendent[70] theatre he caught at the immediate straw of "disorderly conduct."

27   On the sidewalk Soapy began to yell drunken gibberish[71] at the top of his harsh voice. He danced, howled, raved and otherwise disturbed the welkin.[72]

28   The policeman twirled his club, turned his back to Soapy and remarked to a citizen.

29   " 'Tis one of them Yale lads celebratin' the goose egg they give to the Hartford College. Noisy, but no harm. We've instructions to lave them be."

30   Disconsolate, Soapy ceased his unavailing[73] racket.[74] Would never a policeman lay hands on him? In his fancy the Island seemed an unattainable[75] Arcadia.[76] He buttoned his thin coat against the chilling wind.

31   In a cigar store he saw a well-dressed man lighting a cigar at a swinging light. His silk umbrella he had set by the door on entering. Soapy stepped inside, secured the umbrella and sauntered off[77] with it slowly. The man at the cigar light followed hastily.

32   "My umbrella," he said, sternly.

33   "Oh, is it?" sneered Soapy, adding insult to petit larceny.[78] "Well, why don't you call a policeman? I took it. Your umbrella! Why don't you call a cop? There stands one on the corner."

34   The umbrella owner slowed his steps. Soapy did likewise, with a presentiment[79] that luck would again run against him. The policeman looked at the two curiously.

35   "Of course," said the umbrella man—"that is—well, you know how these mistakes occur—I—if it's your umbrella I hope you'll excuse me—I picked it up this morning in a restaurant—If you recognise it as yours, why—I hope you'll—"

---

67. *holding him close, slang*, 68. *songs*, 69. *left*, 70. *decorated*,
71. *nonsensical talk*, 72. *people*, 73. *unproductive*, 74. *noise, slang*,
75. *unreachable*, 76. *region in ancient Greece offering contentment*,
77. *walked off*, 78. *minor theft*, 79. *sense of something about to occur*

36   "Of course it's mine," said Soapy, viciously.

37   The ex-umbrella man retreated. The policeman hurried to assist a tall blonde in an opera cloak across the street in front of a street car that was approaching two blocks away.

38   Soapy walked eastward through a street damaged by improvements. He hurled the umbrella wrathfully[80] into an excavation. He muttered against the men who wear helmets and carry clubs. Because he wanted to fall into their clutches,[81] they seemed to regard him as a king who could do no wrong.

39   At length Soapy reached one of the avenues to the east where the glitter and turmoil[82] was but faint. He set his face down this toward Madison Square, for the homing instinct[83] survives even when the home is a park bench.

40   But on an unusually quiet corner Soapy came to a standstill. Here was an old church, quaint and rambling and gabled. Through one violet-stained window a soft light glowed, where, no doubt, the organist loitered[84] over the keys, making sure of his mastery of the coming Sabbath anthem. For there drifted out to Soapy's ears sweet music that caught and held him transfixed against the convolutions[85] of the iron fence.

41   The moon was above, lustrous and serene; vehicles and pedestrians were few; sparrows twittered sleepily in the eaves[86]— for a little while the scene might have been a country churchyard. And the anthem that the organist played cemented Soapy to the iron fence, for he had known it well in the days when his life contained such things as mothers and roses and ambitions and friends and immaculate[87] thoughts and collars.

42   The conjunction[88] of Soapy's receptive state of mind and the influences about the old church wrought[89] a sudden and wonderful change in his soul. He viewed with swift horror the pit into which he had tumbled, the degraded[90] days, unworthy desires, dead hopes, wrecked faculties and base[91] motives that made up his existence.

43   And also in a moment his heart responded thrillingly to this novel[92] mood. An instantaneous[93] and strong impulse moved him to battle with his desperate fate. He would pull himself out of the mire;[94] he would make a man of himself again; he would conquer the evil that had taken possession of him. There was time; he was comparatively young yet; he would resurrect his old

---

80. *angrily,* 81. *control,* 82. *confusion,* 83. *instinct to return home,*
84. *lingered,* 85. *complicated design,* 86. *edges of the roof,* 87. *clean,*
88. *meeting,* 89. *produced,* 90. *dishonorable,* 91. *primitive,* 92. *new,*
93. *immediate,* 94. *confusion*

eager ambitions and pursue them without faltering.[95] Those solemn but sweet organ notes had set up a revolution in him. Tomorrow he would go into the roaring downtown district and find work. A fur importer had once offered him a place as a driver. He would find him tomorrow and ask for the position. He would be somebody in the world. He would—

44   Soapy felt a hand laid on his arm. He looked quickly around into the broad face of a policeman.

45   "What are you doin' here?" asked the policeman.

46   "Nothin'," said Soapy.

47   "Then come along," said the policeman.

48   "Three months on the island," said the Magistrate in the Police Court the next morning.

---

95. *hesitating*

Understanding the Text: *Main Ideas/Video*

View the Learning Corporation of America film version of the story "The Cop and the Anthem," if it is available in public libraries in your area, or read the story once quickly and answer these questions:

1. Who is Soapy?

2. Where does he want to go and why?

3. How does Soapy plan on getting arrested?

4. Is Soapy a gentleman?

5. How does he feel when he hears the church anthem?

6. O. Henry is famous for his ironic or unexpected endings. Why is Soapy's arrest an example of irony?

If you have viewed the film version of the story, answer these additional questions:

1. How does New York City look in 1904?

2. How does Soapy look at first?

3. How does he look when he goes into a restaurant the second time?

Looking at Language: *Writing Style*

O. Henry's writing style may be described as flowery, because he describes everyday happenings in such a colorful, imaginative style that he will impress and often amuse careful readers. Examine examples of O. Henry's flowery writing style below and match these sentences with the "translations" into simple language in the second column.

1. "The hibernatorial ambitions of Soapy were not of the highest." (paragraph 4)
2. "Three months on the Island was what his soul craved." (paragraph 4)
3. "He scorned the provisions made in the name of charity for the city's dependents." (paragraph 5)
4. "But as Soapy set foot inside the restaurant the head waiter's eye fell upon his frayed trousers and decadent shoes." (paragraph 9)
5. "It seemed that his route to the coveted island was not to be an epicurean one." (10)
6. "Next, upon his left ear on the callous pavement two waiters pitched Soapy." (paragraph 18)
7. "Five blocks Soapy travelled before his courage permitted him to woo capture again." (paragraph 19)
8. "He hurled the umbrella wrathfully into an excavation." (paragraph 38)

a. He threw the umbrella into a hole.
b. Soapy wasn't going to get arrested by not paying to eat.
c. Soapy wanted to spend three months on the Island.
d. Soapy didn't want to spend the winter in paradise.
e. He decided again to try to get arrested after walking a while.
f. The waiter saw Soapy's old pants and shoes when he walked in.
g. Soapy didn't want to accept charity.

🗲Looking at Language: *Vocabulary by Theme*

1. Many vocabulary items in "The Cop and the Anthem" refer to poverty and Soapy's psychological situation. With a partner, examine the items below taken from the text. Define them, consulting a dictionary if necessary. Identify words that are similar in meaning. Then use each word appropriately to complete the sentences that follow.

   insolvency (par. 6)   decadent (par. 9)
   ignoble (par. 9)   mire (par. 43)
   frayed (par. 9)   base (par. 42)
   degraded (par. 42)

   a. Soapy felt bad because he had become a _____ person; he had lost all ambition and disgraced his family.

   b. He wore _____ pants and _____ shoes.

   c. One way he tried to get arrested was to eat in a restaurant and then declare his _____; he thought the owner would then call a policeman because he couldn't pay.

   d. Because Soapy had become a bum, his main concerns were to satisfy his _____ needs, such as food and shelter.

   e. Soapy felt his life was like a _____ because he could not get out of his situation.

   f. Soapy was an _____ character; he had no honor and no purpose in life.

2. Furthermore, one finds in "The Cop and the Anthem" many words that refer to the goal that Soapy is striving for throughout the story: "three months on the Island." Perhaps you have found the vocabulary items in O. Henry's story more difficult than previous stories. The fact that Henry uses synonyms whenever possible, rather than repeat the same word over again, shows his careful attention to word choice. With a partner, examine the words below, which refer to Soapy's "island dream." Define them together, and look up unknown words in the dictionary.

winter quarters (par. 5)   insular haven (par. 23)
winter refuge (par. 8)   cozy warmth (par. 23)
limbo (par. 10)

Literary Concept: *Theme*

Discuss these questions relating to the central ideas, or themes, of "The Cop and the Anthem."

1. On a symbolic level, what central idea does the story present regarding the homeless?

2. Does the story say something about life in a big city?

3. On the universal level, what emotions does Soapy exhibit?

4. What do you think is the main theme of the story?

Culture Point: *The Homeless and the Police*

In "The Cop and the Anthem," O. Henry presents two main character types: the homeless and the police. Examine these passages, which describe both groups, and discuss the questions that follow:

Soapy:
". . . to one of Soapy's proud spirit the gifts of charity are encumbered." ". . . it is better to be a guest of the law, which though conducted by rules, does not meddle unduly with a gentleman's private affairs." (par. 5)
"Soapy had confidence in himself from the lowest button of his vest upward." (par. 8)

The Police:
". . . two yards from the window a large policeman of severe demeanour leaned against a water plug." (par. 19)
"With half an eye Soapy saw that the policeman was watching him fixedly." (par. 21)
". . . he came upon another policeman lounging grandly in front of a transplendent theatre . . . " (par. 26)

1. How does O. Henry characterize Soapy, in general?

2. Does this characterization of a homeless man seem appropriate to you? Do you think most Americans would agree with this portrayal?

3. How does O. Henry portray the different policemen in the story?

4. Do you agree with these portrayals? Do they follow the attitudes that most Americans have toward police, from your observations?

Literary Concept: *Irony*

An ironic situation occurs in literature—as in life—when what is expected or intended does not occur, and what is often most unexpected does occur. As has been mentioned earlier, O. Henry was especially noted for writing stories with ironic endings. Answer the questions below to identify the irony in "The Cop and the Anthem":

1. What does Soapy intend to happen throughout the story?

2. What does he want to happen at the end of the story?

3. What, indeed, does happen at the end of the story?

4. Is this ending unexpected to you?

5. Why is the ending of the story ironic?

READING JOURNAL

Think for a moment about Soapy and others like him who spend their nights on the streets of cities like New York.

Then, write a brief response to one or more of the questions below:

1. Do you pity Soapy?

2. Will Soapy change?

3. Why did Soapy choose to live this life?

4. Do you like this story?

" 'What are you looking for? What do you want?' I
held my breath, then said it. 'Escape.' "

CHAPTER SEVEN

Of Missing Persons

by Jack Finney

About the Author

Jack Finney, a contemporary author, writes fantasies
and science fiction. He won popular acclaim for his
first novel, *The Body Snatchers*, published in 1955 and
made into a popular movie, *The Invasion of the Body
Snatchers*. His stories and novels blend fantasy, humor,
and nostalgia. Finney has also written nonfiction, such
as *Forgotten News: The Crime of the Century and
Other Lost Stories.*

❀The Writer's Perspective

1. Do you believe . . .

   a. that there is life on other planets?
   b. that aliens have visited Earth?
   c. that aliens could be living with us now on Earth?
   d. that it is possible to "time travel" without spaceships?

2. Suppose you had the opportunity to move to a place where you would be happy for the rest of your life and you would have no troubles. What would this "perfect world" of yours be like?

3. Now, suppose you could travel to this place instantly. The only condition to moving there would be that you could never return to your home. You could never see your family and friends again. Would you accept such an offer? What kind of person do you think *would* accept this offer?

4. What is wrong with this world that you would especially like to see changed?

❀At First Glance

1. In paragraph 1, most of the words are italicized. Why?

2. Judging from the first paragraph, what do you think might be in "The Folder"?

3. In paragraph 2, how is life in New York City portrayed?

Of Missing Persons

by Jack Finney

1   *Walk in as though it were an ordinary travel bureau,* the stranger I'd met at a bar had told me. *Ask a few ordinary questions—about a trip you're planning, a vacation, anything like that. Then hint about The Folder a little, but whatever you do, don't mention it directly; wait till he brings it up himself. And if he doesn't, you might as well forget it. If you can. Because you'll never see it; you're not the type, that's all. And if you ask about it, he'll just look at you as though he doesn't know what you're talking about.*

2   I rehearsed it all in my mind, over and over, but what seems possible at night over a beer isn't easy to believe on a raw, rainy day, and I felt like a fool, searching the store fronts for the street number I'd memorized. It was noon hour, West 42nd Street, New York, rainy and windy; and like half the men around me, I walked with a hand on my hatbrim, wearing an old trench coat, head bent into the slanting rain, and the world was real and drab, and this was hopeless.

3   Anyway, I couldn't help thinking, who am I to see The Folder, even if there is one? Name? I said to myself, as though I were already being asked. It's Charley Ewell, and I'm a young guy who works in a bank; a teller. I don't like the job; I don't make much money, and I never will. I've lived in New York for over three years and haven't many friends. What the hell, there's really nothing to say—I see more movies than I want to, read too many books, and I'm sick of meals alone in restaurants. I have ordinary abilities, looks and thoughts. Does that suit you; do I qualify?

4   Now I spotted it, the address in the two-hundred block, an old, pseudo-modernized office building, tired, outdated, refusing to admit it but unable to hide it. New York is full of them west of Fifth.

5   I pushed through the brass-framed glass doors into the tiny lobby, paved with freshly mopped, permanently dirty tile. The green-painted walls were lumpy[1] from old plaster repairs; in a

---

1. *uneven*

chrome frame hung a little wall directory—white celluloid[2] easily-changed letters on a black felt background. There were some twenty-odd names, and I found "Acme Travel Bureau" second on the list, between "A-1 Mimeo" and "Ajax Magic Supplies." I pressed the bell beside the old-style open-grille elevator door; it rang high up in the shaft. There was a long pause, then a thump, and the heavy chains began rattling slowly down toward me, and I almost turned and left—this was insane.

6   But upstairs the Acme office had divorced itself from the atmosphere of the building. I pushed open the pebble-glass door, walked in, and the big square room was bright and clean, fluorescent-lighted. Beside the wide double windows, behind a counter, stood a tall, gray-haired, grave-looking man, a telephone at his ear. He glanced up, nodded to beckon[3] me in, and I felt my heart pumping—he fitted the description exactly. "Yes, United Air Lines," he was saying into the phone. "Flight"—he glanced at a paper on the glass-topped counter—"seven-o-three, and I suggest you check in forty minutes early."

7   Standing before him now, I waited, leaning on the counter, glancing around; he was the man, all right, and yet this was just an ordinary travel agency: big bright posters on the walls, metal floor racks full of folders, printed schedules under the glass on the counter. This is just what it looks like and nothing else, I thought, and again I felt like a fool.

8   "Can I help you?" Behind the counter the tall gray-haired man was smiling at me, replacing the phone, and suddenly I was terribly nervous.

9   "Yes." I stalled for time, unbuttoning my raincoat. Then I looked up at him again and said, "I'd like to—get away." You fool, that's too fast! I told myself. Don't rush it. I watched in a kind of panic to see what effect my answer had had, but he didn't flick an eyelash.

10   "Well, there are a lot of places to go," he said politely. From under the counter he brought out a long, slim folder and laid it on the glass, turning it right side up for me. "Fly to Buenos Aires—Another World!" it said in a double row of pale green letters across the top.

11   I looked at it long enough to be polite. It showed a big silvery plane banking over a harbor at night, a moon shining on the water, mountains in the background. Then I just shook my head; I was afraid to talk, afraid I'd say the wrong thing.

12   "Something quieter, maybe?" He brought out another folder:

---

2. *plastic*, 3. *signal*

thick old tree trunks, rising way up out of sight, sunbeams slanting down through them—"The Virgin Forests of Maine, via Boston and Maine Railroad." "Or"—he laid a third folder on the glass—"Bermuda is nice just now." This one said, "Bermuda, Old World in the New."

13   I decided to risk it. "No," I said, and shook my head. "What I'm really looking for is a permanent place. A new place to live and settle down in." I stared directly into his eyes. "For the rest of my life." Then my nerve failed me, and I tried to think of a way to backtrack.

14   But he only smiled pleasantly and said, "I don't know why we can't advise you on that." He leaned forward on the counter, resting on his forearms, hands clasped; he had all the time in the world for me, his posture conveyed.[4] "What are you looking for; what do you want?"

15   I held my breath, then said it. "Escape."

16   "From what?"

17   "Well—" Now I hesitated; I'd never put it into words before. "From New York, I'd say. And cities in general. From worry. And fear. And the things I read in my newspapers. From loneliness." And then I couldn't stop, though I knew I was talking too much, the words spilling out. "From never doing what I really want to do or having much fun. From selling my days just to stay alive. From life itself—the way it is today, at least." I looked straight at him and said softly, "From the world."

18   Now he was frankly[5] staring, his eyes studying my face intently with no pretense[6] of doing anything else, and I knew in a moment he'd shake his head and say, "Mister, you better get to a doctor." But he didn't. He continued to stare, his eyes examining my forehead now. He was a big man, his gray hair crisp and curling, his lined face very intelligent, very kind; he looked the way ministers should look; he looked the way all fathers should look.

19   He lowered his gaze to look into my eyes and beyond them; he studied my mouth, my chin, the line of my jaw, and I had the sudden conviction[7] that without any difficulty he was learning a great deal about me, more than I knew myself. Suddenly he smiled and placed both elbows on the counter, one hand grasping the other fist and gently massaging it. "Do you like people? Tell the truth, because I'll know if you aren't."

20   "Yes. It isn't easy for me to relax though, and be myself, and make friends."

---

4. *communicated,* 5. *openly,* 6. *disguise,* 7. *belief*

21   He nodded gravely, accepting that. "Would you say you're a reasonably decent kind of man?"

22   "I guess so; I think so." I shrugged.

23   "Why?"

24   I smiled wryly[8]; this was hard to answer. "Well—at least when I'm not, I'm usually sorry about it."

25   He grinned at that, and considered it for a moment or so. Then he smiled—deprecatingly,[9] as though he were about to tell a little joke that wasn't too good. "You know," he said casually, "we occasionally get people in here who seem to be looking for pretty much what you are. So just as a sort of little joke—"

26   I couldn't breathe. This was what I'd been told he would say if he thought I might do.

27   "—we've worked up a little folder. We've even had it printed. Simply for our own amusement, you understand. And for occasional clients like you. So I'll have to ask you to look at it here if you're interested. It's not the sort of thing we'd care to have generally known."

28   I could barely whisper. "I'm interested."

29   He fumbled[10] under the counter, then brought out a long, thin folder, the same size and shape as the others, and slid it over the glass toward me.

30   I looked at it, pulling it closer with a finger tip, almost afraid to touch it. The cover was dark blue, the shade of a night sky, and across the top in white letters it said, "Visit Enchanting Verna!" The blue cover was sprinkled with white dots—stars— and in the lower left corner was a globe, the world, half sur-rounded by clouds. At the upper right, just under the word "Verna," was a star larger and brighter than the others; rays shot out from it, like those from a star on a Christmas card. Across the bottom of the cover it said, "Romantic Verna, where life is the way it *should* be." There was a little arrow beside the legend, meaning Turn the page.

31   I turned, and the folder was like most travel folders inside— there were pictures and text, only these were about "Verna" instead of Paris, or Rome, or the Bahamas. And it was beautifully printed; the pictures looked real. What I mean is, you've seen color stereopticon pictures? Well, that's what these were like, only better, far better. In one picture you could see dew glisten-ing on grass, and it looked wet. In another, a tree trunk seemed to curve out of the page, in perfect detail, and it was a shock to touch it and feel smooth paper instead of the rough actuality of

---

8. *humorously,* 9. *disapprovingly,* 10. *searched*

bark. Miniature human faces, in a third picture, seemed about to speak, the lips moist and alive, the eyeballs shining, the actual texture of skin right there on paper; and it seemed impossible, as you stared, that the people wouldn't move and speak.

32   I studied a large picture spreading across the upper half of two open pages. It seemed to have been taken from the top of a hill; you saw the land dropping away at your feet far down into a valley, then rising up again, way over the other side. The slopes of both hills were covered with forest, and the color was beautiful, perfect; there were miles of green, majestic trees, and you knew as you looked that this forest was virgin, almost untouched. Curving through the floor of the valley, far below, ran a stream, blue from the sky in most places; here and there, where the current broke around massive boulders, the water was foaming white; and again it seemed that if you'd only look closely enough you'd be certain to see that stream move and shine in the sun. In clearings beside the stream there were shake-roofed cabins, some of logs, some of brick or adobe. The caption under the picture simply said, "The Colony."

33   "Fun fooling around with a thing like that," the man behind the counter murmured, nodding at the folder in my hands. "Relieves the monotony. Attractive-looking place, isn't it?"

34   I could only nod dumbly, lowering my eyes to the picture again because that picture told you even more than just what you saw. I don't know how you knew this, but you realized, staring at that forest-covered valley, that this was very much the way America once looked when it was new. And you knew this was only part of a whole land of unspoiled, unharmed forests, where every stream ran pure; you were seeing what people, the last of them dead over a century ago, had once looked at in Kentucky and Wisconsin, and the old Northwest. And you knew that if you could breathe in that air you'd feel it flow into your lungs sweeter than it's been anywhere on earth for a hundred and fifty years.

35   Under that picture was another, of six or eight people on a beach—the shore of a lake, maybe, or the river in the picture above. Two children were squatting on their haunches,[11] dabbling[12] in the water's edge, and in the foreground a half circle of adults were sitting, kneeling, or squatting in comfortable balance on the yellow sand. They were talking, several were smoking, and most of them held half-filled coffee cups; the sun was bright, you knew the air was balmy and that it was morning,

---

11. *buttocks, hips and thighs*, 12. *dipping their hands*

just after breakfast. They were smiling, one woman talking, the others listening. One man had half risen from his squatting position to skip a stone out onto the surface of the water.

36   You knew this: that they were spending twenty minutes or so down on that beach after breakfast before going to work, and you knew they were friends and that they did this every day. You knew—I tell you, you *knew*—that they liked their work, all of them, whatever it was; that there was no forced hurry or pressure about it. And that—well, that's all, I guess; you just knew that every day after breakfast these families spent a leisurely half hour sitting and talking, there in the morning sun, down on that wonderful beach.

37   I'd never seen anything like their faces before. They were ordinary enough in looks, the people in that picture—pleasant, more or less familiar types. Some were young, in their twenties; others were in their thirties; one man and woman seemed around fifty. But the faces of the youngest couple were completely unlined, and it occurred to me then that they had been born there, and that it was a place where no one worried or was ever afraid. The others, the older ones, there were lines in their foreheads, grooves¹³ around their mouths, but you felt that the lines were no longer deepening, that they were healed and untroubled scars. And in the faces of the oldest couple was a look of—I'd say it was a look of permanent *relief*. Not one of those faces bore a trace of malice¹⁴; these people were *happy*. But even more than that, you knew they'd *been* happy, day after day after day for a long, long time, and that they always would be, and they knew it.

38   I wanted to join them. The most desperate longing¹⁵ roared up in me from the bottom of my soul to *be* there—on the beach, after breakfast, with those people in the sunny morning— and I could hardly stand it. I looked up at the man behind the counter and managed to smile. "This is—very interesting."

39   "Yes." He smiled back, then shook his head in amusement. "We've had customers so interested, so carried away,¹⁶ that they didn't want to talk about anything else." He laughed. "They actually wanted to know rates, details, everything."

40   I nodded to show I understood and agreed with them. "And I suppose you've worked out a whole story to go with this?" I glanced at the folder in my hands.

41   "Oh, yes. What would you like to know?"

---

13. *lines,* 14. *hatred,* 15. *desire,* 16. *overcome*

42   "These people," I said softly, and touched the picture of the group on the beach. "What do they do?"

43   "They work; everyone does." He took a pipe from his pocket. "They simply live their lives doing what they like. Some study. We have, according to our little story," he added, and smiled, "a very fine library. Some of our people farm, some write, some make things with their hands. Most of them raise children and—well, they work at whatever it is they really want to do."

44   "And if there isn't anything they really want to do?"

45   He shook his head. "There is always something, for everyone, that he really wants to do. It's just that here there is so rarely time to find out what it is." He brought out a tobacco pouch and, leaning on the counter, began filling his pipe, his eyes level with mine, looking at me gravely. "Life is simple there, and it's serene. In some ways, the good ways, it's like the early pioneering communities here in your country, but without the drudgery[17] that killed people young. There is electricity. There are washing machines, vacuum cleaners, plumbing, modern bathrooms, and modern medicine, very modern. But there are no radios, television, telephones, or automobiles. Distances are small, and people live and work in small communities. They raise or make most of the things they use. Every man builds his own house, with all the help he needs from his neighbors. Their recreation is their own, and there is a great deal of it, but there is no recreation for sale, nothing you buy a ticket to. They have dances, card parties, weddings, christenings, birthday celebrations, harvest parties. There are swimming and sports of all kinds. There is conversation, a lot of it, plenty of joking and laughter. There is a great deal of visiting and sharing of meals, and each day is well filled and well spent. There are no pressures, economic or social, and life holds few threats. Every man, woman and child is a happy person." After a moment he smiled. "I'm repeating the text, of course, in our little joke."

46   "Of course," I murmured, and looked down at the folder again, turning a page. "Homes in The Colony," said a caption, and there, true and real, were a dozen or so pictures of the interiors of what must have been the cabins I'd seen in the first photograph, or others like them. There were living rooms, kitchens, dens, patios. Many of the homes seemed to be furnished in a kind of Early American style, except that it looked—authentic, as though those rocking chairs, cupboards, tables and

---

17. *hard work*

hooked rugs had been made by the people themselves, taking their time and making them well and beautifully. Others of the interiors seemed modern in style; one showed a definite Oriental influence.

47   All of them had, plainly and unmistakably, one quality in common: You knew as you looked at them that these rooms were *home*, really home, to the people who lived in them. On the wall of one living room, over the stone fireplace, hung a hand-stitched motto; it said, "There Is No Place Like Home," but the words didn't seem quaint or amusing, they didn't seem old-fashioned, resurrected[18] or copied from a past that was gone. They seemed real; they belonged; those words were nothing more or less than a simple expression of true feeling and fact.

48   "Who are you?" I lifted my head from the folder to stare into the man's eyes.

49   He lighted his pipe, taking his time, sucking the match flame down into the bowl, eyes glancing up at me. "It's in the text," he said then, "on the back page. We—that is to say, the people of Verna, the original inhabitants—are people like yourself. Verna is a planet of air, sun, land and sea, like this one. And of the same approximate temperature. So life evolved[19] there, of course, just about as it has here, though rather earlier; and we are people like you. There are trivial[20] anatomical[21] differences, but nothing important. We read and enjoy your James Thurber, John Clayton, Rabelais, Allen Marple, Hemingway, Grimm, Mark Twain, Alan Nelson. We like your chocolate, which we didn't have, and a great deal of your music. And you'd like many of the things we have. Our thoughts, though, and the great aims and directions of our history and development have been—drastically[22] different from yours." He smiled and blew out a puff of smoke. "Amusing fantasy, isn't it?"

50   "Yes," I knew I sounded abrupt, and I hadn't stopped to smile; the words were spilling out. "And where is Verna?"

51   "Light years away, by your measurements."

52   I was suddenly irritated, I didn't know why. "A little hard to get to, then, wouldn't it be?"

53   For a moment he looked at me; then he turned to the window beside him. "Come here," he said, and I walked around the counter to stand beside him. "There, off to the left"—he put a hand on my shoulder and pointed with his pipe stem—"are

18. *brought back into use*, 19. *changed*, 20. *unimportant*, 21. *bodily*, 22. *significantly*

two apartment buildings, built back to back. The entrance to one is on Fifth Avenue, the entrance to the other on Sixth. See them? In the middle of the block; you can just see their roofs."

54   I nodded, and he said, "A man and his wife live on the fourteenth floor of one of those buildings. A wall of their living room is the back wall of the building. They have friends on the fourteenth floor of the other building, and a wall of *their* living room is the back wall of *their* building. These two couples live, in other words, within two feet of one another, since the back building walls actually touch."

55   The big man smiled. "But when the Robinsons want to visit the Bradens, they walk from their living room to the front door. They then walk down a long hall to the elevators. They ride fourteen floors down; then, in the street, they must walk around to the next block. And the city blocks there are long; in bad weather they have sometimes actually taken a cab. They walk into the other building, they go on through the lobby, ride up fourteen floors, walk down a hall, ring a bell, and are finally admitted into their friends' living room—only two feet from their own."

56   The big man turned back to the counter, and I walked around to the other side again. "All I can tell you," he said then, "is that the way the Robinsons travel is like space travel, the actual physical crossing of those enormous distances." He shrugged, "But if they could only step through those two feet of wall without harming themselves or the wall—well, that is how we 'travel.' We don't cross space, we avoid it." He smiled. "Draw a breath here—and exhale it on Verna."

57   I said softly, "And that's how they arrived, isn't it? The people in the picture. You took them there." He nodded, and I said, "Why?"

58   He shrugged. "If you saw a neighbor's house on fire, would you rescue his family, if you could? As many as you could, at least?"

59   "Yes."

60   "Well—so would we."

61   "You think it's that bad, then? With us?"

62   "How does it look to you?"

63   I thought about the headlines in my morning paper, that morning and every morning. "Not so good."

64   He just nodded and said, "We can't take you all, can't even take very many. So we've been selecting a few."

65   "For how long?"

66   "A long time." He smiled. "One of us was a member of Lincoln's cabinet. But it was not until just before your First World War that we felt we could see what was coming; until then we'd been merely observers. We opened our first agency in Mexico City in nineteen thirteen. Now we have branches in every major city."

67   "Nineteen thirteen," I murmured, as something caught in my memory. "Mexico. Listen! Did—"

68   "Yes." He smiled, anticipating my question. "Ambrose Bierce joined us that year, or the next. He lived until nineteen thirty-one, a very old man, and wrote four more books, which we have." He turned back a page in the folder and pointed to the cabin in the first large photograph. "That was his home."

69   "And what about Judge Crater?"

70   "Crater?"

71   "Another famous disappearance; he was a New York judge who simply disappeared some years ago."

72   "I don't know. We had a judge, I remember, from New York City, some twenty-odd years ago, but I can't recall his name."

73   I leaned across the counter toward him, my face, very close to his, and I nodded. "I like your little joke," I said. "I like it very much, more than I can possibly tell you." Very softly I added, "When does it stop being a joke?"

74   For a moment he studied me; then he spoke. "Now. If you want it to."

75   *You've got to decide on the spot*, the middle-aged man at the Lexington Avenue bar had told me, *because you'll never get another chance. I know; I've tried.* Now I stood there thinking; there were people I'd hate never to see again, and a girl I was just getting to know, and this was the world I'd been born in. Then I thought about leaving that room, going back to my job, then back to my room at night. And finally I thought of the deep green valley in the picture and the little yellow beach in the morning sun. "I'll go," I whispered. "If you'll have me."

76   He studied my face. "Be sure," he said sharply. "Be certain. We want no one there who won't be happy, and if you have any least doubt, we'd prefer that—"

77   "I'm sure," I said.

78   After a moment the gray-haired man slid open a drawer under the counter and brought out a little rectangle of yellow cardboard. One side was printed, and through the printing ran a

band of light green; it looked like a railroad ticket to White Plains or somewhere. The printing said, "Good, when validated, for ONE TRIP TO VERNA. Nontransferable. One way only."

79   "Ah—how much?" I said, reaching for my wallet, wondering if he wanted me to pay.

80   He glanced at my hand on my hip pocket. "All you've got. Including your small change." He smiled. "You won't need it anymore, and we can use your currency for operating expenses. Light bills, rent, and so on."

81   "I don't have much."

82   "That doesn't matter." From under the counter he brought out a heavy stamping machine, the kind you see in railroad ticket offices. "We once sold a ticket for thirty-seven hundred dollars. And we sold another just like it for six cents." He slid the ticket into the machine, struck the lever[23] with his fist, then handed the ticket to me. On the back, now, was a freshly printed rectangle of purple ink, and within it the words, "Good this day only," followed by the date. I put two five-dollar bills, a one, and seventeen cents in change on the counter. "Take the ticket to the Acme Depot," the gray-haired man said, and, leaning across the counter, began giving me directions for getting there.

83   It's a tiny hole in the wall, the Acme Depot; you may have seen it—just a little store front on one of the narrow streets west of Broadway. On the window is painted, not very well, "Acme." Inside, the walls and ceiling, under layers of old paint, are covered with the kind of stamped tin you see in old buildings. There's a worn wooden counter and a few battered[24] chrome and imitation red leather chairs. There are scores of places like the Acme Depot in that area—little theater-ticket agencies, obscure busline offices, employment agencies. You could pass this one a thousand times and never really see it; and if you live in New York, you probably have.

84   Behind the counter, when I arrived, stood a shirt-sleeved man, smoking a cigar stump and working on some papers; four or five people silently waited in the chairs. The man at the counter glanced up as I stepped in, looked down at my hand for my ticket, and when I showed it, nodded at the last vacant chair, and I sat down.

85   There was a girl beside me, hands folded on her purse. She was pleasant-looking, rather pretty; I thought she might have been a stenographer. Across the narrow little office sat a young Negro in work clothes, his wife beside him holding their little girl

---

23. *bar,* 24. *worn*

in her lap. And there was a man of around fifty, his face averted from the rest of us, staring out into the rain at passing pedestrians. He was expensively dressed and wore a gray Homburg;[25] he could have been the vice-president of a large bank, I thought, and I wondered what his ticket had cost.

86   Maybe twenty minutes passed, the man behind the counter working on some papers; then a small battered old bus pulled up at the curb outside, and I heard the hand brake set. The bus was a shabby[26] thing, bought third- or fourthhand and painted red and white over the old paint, the fenders lumpy from countless pounded-out dents, the tire treads worn almost smooth. On the side, in red letters, it said "Acme," and the driver wore a leather jacket and the kind of worn cloth cap that cab drivers wear. It was precisely the sort of obscure[27] little bus you see around there, ridden always by shabby, tired, silent people, going no one knows where.

87   It took nearly two hours for the little bus to work south through the traffic, toward the tip of Manhattan, and we all sat, each wrapped in his own silence and thoughts, staring out the rain-spattered windows; the little girl was asleep. Through the streaking glass beside me I watched drenched[28] people huddled at city bus stops, and saw them rap angrily on the closed doors of buses jammed to capacity, and saw the strained, harassed faces of the drivers. At Fourteenth Street I saw a speeding cab splash a sheet of street-dirty water on a man at the curb, and saw the man's mouth writhe[29] as he cursed. Often our bus stood motionless, the traffic light red, as throngs[30] flowed out into the street from the curb, threading their way around us and the other waiting cars. I saw hundreds of faces, and not once did I see anyone smile.

88   I dozed; then we were on a glistening[31] black highway somewhere on Long Island. I slept again, and awakened in darkness as we jolted[32] off the highway onto a muddy double-rut[33] road, and I caught a glimpse of a farmhouse, the windows dark. Then the bus slowed, lurched[34] once, and stopped. The hand brake set, the motor died, and we were parked beside what looked like a barn.

89   It *was* a barn . . . .The driver walked up to it, pulled the big sliding wood door open, its wheels creaking[35] on the rusted old trolley[36] overhead, and stood holding it open as we filed in.

---

25. *hat,* 26. *worn,* 27. *undistinguishable,* 28. *soaked,* 29. *twist,* 30. *crowds,*
31. *shining,* 32. *turned suddenly,* 33. *double-track,* 34. *moved forward,*
35. *squeaking,* 36. *track*

Then he released it, stepping inside with us, and the big door slid closed of its own weight. The barn was damp, old, the walls no longer plumb,[37] and it smelled of cattle; there was nothing inside on the packed-dirt floor but a bench of unpainted pine, and the driver indicated it with the beam of a flashlight. "Sit here, please," he said quietly. "Get your tickets ready." Then he moved down the line, punching each of our tickets, and on the floor I caught a momentary glimpse, in the shifting beam of his light, of tiny mounds of countless more round bits of cardboard, like little drifts of yellow confetti.[38] Then he was at the door again, sliding it open just enough to pass through, and for a moment we saw him silhouetted[39] against the night sky. "Good luck," he said. "Just wait where you are." He released the door; it slid closed, snipping[40] off the wavering[41] beam of his flashlight; and a moment later we heard the motor start and the bus lumber[42] away in low gear.

90   The dark barn was silent now, except for our breathing. Time ticked away, and I felt an urge, presently, to speak to whoever was next to me. But I didn't quite know what to say, and I began to feel embarrassed, a little foolish, and very aware that I was simply sitting in an old and deserted barn. The seconds passed, and I moved my feet restlessly; presently I realized that I was getting cold and chilled. Then suddenly I knew—and my face flushed in violent anger and a terrible shame. We'd been tricked! Bilked[43] out of our money by our pathetic[44] will to believe an absurd and fantastic fable and left, now, to sit there as long as we pleased, until we came to our senses finally, like countless others before us, and made our way home as best we could. It was suddenly impossible to understand or even remember how I could have been so gullible, and I was on my feet, stumbling through the dark across the uneven floor, with some notion[45] of getting to a phone and the police. The big barn door was heavier than I'd thought, but I slid it back, took a running step through it, then turned to shout back to the others to come along.

91   You have seen how very much you can observe in the fractional instant of a lightning flash—an entire landscape sometimes, every detail etched[46] on your memory, to be seen and studied in your mind for long moments afterward. As I turned back toward the opened door the inside of that barn came alight. Through every wide crack of its walls and ceiling and through the big dust-coated windows in its side streamed

---

37. *straight*, 38. *bits of paper*, 39. *outlined*, 40. *cutting*, 41. *moving*,
42. *move slowly*, 43. *cheated*, 44. *pitiful*, 45. *idea*, 46. *marked*

the light of an intensely brilliant blue and sunny sky, and the air pulling into my lungs as I opened my mouth to shout was sweeter than any I had ever tasted in my life. Dimly, through a wide, dust-smeared window of that barn, I looked—for less than the blink of any eye—down into a deep majestic V of forest-covered slope, and I saw, tumbling through it, far below, a tiny stream, blue from the sky, and at that stream's edge between two low roofs a yellow patch of sun-drenched beach. And then, that picture engraved on my mind forever, the heavy door slid shut, my fingernails rasping[47] along the splintery[48] wood in a desperate effort to stop it—and I was standing alone in a cold and rain-swept night.

92   It took four or five seconds, no longer, fumbling at that door, to heave it open again. But it was four or five seconds too long. The barn was empty, dark. There was nothing inside but a worn pine bench—and in the flicker of the lighted match in my hand, tiny drifts of what looked like damp confetti on the floor. As my mind had known even as my hands scratched at the outside of that door, there was no one inside now; and I knew where they were—knew they were walking, laughing aloud in a sudden wonderful and eager ecstasy,[49] down into that forest-green valley, toward home.

93   I work in a bank, in a job I don't like; and I ride to and from it in the subway, reading the daily papers, the news they contain. I live in a rented room, and in the battered[50] dresser under a pile of my folded handkerchiefs is a little rectangle of yellow cardboard. Printed on its face are the words, "Good, when validated, for one trip to Verna," and stamped on the back is a date. But the date is gone, long since, the ticket void, punched in a pattern of tiny holes.

94   I've been back to the Acme Travel Bureau. The first time the tall gray-haired man walked up to me and laid two five-dollar bills, a one, and seventeen cents in change before me. "You left this on the counter last time you were here," he said gravely. Looking me squarely in the eyes, he added bleakly,[51] "I don't know why." Then some customers came in, he turned to greet them, and there was nothing for me to do but leave.

95   *Walk in as though it were the ordinary travel agency it seems—you can find it, somewhere, in any city you try! Ask a few ordinary questions—about a trip you're planning, a vacation, anything you like. Then hint about The Folder a little, but don't mention it directly. Give him time to size you up and*

---

47. *scratching,* 48. *cracked,* 49. *joy,* 50. *worn,* 51. *coldly*

offer it himself. And if he does, if you're the type, if you can believe—then make up your mind and stick to it! Because you won't ever get a second chance. I know, because I've tried. And tried. And tried.

Understanding the Text: *Main Ideas*

Answer these questions to check your understanding of the main ideas.

1. Who is Charley Ewell?

2. What does he want?

3. What is Verna?

4. What does Charley decide to do?

5. Does he go to Verna?

6. What happens at the end of the story?

Understanding the Text: *Scanning for Details*

With a partner, complete the following sentences and answer the questions, which focus on details in the text. If you cannot recall the information, scan the text for the details. The sentences follow the chronological order of the story's plot.

1. Charley Ewell, the narrator, worked in a _____.

2. To learn about The Folder, Ewell visited _____. (Give the exact name.)

3. The man who worked in the office was described physically as

    _____.

4. The pictures of Verna that the man showed Charley portrayed

    _____.

(Give specific description.)

5. The people of Verna, according to the man, work _____

_____.

6. According to the travel agent, how long had the people of Verna had travel agencies on Earth to recruit settlers to their

planet? _____

_____

7. How much did Charley Ewell pay for his one-way ticket to

Verna? _____

_____

8. From Manhattan, the bus to Verna drove its passengers to

_____

_____.

(Describe the place.)

9. After Charley ran out of the barn, the other passengers

_____

_____.

✺ Literary Concepts: *Fantasy, Narrator, Irony*

1. Fantasy

"Of Missing Persons," like other stories by Jack Finney, can be called a fantasy because in it, Finney creates a nonexistent or unreal world. At least, we do not know for certain that a world such as Verna exists. However, Finney gives Verna specific physical characteristics, and gives Vernans particular qualities, making his story fantastic. Many times, fantasy writers use the unreal world as a way of criticizing the real world.

Discuss the questions below, which deal with fantasy:

a. Although this story is classified as an example of fantasy, do you think the story is incredible?
b. Do you think Finney uses his descriptions of Verna to criticize Earth?

      c. Have you read any other fantasy stories or seen fantastic films?

2. Narrator

      a. Who is the *narrator*?

      b. Who is he talking to when he "speaks" in italic type in the first and last paragraphs of the story?

3. Irony

      a. What does Charley Ewell intend to do in the story? What, in fact, happens to him in the end of the story?

      b. Do you think the ending of the story has a "twist," like "The Cop and the Anthem"? Is the ending *ironic*? Did you expect this ending?

❋ Understanding the Text: *Drawing Inferences*

In small groups, discuss the questions below, which require you to draw inferences, or conclusions, about the story.

1. What made Charley Ewell leave the barn and run away?

2. How was he different from the other passengers on the bus to Verna?

3. Why does Charley keep the ticket in his drawer?

4. Do you believe the events in this story are possible?

5. Has this story made you think about how satisfied you are with your own life? Would you like to change your life in any way?

6. What message do you think the author, Jack Finney, was trying to give to his readers?

❋ Looking at Language: *Guessing Vocabulary in Context*

The context of sentences can aid you in guessing the meanings of unfamiliar words, as you have learned in reading studies. With a partner, practice this skill by reading the sentences below and defining the italicized words. With each sentence, write any words or ideas in the context that helped you guess the meaning.

1. "Now he was frankly staring, his eyes studying my face *intently* with no pretense of doing anything else . . . "

   Intently probably means _____.

   Context Clues: _____

2. "He *fumbled* under the counter, then brought out a long, thin folder, the same size and shape as the others, and slid it over the glass toward me."
   "It took four or five seconds, no longer, *fumbling* at that door, to heave it open again."

   The word *fumble* in these sentences means _____

   _____.

   Context Clues: _____

3. "Life is simple there, and it's serene. In some ways, the good ways, it's like the early pioneering communities here in your country, but without the *drudgery* that killed people young. There is electricity. There are washing machines, vacuum cleaners, plumbing . . . "

   Here, the word *drudgery* probably means _____

   _____.

   Context Clues: _____

4. "The bus was a *shabby* thing, bought third- or fourthhand and painted red and white over the old paint . . . "

   Shabby probably means _____.

   Context Clues: _____

5. "Often our bus stood motionless, the traffic light red, as *throngs* flowed out into the street from the curb, threading their way around us and other waiting cars. I saw hundreds of faces, and not once did I see anyone smile."
   From the context, you can guess that throngs here refers to

   _____.

   Context Clues: _____

6. "Then suddenly I knew—and my face *flushed in violent anger* and a terrible shame. We'd been tricked! Bilked out of our money by our pathetic will to believe an absurd and fantastic fable . . . ''

The phrase *flushed in violent anger* probably means _____

_____.

7. "You have seen how very much you can observe in the fractional instant of a lightning flash—an entire landscape sometimes, every detail *etched* on your memory, to be seen and studied in your mind for long moments afterward.

Etched probably means _____.

Context Clues: _____

Looking at Language: *Vocabulary by Theme*

"Of Missing Persons" portrays city-dwelling Americans in a fairly negative way, as unhappy, unsmiling, and harassed by work and city life in general. In groups, discuss these questions, which deal with the way author Jack Finney describes Americans in contrast to Vernans.

1. Begin with paragraphs 86 and 87. Look for words that describe the way New Yorkers look or act. List them along with their meanings. Look up any unknown words in the dictionary.

2. Now scan paragraph 37 for words that describe how Vernans feel and look. List these words and use a dictionary to help you with definitions.

3. In your group, compare the two groups of words. Are the people of your country more like New Yorkers or more like Vernans?

4. Discuss whether you think Finney's portrayal of New Yorkers is accurate. Are only New Yorkers like this?

READING JOURNAL: FREEWRITING

Imagine that you could travel, with or without your family and friends, to a perfect world. What would this world be like? Who would be there? What would it look like? What would you do?

Describe this place and your life there. Write for three minutes without stopping. Then read what you have read. Write again for three minutes nonstop to add more details and refine your ideas. Then share your paper with a classmate and compare your "perfect worlds."

Also in your journal, answer these questions:

1. Do you believe this story is possible?

2. Do you like this story?

VIDEO

Jack Finney's popular novel, *Invasion of the Body Snatchers*, has so captured the interest of audiences that there are two film versions of the story, one made in 1956 starring Kevin McCarthy and Dana Wynter, and the other made in 1978 starring Donald Sutherland and Brooke Adams. The novel describes an invasion by aliens who "snatch" the bodies of Earth victims, and while the theme is not the same as "Of Missing Persons," viewing either film version will give you another example of fantasy.

Acquainted with the Night

by Robert Frost

About the Author

Robert Frost (1874–1963) is often ranked as America's leading poet. His poems are deceptively accessible; they sound like conversation, but contain wisdom, humor, and down-to-earth philosophy. Many of Frost's poems reflect his love of nature. He was awarded the Pulitzer prize for poetry four times for his collections of poems, *New Hampshire* (1924), *Collected Poems* (1931), *A Further Range* (1937), and *A Witness Tree*

(1943). He was born in San Francisco, lived in New England, and supported himself by farming and teaching.

Reading Poetry

Poetry has been an important form of literature since ancient times. Throughout the world, people have used the special language of poetry—patterns of rhythmical verse that appeal to the ear as well as the imagination—to relate their experiences about life. In this way, poetry is very similar to prose, or the story form of literature.

However, poetry also differs from prose. Naturally you can distinguish poetry by the way it looks on the page and the way it sounds when you read it aloud. From the length of most poems, you can see that the information contained in one word or line is much more intense than in one word or line of a story. Second, there is a distinctive rhythm and sound to poems.

Poems in English may be different from those of your culture, but like all poems, they should be read aloud, slowly, repeatedly, so that you get the feel of the language and the patterns of its sounds.

In the first reading of the poems that follow, read each aloud, very slowly. Pay attention to the rhythm of each line and stress words or phrases with important meaning. Ask your instructor to read this first poem aloud for you. Mark the intonation and stress as she or he reads. After several readings, focus on the content of the poem by identifying word meanings and discerning the messages.

At First Glance

1. Read the title of the poem. What do you think it means to be "acquainted with the night"?

2. The first verse of the poem tells us that the narrator of the poem "[has] outwalked the furthest city light." What kind of person do you think would often walk on streets at night? Who do you think the narrator could be?

Acquainted with the Night

by Robert Frost

1   *I* have been one acquainted with the night.
    I have walked out in rain—and back in rain.
    I have outwalked the furthest city light.

2   I have looked down the saddest city lane.
    I have passed by the watchman on his beat
    And dropped my eyes, unwilling to explain.

3   I have stood still and stopped the sound of feet
    When far away an interrupted cry
    Came over houses from another street,

4   But not to call me back or say good-by;
    And further still at an unearthly height
    One luminary clock against the sky

5   Proclaimed the time was neither wrong nor right.
    I have been one acquainted with the night.

Understanding the Text: *Analysis*

Read the poem and answer the questions about each verse.

1. In verse 1, Frost writes that the narrator has "outwalked the furthest city light." Why do you think the narrator would measure his walking in these terms, as far as "the furthest city light"?

2. In verse 2, the narrator says he/she has "passed by the watchman on his beat and dropped [his/her] eyes." What would make a person "drop his/her eyes" when he/she met a security guard?

3. Verse 3 describes the narrator standing "still and [stopping] the sound of feet." Why does a person sometimes stop and stand still when he or she walks? Why does another person stop when he or she hears someone walking behind him?

4. In verse 4, Frost writes of "one luminary clock against the sky." What do you think he is referring to here?

5. The last verse says that the clock tells the narrator "the time was neither wrong nor right." How does a person feel when he says that a certain time of day is "neither wrong nor right"?

6. Finally, what kind of person do you think the narrator is?

Literary Concept: *Tone*

Poets must choose their words especially carefully, since poems are such compact forms of literature. By using particular descriptive words, poets, storytellers, can express their attitude, or set a mood that tells how they feel about their subject. Tone can be explained as the attitude or mood of a writer as depicted in language choice and content.

One can define the tone of this poem by examining the words Frost uses to depict a city at night. Read over the following descriptive lines and complete the sentences below which comment on the tone of the poem. Express the tone with an adjective that describes the feeling the writer conveys about his subject.

Descriptive Lines:

"I have walked out in rain . . . " (verse 1)
"I have looked down the saddest city lane . . . " (verse 2)
". . . an interrupted cry came over houses . . . " (verse 3)
". . . at an unearthly height one luminary clock against the sky . . . " (verse 4)

The tone of "Acquainted with the Night" is expressed through the details and words Robert Frost uses to describe nights

spent in a city. The tone of this poem is _____

(adjective/s). The poem makes the reader feel _____

_____.

Dream Deferred

by Langston Hughes

About the Author

Langston Hughes (1902–1967) was an American poet, novelist, and playwright who wrote about the state of African Americans in the United States. He was a prominent participant in the Harlem Renaissance, a period in the 1920s–1930s when African American art thrived in New York City's Harlem neighborhood. Hughes's writing reflected two themes: his love of country and his devotion to his race. His works include the books of poems, *The Weary Blues* (1926), *The Dream Keeper* (1932), and *Freedom's Plow* (1943);

and the novel *Not Without Laughter* (1930). He was born in Joplin, MO.

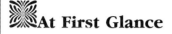At First Glance

1. What is Harlem?

2. The first line of this poem is,
   "What happens to a dream deferred?"
   What does "deferred" mean?
   What things can be deferred?

Prereading Vocabulary

Guess the meanings of the words below, which appear in Hughes' poem.

1. fester = _____
   If you don't clean and care for a sore, it may fester.

2. crust = _____

   syrup = _____
   If syrup is left uncovered for a long time, it will develop a sugary crust.

3. sag = _____
   The man's back is sagging because he is carrying a heavy load.

Dream Deferred

by Langston Hughes

*W*hat happens to a dream deferred?
  Does it dry up
  like a raisin in the sun?
  Or fester like a sore—
  And then run?
  Does it stink like rotten meat?
  Or crust and sugar over—
  like a syrupy sweet?
  Maybe it just sags
  like a heavy load.

Or does it explode?

Literary Concept: *Figurative Language—Similes*

Langston Hughes's poem contains many good examples of similes, one type of figurative or comparative language that readers often find in serious writing. Similes are comparisons introduced by "like" or "as" between objects that are not usually compared to one another. The purpose of using figurative language is to create a mental image in one's mind. For example, a young person on a date may tell his or her partner that he or she has "eyes like pools of water." This is a simile, a type of figurative language, because this person's eyes are not really pools. The purpose of using this comparison is to create a mental image; calling eyes pools of water makes us think of clear, deep eyes that seem as deep as water.

Likewise, Hughes includes similes in his poem when he compares a dream deferred to common things. Below are examples of the similes (comparisons introduced by like) in his poem. Read each line over carefully. Then write down the mental image that you get when you think about the lines in comparison to a lost dream.

1. "Does it [a dream deferred] dry up like a raisin in the sun?"

2. "Or fester like a sore—"

3. "Or crust and sugar over—like a syrupy sweet?"

4. "Maybe it [a dream deferred] just sags like a heavy load."

Understanding the Text: *Making Comparisons*

Compare the two poems in this chapter. Mark which statements below refer to "Acquainted with the Night" and which apply to "Dream Deferred." Discuss your responses with a partner.

This poem has a serious message.
The tone of this poem is sad.
The tone of this poem is bitter.
This poem contains a great deal of figurative language.
This poem makes a strong impact on its readers.

READING JOURNAL

In your journal, answer one or more of these questions.

1. Do you like poetry?

2. Are poems more difficult to understand than stories?

3. Write about which of these two poems you like best and explain why.

VIDEO

Another well-known African American writer, Lorraine Hansberry, wrote *A Raisin in the Sun* (1958), a play that depicts the struggles of an African American family in Chicago's Southside, whose title was based on this poem. A commercial film was made from this play in 1961 starring Sidney Poitier and Ruby Dee. You may want to view this film and compare the main idea of the poem with that of the play/film.

Projects: UNIT THREE

Project I: Dramatization

Dramatization means to act out a story. In this unit, you have read two engaging stories whose endings are left unknown. For this project, you and a partner will assume the roles of characters from a story and act out a scene from the endings of the story. You will assume the role of a character, as you may have done in the Literary Party project in Unit 2, and act as that character would, according to your knowledge of the character.

Choose one of the situations below and dramatize what you think could happen with your partner. You and your partner will need to "invent" the action and dialogue in your scene based on the information you know of the character(s) from the story. Rehearse your dramatizations with your partner and be prepared to perform them. You may write your dialogue on paper (but memorize it for class performance) or deliver your lines extemporaneously.

DRAMATIZATION SITUATIONS:

1. Imagine that you are Soapy, the bum in "The Cop and the Anthem," and your partner is the magistrate who sentences you to three months in prison. What arguments do you give to the judge? What is the judge's reaction and what does he say?
2. To take "The Cop and the Anthem" a step further, imagine that you are Soapy and your partner is a fellow bum and prison inmate. You two have just been released from prison. It's spring in New York City. What do you do?
3. Suppose that you are Charley Ewell, the disillusioned bank teller in "Of Missing Persons." You are unhappy, so you return to the Acme Travel Agency and implore the agent, played by your partner, to allow you to go to Verna.
4. You are Charley Ewell, and your partner is Charley's new girlfriend (who was mentioned in the story). Of course, you are disappointed at having lost your chance to travel to Verna. You explain what happened to your girlfriend. What is her reaction and recommendations?

Project II: Written Character Analysis

Often, students of literature are asked to write about a story or a character they have encountered. This is an opportunity for you to convey your ideas about what you have read. When you write about literature, you can write about many different aspects of a story or a character. You can analyze the "hidden meaning" of a story or an event in a story, or you can probe a character's behavior. For this project, you will begin with a simple assignment. You will write a short essay describing a character from a story or stories in Units One or Two. (The assignment is explained in detail on the next page.)

Writing about literature is not as difficult as you may think. In fact, it is similar to writing about nonliterature. The standard essay format is used with an introduction, thesis statement, body paragraphs, and conclusion. (A suggested plan for organizing your essay is also given on the next page.) Furthermore, the ideas in the body are supported with examples or "evidence" from the stories. **Direct quotations** or **paraphrases** of the information in the stories are used to substantiate your ideas.

There is no **one** correct way to analyze or interpret a story. You can bring your unique ideas to each story you read, because each story should say something different to each of you. The important thing is that your essay must include ample evidence from the stories to support your ideas.

To prepare for this assignment, you will work through some prewriting activities and read and analyze a sample essay that describes a character from a story.

A. PREWRITING PRACTICE

To begin, you will practice taking information from a story and using it as support for ideas in an interpretive essay. Information taken from a text will serve the same function as facts, examples, and other support do in a nonliterature essay.

Work in small groups to answer the questions below.

Each group will complete a sentence that describes one character from the stories. Group members must agree on one "answer" to the sentence, and work together to find support from the story.

Support can include **direct quotations** or **paraphrases** (restatements) of information from the stories. This information should "prove" your description of the character.

You must also identify the place in the story (page number or general location, i.e., beginning, middle, end) where you found the support.

Later, you will compile these sentences into practice paragraphs that could be used in essays describing characters.

GROUP A:

In "Of Missing Persons," the narrator can be characterized as a ____ young man.
(Add one word to describe the narrator's **personality.**)

Support: Page or Place:

1. _____   1. _____

2. _____   2. _____

3. _____   3. _____

GROUP B:

In "Butch Minds the Baby," Big Butch can be described as a ____ father.
(Add one word to describe his behavior as a father.)

Support: Page or Place:

1. _____   1. _____

2. _____   2. _____

3. _____   3. _____

GROUP C:

In "The Cop and the Anthem," Soapy considers himself to be

_____.

(Add one word to describe Soapy's **self-image.**)

Support: Page or Place:

1. _____   1. _____

2. _____   2. _____

3. _____   3. _____

B. WRITING ASSIGNMENT

Your first formal writing assignment will be to write a short essay about a character or characters from the stories you have read.

Choose one assignment below:

1. Describe two or three major strengths or weaknesses in the personality of one character from the stories you have read. Use examples of his or her behavior to **show** that he or she possesses these qualities.
2. Find two similar characters from the stories you have read. Explain how each character is similar. What personality traits do they share? How do they deal with their problems in similar ways? Use information from both stories to show how the two characters are similar.
3. Describe one character's hopes or dreams. How does he or she attempt to realize his or her dreams? Does he or she succeed or fail? Why?

SUGGESTED PLAN TO ORGANIZE YOUR ESSAY:

I. Introduction

Name of story/stories and authors
Brief summary sentence that suggests story content(s)
Introduction of character(s)
Thesis Statement: Your ideas about the character(s)

II. Topic Sentence: First major point about character(s)

Support: specific action/behavior/characteristics of character that show he/she possesses this quality
Brief plot/character explanation

III. Topic Sentence: Second major point about character(s)

Support
Brief plot/character explanation

IV. Topic Sentence: Third major point about character(s)

Support
Brief plot/character explanation

V. Conclusion

Your opinion of character(s) and why you feel this way,
Your opinion of why character(s) behaves this way, or
Your opinion of writer(s)'s portrayal of character(s)

C. PARAGRAPH PRACTICE

Write a practice paragraph that describes the character your group discussed in the previous exercise. Follow these guidelines:

a. The Topic Sentence of your paragraph will be the first sentence in the previous exercise, which contains the word you chose to describe the character.

b. The sentences that contain supporting information from the story will constitute the Body of your paragraph. This support can be in the form of direct quotes (full or partial quotes) taken exactly from the text, or paraphrases (in your words) of the information from the story. Try to use at least one direct quote in your paragraph. Use connecting words between each sentence of support.

c. Then, add a Return, or concluding, sentence that reiterates your idea about the character.

D. ANALYSIS OF SAMPLE ESSAY

Read the sample essay below, which describes a character from a story you will read in Unit 4. Use this model to help you write your essay.

The Wife in Chopin's "The Story of an Hour"

Kate Chopin's "The Story of an Hour" reveals the secret feelings of a traditional, nineteenth-century American wife trapped in a confining marriage. Louise Mallard appears to be a happily married woman, but when she is faced with the death of her husband, you learn that she has always dreamed of being free of him.

In the beginning of the story, Mrs. Mallard is presented as a typical happily married woman. In fact, her friends and family use "great care . . . to break to her as gently as possible the news of her husband's death." Mrs. Mallard's reaction is also that of a woman who loves her husband: "She wept at once, with sudden, wild abandonment, in her sister's arms," Chopin writes. "When the storm of grief had spent itself she went away to her room alone. She would have no one follow her." From this, we gather that Mrs. Mallard loved her husband and is deeply saddened by his death.

However, later in the story, we discover that the wife is actually happy about her husband's death because she yearns for her freedom. As the young wife sits alone in her room, her true feelings emerge: "She was beginning to recognize this thing that was approaching to possess her, and she was striving to beat it back with her will . . . " the author writes. "When she abandoned herself a little whispered word escaped her slightly parted lips. She said it over and over under her breath: 'free, free, free!' "

At this point, Mrs. Mallard imagines how free she will be without her husband. She looks "beyond that bitter moment" of her husband's funeral to a "long procession of years to come

---

that would belong to her absolutely. And she open[s] and spread[s] her arms out to them in welcome." Now, as the young wife contemplates her life ahead, her feelings for her dead husband are unimportant to her: "She had loved him— sometimes. Often she had not. What did it matter!" Here, the woman reveals that her own freedom is now more important to her than her husband was.

From this story, we learn a great deal about the secret feelings that this woman has about her marriage and her husband, feelings that she does not reveal even to her closest family and friends. Mrs. Mallard can provide us with an important lesson about marriage in general: if married couples conceal their unhappiness, the results could be disastrous.

ANALYSIS QUESTIONS:

Discuss the sample essay in a group by answering these questions:

1. What information do you find in the introduction?
2. Have you ever read "The Story of an Hour"? Can you generally understand what the story is about from the essay about the wife?
3. What does the Thesis Statement say about the character?
4. Are connecting words used to introduce paragraphs?
5. These connecting words tell us that the analysis of the character is organized in the order of ____.
6. Are many direct quotations used as support in body paragraphs? Do you find much paraphrase?
7. Can you guess if the quotations used as support are complete or partial quotations? Also, why are brackets used in the quote in paragraph 4? (You can consult "The Story of an Hour" in Chapter 9.)
8. What verb tense is the essay written in? Why?
9. Does the conclusion restate the Thesis Statement? What additional information is given in this paragraph?

UNIT FOUR

The Unforeseen

In each story in Unit Four, there exists an unknown quantity: a world of deception in "The Rule of Names," and inner emotional struggles in "The Story of an Hour" and "The Magic Barrel." The stories herein do not contain clear plots; rather, they move in unforeseen directions, requiring students to read carefully to follow the story line and discern themes and other literary elements. A poem in this unit, "A Dream within a Dream," carries on the abstract quality of the writing in this unit. Furthermore, students are encouraged to expand their literary experience by writing their own story or poem.

". . . the name is the thing," he said in his shy, soft, husky voice, *"and the truename is the true thing. To speak the name is to control the thing."*

CHAPTER EIGHT

The Rule of Names

by Ursula K. Le Guin

About the Author

Ursula K. Le Guin, born in Berkeley, California, in 1929, is a leading American fantasy and science fiction writer, recognized for creating a variety of imaginary worlds in novels and short stories. Her novel *The Left Hand of Darkness* (1970) won the Hugo and Nebula Awards, and other Le Guin novels have received writing awards, including *A Wizard of Earthsea* (1969) and *The Farthest Shore* (1973). In her fiction, Le Guin has created diverse worlds of the present and the future: an island world called Earthsea, a Hainish world of

planets, an imaginary European country, Orsinia, and the American West Coast in the near future.

At First Glance

1. Read the title and the first line of the story. What do you think is "The Rule of Names"?

2. Finish reading the first paragraph of the story. What kind of person do you think Mr. Underhill is? Where do you think he lives?

3. In paragraph 2, we learn Mr. Underhill is a wizard. What is a wizard? What does he do? Is he generally thought of as a good or a bad force?

The Writer's Perspective

1. As you have found from the author description, Le Guin writes fantasy stories. What type of story do you expect this tale of a wizard named Mr. Underhill to be? adventure? mystery? love story?

2. If you read "Of Missing Persons" by Jack Finney in the previous unit, think about the characteristics of the fantasy world Finney created. What was his fantasy world like? As you read, compare Le Guin's fantasy world with Finney's.

3. What kind of fantasy stories exist in your culture? As you read, compare those types of stories with this one.

The Rule of Names

by Ursula K. Le Guin

1   *M*r. Underhill came out from under his hill, smiling and breathing hard. Each breath shot out of his nostrils as a double puff of steam, snow-white in the morning sunshine. Mr. Underhill looked up at the bright December sky and smiled wider than ever, showing snow-white teeth. Then he went down to the village.

2   "Morning, Mr. Underhill," said the villagers as he passed them in the narrow street between houses with conical, overhanging roofs like the fat red caps of toadstools.[1] "Morning, morning!" he replied to each. (It was of course bad luck to wish anyone a *good* morning; a simple statement of the time of day was quite enough, in a place so permeated with Influences as Sattins Island, where a careless adjective might change the weather for a week.) All of them spoke to him, some with affection, some with affectionate disdain.[2] He was all the little island had in the way of a wizard, and so deserved respect—but how could you respect a little fat man of fifty who waddled along with his toes turned in, breathing steam and smiling? He was no great shakes as a workman either. His fireworks were fairly elaborate but his elixirs were weak. Warts he charmed off frequently reappeared after three days; tomatoes he enchanted grew no bigger than cante-loupes; and rare times when a strange ship stopped at Sattins Harbor, Mr. Underhill always stayed under his hill—for fear, he explained, of the evil eye. He was, in other words, a wizard the way walleyed[3] Gan was a carpenter: by default. The villagers made do with badly-hung doors and inefficient spells, for this generation, and relieved their annoyance by treating Mr. Under-hill quite familiarly, as a mere fellow-villager. They even asked him to dinner. Once he asked some of them to dinner, and served a splendid repast,[4] with silver, crystal, damask, roast goose, sparkling Andrades '639, and plum pudding with hard sauce; but he was so nervous all through the meal that it took the joy out of it, and besides, everybody was hungry again half

---

1. *wild mushroom-like plants*, 2. *hatred*, 3. *bulging-eyed*, 4. *dinner*

an hour afterward. He did not like anyone to visit his cave, not even the anteroom,[5] beyond which in fact nobody had ever got. When he saw people approaching the hill he always came trotting out to meet them. "Let's sit out here under the pine trees!" he would say, smiling and waving towards the fir grove, or if it was raining, "Let's go have a drink at the inn, eh?" though everybody knew he drank nothing stronger than well-water.

3   Some of the village children, teased by that locked cave, poked and pried and made raids while Mr. Underhill was away; but the small door that led into the inner chamber was spell-shut, and it seemed for once to be an effective spell. Once a couple of boys, thinking the wizard was over on the West Shore curing Mrs. Ruuna's sick donkey, brought a crowbar and a hatchet up there, but at the first whack of the hatchet on the door there came a roar of wrath from inside, and a cloud of purple steam. Mr. Underhill had got home early. The boys fled. He did not come out, and the boys came to no harm, though they said you couldn't believe what a huge hooting howling hissing horrible bellow that little fat man could make unless you'd heard it.

4   His business in town this day was three dozen fresh eggs and a pound of liver; also a stop at Seacaptain Fogeno's cottage[6] to renew the seeing-charm on the old man's eyes (quite useless when applied to a case of detached retina, but Mr. Underhill kept trying), and finally a chat with old Goody Guld, the concertina[7]-maker's widow. Mr. Underhill's friends were mostly old people. He was timid with the strong young men of the village, and the girls were shy of him. "He makes me nervous, he smiles so much," they all said, pouting, twisting silky ringlets round a finger. "Nervous" was a newfangled word, and their mothers all replied grimly, "Nervous my foot, silliness is the word for it. Mr. Underhill is a very respectable wizard!"

5   After leaving Goody Guld, Mr. Underhill passed by the school, which was being held this day out on the common.[8] Since no one on Sattins Island was literate, there were no books to learn to read from and no desks to carve initials on and no black-boards to erase, and in fact no schoolhouse. On rainy days the children met in the loft of the Communal Barn, and got hay in their pants; on sunny days the schoolteacher, Palani, took them anywhere she felt like. Today, surrounded by thirty interested

5. *entry room,* 6. *small, quaint house,* 7. *accordian,* 8. *town square*

children under twelve and forty uninterested sheep under five, she was teaching an important item on the curriculum: the Rules of Names. Mr. Underhill, smiling shyly, paused to listen and watch. Palani, a plump, pretty girl of twenty, made a charming picture there in the wintry sunlight, sheep and children around her, a leafless oak above her, and behind her the dunes and sea and clear, pale sky. She spoke earnestly, her face flushed pink by wind and words. "Now you know the Rules of Names, already, children. There are two, and they're the same on every island in the world. What's one of them?"

6   "It ain't polite to ask anybody what his name is," shouted a fat, quick boy, interrupted by a little girl shrieking, "You can't never tell your own name to nobody my ma says!"

7   "Yes, Suba. Yes, Popi dear, don't screech. That's right. You never ask anybody his name. You never tell your own. Now think about that a minute and then tell me why we call our wizard Mr. Underhill." She smiled across the curly heads and the woolly backs at Mr. Underhill, who beamed, and nervously clutched his sack of eggs.

8   " 'Cause he lives under a hill!" said half the children.

9   "But is it his truename?"

10   "No!" said the fat boy, echoed by little Popi shrieking, "No!"

11   "How do you know it's not?"

12   " 'Cause he came here all alone and so there wasn't anybody knew his truename so they couldn't tell us, and *he* couldn't—"

13   "Very good, Suba. Popi, don't shout. That's right. Even a wizard can't tell his truename. When you children are through school and go through the Passage, you'll leave your childnames behind and keep only your truenames, which you must never ask for and never give away. Why is that the rule?"

14   The children were silent. The sheep bleated gently. Mr. Underhill answer the question: "Because the name is the thing," he said in his shy, soft, husky voice, "and the truename is the true thing. To speak the name is to control the thing. Am I right, Schoolmistress?"

15   She smiled and curtseyed,[9] evidently a little embarrassed by his participation. And he trotted off towards his hill, clutching his eggs to his bosom. Somehow the minute spent watching Palani and the children had made him very hungry. He locked

---

9. *bowed*

his inner door behind him with a hasty incantation, but there must have been a leak or two in the spell, for soon the bare anteroom of the cave was rich with the smell of frying eggs and sizzling liver.

16   The wind that day was light and fresh out of the west, and on it at noon a little boat came skimming the bright waves into Sattins Harbor. Even as it rounded the point a sharp-eyed boy spotted it, and knowing, like every child on the island, every sail and spar of the forty boats of the fishing fleet, he ran down the street calling out, "A foreign boat, a foreign boat!" Very seldom was the lonely isle visited by a boat from some equally lonely isle of the East Reach, or an adventurous trade from the Archipelago. By the time the boat was at the pier half the village was there to greet it, and fishermen were following it homewards, and cowherds and clam-diggers and herb-hunters were puffing up and down all thē rocky hills, heading towards the harbor.

17   But Mr. Underhill's door stayed shut.

18   There was only one man aboard the boat. Old Seacaptain Fogeno, when they told him that, drew down a bristle of white brows over his unseeing eyes. "There's only one kind of man," he said, "that sails the Outer Reach alone. A wizard, or a warlock, or a Mage . . . "

19   So the villagers were breathless hoping to see for once in their lives a Mage, one of the mighty White Magicians of the rich, towered, crowded inner islands of the Archipelago. They were disappointed, for the voyager was quite young, a handsome black-bearded fellow who hailed them cheerfully from his boat, and leaped ashore like any sailor glad to have made port. He introduced himself at once as a sea-peddlar. But when they told Seacaptain Fogeno that he carried an oaken walking-stick around with him, the old man nodded. "Two wizards in one town," he said. "Bad!" And his mouth snapped shut like an old carp's.[10]

20   As the stranger could not give them his name, they gave him one right away: Blackbeard. And they gave him plenty of attention. He had a small mixed cargo of cloth and sandals and piswi feathers for trimming cloaks and cheap incense and levity stones and fine herbs and great glass beads from Venway—the usual peddlar's lot. Everyone on Sattins Island came to look, to chat with the voyager, and perhaps to buy something—'Just to remember him by!" cackled Goody Guld, who like all the women and girls of the village was smitten with Blackbeard's bold good looks. All the boys hung round him too, to hear him tell of his

10. *type of fish*

voyages to far, strange islands of the Reach or describe the great rich islands of the Archipelago, the Inner Lanes, the roadsteads white with ships, and the golden roofs of Havnor. The men willingly listened to his tales; but some of them wondered why a trader should sail alone, and kept their eyes thoughtfully upon his oaken staff.[11]

21   But all this time Mr. Underhill stayed under his hill.

22   "This is the first island I've ever seen that had no wizard," said Blackbeard one evening to Goody Guld, who had invited him and her nephew and Palani in for a cup of rushwash tea. "What do you do when you get a toothache, or the cow goes dry?"

23   "Why, we've got Mr. Underhill!" said the old woman.

24   "For what that's worth," muttered her nephew Birt, and then blushed purple and spilled his tea. Birt was a fisherman, a large, brave, wordless young man. He loved the schoolmistress, but the nearest he had come to telling her of his love was to give baskets of fresh mackerel to her father's cook.

25   "Oh, you do have a wizard?" Blackbeard asked. "Is he invisible?"

26   "No, he's just very shy," said Palani. "You've only been here a week, you know, and we see so few strangers here. . . ." She also blushed a little, but did not spill her tea.

27   Blackbeard smiled at her. "He's a good Sattinsman, then, eh?"

28   "No," said Goody Guld, "no more than you are. Another cup, nevvy? keep it in the cup this time. No, my dear, he came in a little bit of a boat, four years ago was it? just a day after the end of the shad run, I recall, for they was taking up the nets over in East Creek, and Pondi Cowherd broke his leg that very morn-ing—five years ago it must be. No, four. No, five it is, 'twas the year the garlic didn't sprout. So he sails in on a bit of a sloop[12] loaded full up with great chests and boxes and says to Seacaptain Fogeno, who wasn't blind then, though old enough goodness knows to be blind twice over, 'I hear tell,' he says, 'you've got no wizard nor warlock at all, might you be wanting one?' 'Indeed, if the magic's white!' says the Captain, and before you could say cuttlefish Mr. Underhill had settled down in the cave under the hill and was charming the mange off Goody Beltow's cat. Though the fur grew in grey, and 'twas an orange cat. Queer-looking thing it was after that. It died last winter in the cold spell. Goody Beltow took on so at that cat's death, poor thing, worse than when her man was drowned on the Long Banks, the year of the

---

11. *stick,* 12. *sailboat*

long herring-runs, when nevvy Birt here was but a babe in petti-
coats." Here Birt spilled his tea again, and Blackbeard grinned, but
Goody Guld proceeded undismayed, and talked on till nightfall.

29   Next day Blackbeard was down at the pier, seeing after the
sprung board in his boat which he seemed to take a long time
fixing, and as usual drawing the taciturn[13] Sattinsmen into talk.
"Now which of these is your wizard's craft?" he asked. "Or has
he got one of those the Mages fold up into a walnut shell when
they're not using it?"

30   "Nay," said a stolid[14] fisherman. "She's oop in his cave, under
hill."

31   "He carried the boat he came in up to this cave?"

32   "Aye. Clear oop. I helped. Heavier as lead she was. Full oop
with great boxes, and they full oop with books o' spells, he says.
Heavier as lead she was." And the stolid fisherman turned his
back, sighing stolidly. Goody Guld's nephew, mending a net
nearby, looked up from his work and asked with equal stolidity,
"Would ye like to meet Mr. Underhill, maybe?"

33   Blackbeard returned Birt's look. Clever black eyes met candid
blue ones for a long moment; then Blackbeard smiled and said,
"Yes. Will you take me up to the hill, Birt?"

34   "Aye, when I'm done with this," said the fisherman. And when
the net was mended, he and the Archipelagan set off up the
village street towards the high green hill above it. But as they
crossed the common Blackbeard said, "Hold on a while, friend
Birt. I have a tale to tell you, before we meet your wizard."

35   "Tell away," says Birt, sitting down in the shade of a live-oak.

36   "It's a story that started a hundred years ago, and isn't
finished yet—though it soon will be, very soon. . . . In the very
heart of the Archipelago, where the islands crowd thick as flies
on honey, there's a little isle called Pendor. The sealords of
Pendor were mighty men, in the old days of war before the
League. Loot and ransom and tribute came pouring into Pendor,
and they gathered a great treasure there, long ago. Then from
somewhere away out in the West Reach, where dragons breed on
the lava isles, came one day a very mighty dragon. Not one of
those overgrown lizards most of you Outer Reach folk call
dragons, but a big, black, winged, wise, cunning monster, full of
strength and subtlety, and like all dragons loving gold and
precious stones above all things. He killed the Sealord and his
soldiers, and the people of Pendor fled in their ships by night.
They all fled away and left the dragon coiled up in Pendor

---

13. *untalkative,* 14. *emotionless*

Towers. And there he stayed for a hundred years, dragging his scaly belly over the emeralds and sapphires and coins of gold, coming forth only once in a year or two when he must eat. He'd raid nearby islands for his food. You know what dragons eat?"

37   Birt nodded and said in a whisper, "Maidens."

38   "Right," said Blackbeard. "Well, that couldn't be endured forever, nor the thought of him sitting on all that treasure. So after the League grew strong, and the Archipelago wasn't so busy with wars and piracy, it was decided to attack Pendor, drive out the dragon, and get the gold and jewels for the treasury of the League. They're forever wanting money, the League is. So a huge fleet gathered from fifty islands, and seven Mages stood in the prows of the seven strongest ships, and they sailed towards Pendor. . . . They got there. They landed. Nothing stirred. The houses all stood empty, the dishes on the tables full of a hundred years' dust. The bones of the old Sealord and his men lay about in the castle courts and on the stairs. And the Tower rooms reeked of dragon. But there was no dragon. And no treasure, not a diamond the size of a poppyseed, not a single silver bead . . . Knowing that he couldn't stand up to seven Mages, the dragon had skipped out. They tracked him, and found he'd flown to a deserted island up north called Udrath; they followed his trail there, and what did they find? Bones again. His bones—the dragon's. But no treasure. A wizard, some unknown wizard from somewhere, must have met him singlehanded, and defeated him—and then made off with the treasure, right under the League's nose!"

39   The fisherman listened, attentive and expressionless.

40   "Now that must have been a powerful wizard and a clever one, first to kill a dragon, and second to get off without leaving a trace. The lords and Mages of the Archipelago couldn't track him at all, neither where he'd come from nor where he'd made off to. They were about to give up. That was last spring; I'd been off on a three-year voyage up in the North Reach, and got back about that time. And they asked me to help them find the unknown wizard. That was clever of them. Because I'm not only a wizard myself, as I think some of the oafs[15] here have guessed, but I am also a descendant of the Lords of Pendor. That treasure is mine. It's mine, and knows that it's mine. Those fools of the League couldn't find it, because it's not theirs. It belongs to the House of Pendor, and the great emerald, the star of the hoard, Inalkil the Greenstone, knows its master. Behold!" Blackbeard raised his oaken staff and cried aloud, "Inalkil!" The tip of the

15. *stupid persons*

staff began to glow green, a fiery green radiance, a dazzling haze the color of April grass, and at the same moment the staff tipped in the wizard's hand, leaning, slanting till it pointed straight at the side of the hill above them.

41   "It wasn't so bright a glow, far away in Havnor," Blackbeard murmured, "but the staff pointed true. Inalkil answered when I called. The jewel knows its master. And I know the thief, and I shall conquer him. He's a mighty wizard, who could overcome a dragon. But I am mightier. Do you want to know why, oaf? Because I know his name!"

42   As Blackbeard's tone got more arrogant, Birt had looked duller and duller, blanker and blanker; but at this he gave a twitch, shut his mouth, and stared at the Archipelagan. "How did you . . . learn it?" he asked very slowly.

43   Blackbeard grinned, and did not answer.

44   "Black magic?"

45   "How else?"

46   Birt looked pale, and said nothing.

47   "I am the Sealord of Pendor, oaf, and I will have the gold my fathers won, and the jewels my mothers wore, and the Greenstone! For they are mine. —Now, you can tell your village boobies[16] the whole story after I have defeated this wizard and gone. Wait here. Or you can come and watch, if you're not afraid. You'll never get the chance again to see a great wizard in all his power." Blackbeard turned, and without a backward glance strode off up the hill towards the entrance to the cave.

48   Very slowly, Birt followed. A good distance from the cave he stopped, sat down under a hawthorn tree, and watched. The Archipelegan had stopped; a stiff, dark figure alone on the green swell of the hill before the gaping cave-mouth, he stood perfectly still. All at once he swung his staff up over his head, and the emerald radiance shone about him as he shouted, "Thief, thief of the Hoard of Pendor, come forth!"

49   There was a crash, as of dropped crockery, from inside the cave, and a lot of dust came spewing out. Scared, Birt ducked. When he looked again he saw Blackbeard still standing motionless, and at the mouth of the cave, dusty and dishevelled,[17] stood Mr. Underhill. He looked small and pitiful, with his toes turned in as usual, and his little bowlegs in black tights, and no staff—he never had had one, Birt suddenly thought. Mr. Underhill spoke. "Who are you?" he said in his husky little voice.

50   "I am the Sealord of Pendor, thief, come to claim my treasure!"

16. *slang, stupid persons,*   17. *messy*

51   At that, Mr. Underhill slowly turned pink, as he always did when people were rude to him. But he then turned something else. He turned yellow. His hair bristled out, he gave a coughing roar—and was a yellow lion leaping down the hill at Blackbeard, white fangs gleaming.

52   But Blackbeard no longer stood there. A gigantic tiger, color of night and lightning, bounded to meet the lion . . . .

53   The lion was gone. Below the cave all of a sudden stood a high grove of trees, black in the winter sunshine. The tiger, checking himself in mid-leap just before he entered the shadow of the trees, caught fire in the air, became a tongue of flame lashing out at the dry black branches.

54   But where the trees had stood a sudden cataract leaped from the hillside, an arch of silvery crashing water, thundering down upon the fire. But the fire was gone. . . .

55   For just a moment before the fisherman's staring eyes two hills rose—the green one he knew, and a new one, a bare, brown hillock ready to drink up the rushing waterfall. That passed so quickly it made Birt blink, and after blinking he blinked again, and moaned, for what he saw now was a great deal worse. Where the cataract had been there hovered a dragon. Black wings darkened all the hill, steel claws reached groping, and from the dark, scaly, gaping lips fire and steam shot out.

56   Beneath the monstrous creature stood Blackbeard, laughing.

57   "Take any shape you please, little Mr. Underhill!" he taunted. "I can match you. But the game grows tiresome. I want to look upon my treasure, upon Inalkil. Now, big dragon, little wizard, take your true shape. I command you by the power of your true name—Yevaud!"

58   Birt could not move at all, not even to blink. He cowered,[18] staring whether he would or not. He saw the black dragon hang there in the air above Blackbeard. He saw the fire lick like many tongues from the scaly mouth, the steam jet from the red nostrils. He saw Blackbeard's face grow white, white as chalk, and the beard-fringed lips trembling.

59   "Your name is Yevaud!"

60   "Yes," said a great, husky, hissing voice. "My truename is Yevaud and my true shape is this shape."

61   "But the dragon was killed—they found dragon-bones on Udrath Island—"

62   "That was another dragon," said the dragon, and then stooped like a hawk, talons outstretched. And Birt shut his eyes.

18. *shrank away in fear*

63   When he opened them the sky was clear, the hillside empty, except for a reddish-blackish trampled spot, and a few talon-marks in the grass.

64   Birt the fisherman got to his feet and ran. He ran across the common, scattering sheep to right and left, and straight down the village street to Palani's father's house. Palani was out in the garden weeding the nasturtiums. "Come with me!" Birt gasped. She stared. He grabbed her wrist and dragged her with him. She screeched a little, but did not resist. He ran with her straight to the pier, pushed her into his fishing-sloop the *Queenie*, untied the painter, took up the oars and set off rowing like a demon. The last that Sattins Island saw of him and Palani was the *Queenie*'s sail vanishing in the direction of the nearest island westward.

65   The villagers thought they would never stop talking about it, how Goody Guld's nephew Birt had lost his mind and sailed off with the schoolmistress on the very same day that the peddlar Blackbeard disappeared without a trace, leaving all his feathers and beads behind. But they did stop talking about it, three days later. They had other things to talk about, when Mr. Underhill finally came out of his cave.

66   Mr. Underhill had decided that since his truename was no longer a secret, he might as well drop his disguise. Walking was a lot harder than flying, and besides, it was a long, long time since he had had a real meal.

Understanding the Text: *Recalling Main Ideas/Drawing Inferences*

Answer the questions below in a small group. Discuss your answers with the rest of the class.

1. What is the real identity of Mr. Underhill?

2. Scan the beginning of the story and write down clues to Mr. Underhill's real identity.

3. What powers does Mr. Underhill possess?

4. Who is Blackbeard? What powers does he have?

5. Why has Mr. Underhill come to Sattins Island?

6. Why has Blackbeard come to Sattins Island?

7. In the battle at the end of the story, who is the winner?

8. Will Mr. Underhill remain on the island?

Understanding the Text: *Analysis*

Answer these questions with your group:

1. In paragraph 2, the author explains that on Sattins Island people don't say "Good morning!" because it is "a place so permeated with Influences" that "a careless adjective might change the weather for a week." What does the author mean to say about the island?

2. Also in paragraph 2, we learn that this island, like all others, needs a wizard. Why do the villagers need a wizard? What kind of tasks does he perform?

3. What strange characteristic does Mr. Underhill have, as described in paragraph 2?

4. In paragraph 5, what do you learn about education on Sattins Island?

5. Reread paragraphs 5 through 14. Then, explain in your own words the Rules of Names.

6. Why do you think this society has such rules about names?

7. What do you learn in paragraph 18 about the identity of the stranger who visits the island?

8. Who is Birt? How is he described, in paragraph 24?

9. In paragraph 28, when Goody Guld recalls Mr. Underhill's arrival to the island, what do we learn about life on Sattins Island? What is important in the island's history?

10. How are Sattinsmen depicted, in paragraphs 29 and 30?

11. Summarize the tale that Blackbeard tells, beginning in paragraph 36.

12. In paragraph 42, how does Birt feel as Blackbeard tells him the story?

13. In paragraph 48, does Birt decide to stay and watch the wizard battle or does he run away?

14. In paragraph 51, after Blackbeard confronts Mr. Underhill, what does Mr. Underhill do?

15. What does Blackbeard do, in paragraph 52?

16. What forms do the two wizards transform themselves into in paragraphs 53 and 54?

17. Finally, Mr. Underhill assumes his real shape in paragraph 55. How is he described in this paragraph?

18. In paragraph 57, Blackbeard confidently calls Mr. Underhill by his truename. However, in paragraph 58, Blackbeard trembles and his "face grow[s] white, white as chalk." Why does Blackbeard's emotional state change suddenly?

19. In paragraph 63, Birt opens his eyes after the confrontation to see "the hillside empty, except for a reddish-blackish trampled spot, and a few talon-marks in the grass." What has happened?

20. Finally, what does Birt do in paragraph 64?

21. Why do you think Birt does what he does in the end?

22. In the last two paragraphs, the villagers are talking about Birt's sudden departure. Then, the last line of the story says: "Walking was a lot harder than flying, and besides, it was a long, long time since he had had a real meal." What do you think happened then?

Literary Concepts: *Setting, Fantasy*

Ursula K. Le Guin's "The Rule of Names" is categorized as a fantasy tale because she creates an unreal world, as Jack Finney did in "Of Missing Persons." Finney's world was clearly defined as being outside the planet Earth, and the time was, at least, roughly set by his description of Earth life. However, in this story, Le Guin gives no definition of where her world is, nor when the story occurs. To understand more about the story and its characters, first examine the setting and then analyze your reactions to the fantasy world of the story.

1. Setting

   Sattins Island is a world created by the author, so the reader must piece together clues to determine the nature of the place. For instance, the first two paragraphs tell us the setting is a village with narrow streets and cone-shaped houses. Other details in these paragraphs and others give us clues about the island, its inhabitants, and life-style. As for the time of the story, the reader can only guess.

   With your partner, scan paragraphs 1 and 2 and other parts of the story to determine the setting.

   a. Describe Sattins Island.

   Size: _____

   Geographical description: _____

   Chief industries: _____

   Method of transportation: _____

   b. When do you guess the story took place? _____

   c. Is Sattins Island on Earth or elsewhere? _____

2. Fantasy

   Discuss these questions with your partner about Le Guin's fantasy world:

   a. What unreal elements in the story tell you this is a fantasy world?
   b. Do you believe such a world, including its inhabitants, could exist?

Looking at Language: *Participial Phrases*

In this story, we find many present and past participles used to combine ideas in sentences. The first line of the story provides an example: "Mr. Underhill came out from under his hill, smiling and breathing hard." Here, the author has combined three simple actions into one sentence by using phrases beginning with the present participles "smiling" and "breathing." As you know, the use of participial phrases, rather than another method of combining ideas in sentences, creates the variety in

sentence patterns that makes writing interesting. Of course, as you have studied, the subject of the actions in the main clause and in the participial phrase must be the same.

1. With a partner, examine the sentences below, which are taken from the story, and identify the participial phrases. Discuss why present (+ing) or past (+ed) participles are used.

    a. "Some of the village children, teased by that locked cave, poked and pried and made raids while Mr. Underhill was away . . . " (paragraph 3)
    b. " 'He makes me nervous, he smiles so much,' they all said, pouting, twisting silky ringlets round a finger." (paragraph 4)
    c. "After leaving Goody Guld, Mr. Underhill passed by the school . . . " (paragraph 5)
    d. "Mr. Underhill, smiling shyly, paused to listen and watch." (paragraph 5)
    e. "She spoke earnestly, her face flushed pink by wind and words." (paragraph 5)

2. Now with your partner, rewrite these sentences from the story, replacing standard verbs with participial phrases. Remember that the subject of the verbs must be the same for the main part of the sentence and the participial phrase.

    a. ". . . but some of them wondered why a trader should sail alone, and kept their eyes thoughtfully upon his oaken staff." (paragraph 20)
    b. " 'For what that's worth,' muttered her nephew Birt, and then blushed purple and spilled his tea." (paragraph 24)
    c. ". . . Goody Guld proceeded undismayed, and talked on till nightfall." (paragraph 28)
    d. "Blackbeard grinned, and did not answer." (paragraph 43)
    e. "He grabbed her wrist and dragged her with him." (paragraph 64)

❋Looking at Language: *Vocabulary by Theme—Antonyms*

In the last half of "The Rule of Names," you find contrasts drawn between the Sattinsmen, particularly Birt, and the wizard Blackbeard. Beginning in paragraph 29, you can find numerous descriptive adjectives, which differ from those used to depict the common villagers and wizards.

To expand your vocabulary, complete the list of vocabulary items below with your partner by supplying antonyms that could be used to describe the two types of characters. Words that come from the story are supplied to begin your list. In the column next to the given word, write an antonym. The antonym may be one you and your partner generate, or may be found in other places in the story. If you are unsure of the given words' meanings, consult a dictionary. Compare your lists with the class, and add other words that describe the characters.

Birt and the Villagers	Blackbeard, the Wizard
taciturn (par. 29)	_____
stolid (par. 30)	_____
_____	clever (par. 33)
candid (par. 33)	_____
expressionless (par. 39)	_____
_____	arrogant (par. 42)
dull (par. 42)	_____

Culture Point: *Monsters and Myths*

The notion of dragons and other mythical creatures has been present in cultures throughout the world since ancient times. For example, dragons described in tales of Greece, Norway, Germany, and England were similar to Le Guin's winged, fire-breathing serpent. Such monsters swallowed ships and men in a single gulp, and preyed on young maidens. The dragon also symbolized sin in early Christian religion. Thus, a legend arose that a brave soldier who became a Christian saint, or holy person, Saint George, killed a dragon to save a king's daughter. Saint George's mythical slaying of the dragon has been portrayed by many artists, including the Italian painter Raphael.

Share your culture's ideas about mythical creatures by answering these questions in a small group.

1. Have dragons or other monsters existed in stories or other art forms in your culture? Explain.

2. Have you read a particular story from your culture about a monster? Describe it.

3. Why do you think people create myths involving monsters?

READING JOURNAL

In your Reading Journal, answer one or more of these questions about "The Rule of Names."

1. Why do you think people didn't give their real names?

2. Do you ever imagine worlds full of dragons and wizards? What takes place in these worlds?

3. If you have read another story about monsters or wizards, tell briefly what it was about.

4. Do you like this story?

VIDEO

Fantasy is the subject of many films whose subjects are similar to "The Rule of Names." In your class or outside, you may wish to view a film such as *Clash of the Titans* (1981), *Dragonslayer* (1981), or *Conan the Barbarian* (1982) to compare the mythological monsters and wizards on screen with those in Le Guin's story. Moreover, Japanese movies such as the *Gamera* series (*Gamera Versus Barugon, Gamera Versus Gaos, Gamera Versus Zigra*) present monsters in both good and bad lights, not unlike the "white magic" and "black magic" wizards mentioned in "The Rule of Names."

"She breathed a quick prayer that life might be long. It was only yesterday that she had thought with a shudder that life might be long."

CHAPTER NINE

The Story of an Hour

by Kate Chopin

About the Author

Kate Chopin (1851–1904) was born in St. Louis, Missouri. She lived for many years in Louisiana, where she married a cotton broker. After her husband's death, Chopin returned to St. Louis with her children and started writing. She wrote "The Story of an Hour" in 1894, along with other short stories and novels. Her most famous novel *The Awakening* (1899), was controversial because it dealt sympathetically with adultery. The themes of women's emotions and wives' domination by husbands runs throughout her writing.

At First Glance

1. What information does the title "The Story of an Hour" give you about this text?

2. Read the first paragraph of the story. How do you think people imagined Mrs. Mallard would feel when she learned of her husband's death?

3. Read the list of words below, which describe the feelings and events in the life of the main character of this story. With a partner, discuss the words you know and look up the unfamiliar words in a dictionary. Which words describe positive feelings and which describe negative feelings? What do they suggest about the story?

   storm of grief   vacant stare
   exalted   self-assertion
   sob   bitter moment
   illumination   triumph

The Writer's Perspective

1. Kate Chopin wrote this story at the turn of the twentieth century. What do you think the relationship was like between an American husband and wife around the year 1900?

2. Chopin is recognized as an early "women's liberationist." What does women's liberation mean? What do women want to be liberated from?

3. Do you agree with the goals and ideas of the women's liberation movement?

4. Have women become more "liberated" in your culture? How?

5. What do you see as the ideal roles of a husband and wife?

The Story of an Hour

by Kate Chopin

1   *K*nowing that Mrs. Mallard was afflicted with a heart trouble, great care was taken to break to her as gently as possible the news of her husband's death.

2   It was her sister Josephine who told her, in broken sentences; veiled[1] hints that revealed in half concealing. Her husband's friend Richards was there, too, near her. It was he who had been in the newspaper office when intelligence of the railroad disaster was received, with Brently Mallard's name leading the list of "killed." He had only taken the time to assure himself of its truth by a second telegram, and hastened to forestall[2] any less careful, less tender friend in bearing the sad message.

3   She did not hear the story as many women have heard the same, with a paralyzed inability to accept its significance. She wept at once, with sudden, wild abandonment, in her sister's arms. When the storm of grief had spent itself she went away to her room alone. She would have no one follow her.

4   There stood facing the open window, a comfortable, roomy armchair. Into this she sank, pressed down by a physical exhaustion that haunted her body and seemed to reach into her soul.

5   She could see in the open square before her house the tops of trees that were all aquiver[3] with the new spring life. The delicious breath of rain was in the air. In the street below a peddler was crying his wares. The notes of a distant song which some one was singing reached her faintly, and countless sparrows were twittering in the eaves.

6   There were patches of blue sky showing here and there through the clouds that had met and piled one above the other in the west facing her window.

7   She sat with her head thrown back upon the cushion of the chair, quite motionless, except when a sob came up into her throat and shook her, as a child who had cried itself to sleep continues to sob in its dreams.

---

1. *concealed*, 2. *prevent*, 3. *shaking*

8   She was young, with a fair, calm face, whose lines bespoke repression and even a certain strength. But now there was a dull stare in her eyes, whose gaze was fixed away off yonder on one of those patches of blue sky. It was not a glance of reflection, but rather indicated a suspension of intelligent thought.

9   There was something coming to her and she was waiting for it, fearfully. What was it? She did not know; it was too subtle and elusive[4] to name. But she felt it, creeping out of the sky, reaching toward her through the sounds, the scents, the color that filled the air.

10   Now her bosom rose and fell tumultuously.[5] She was beginning to recognize this thing that was approaching to possess her, and she was striving to beat it back with her will—as powerless as her two white slender hands would have been.

11   When she abandoned herself a little whispered word escaped her slightly parted lips. She said it over and over under her breath: "Free, free, free!" The vacant stare and the look of terror that had followed it went from her eyes. They stayed keen and bright. Her pulses beat fast, and the coursing blood warmed and relaxed every inch of her body.

12   She did not stop to ask if it were or were not a monstrous joy that held her. A clear and exalted perception enabled her to dismiss the suggestion as trivial.

13   She knew that she would weep again when she saw the kind, tender hands folded in death; the face that had never looked save with love upon her, fixed and gray and dead. But she saw beyond that bitter moment a long procession of years to come that would belong to her absolutely. And she opened and spread her arms out to them in welcome.

14   There would be no one to live for during those coming years; she would live for herself. There would be no powerful will bending hers in that blind persistence with which men and women believe they have a right to impose a private will upon a fellow-creature. A kind intention or a cruel intention made the act seem no less a crime as she looked upon it in that brief moment of illumination.

15   And yet she had loved him—sometimes. Often she had not. What did it matter! What could love, the unsolved mystery, count for in face of this possession of self-assertion which she suddenly recognized as the strongest impulse of her being!

16   "Free! Body and soul free!" she kept whispering.

---

4. *difficult to detect,* 5. *violently*

17 Josephine was kneeling before the closed door with her lips to the keyhole, imploring for admission. "Louise, open the door! I beg; open the door—you will make yourself ill. What are you doing, Louise? For heaven's sake open the door."

18 "Go away. I am not making myself ill." No; she was drinking in a very elixir[6] of life through that open window.

19 Her fancy was running riot along those days ahead of her. Spring days, and summer days, and all sorts of days that would be her own. She breathed a quick prayer that life might be long. It was only yesterday she had thought with a shudder[7] that life might be long.

20 She arose at length and opened the door to her sister's importunities. There was a feverish triumph in her eyes, and she carried herself unwittingly like a goddess of Victory. She clasped her sister's waist, and together they descended the stairs. Richards stood waiting for them at the bottom.

21 Some one was opening the front door with a latchkey. It was Brently Mallard who entered, a little travel-stained, composedly carrying his gripsack and umbrella. He had been far from the scene of accident, and did not even know there had been one. He stood amazed at Josephine's piercing cry; at Richards' quick motion to screen him from the view of his wife.

22 But Richards was too late.

23 When the doctors came they said she had died of heart disease—of joy that kills.

---

6. *medicine*, 7. *tremble*

Understanding the Text: *Analysis*

After you have read the story carefully, answer these questions on the main ideas.

1. In paragraph 2, who tells Mrs. Mallard of her husband's death? Who confirms Mr. Mallard's death?

2. This news is told to Mrs. Mallard "in broken sentences; veiled hints that revealed in half concealing." Explain in your words what this means. Why is the news of Mr. Mallard's death told to his wife in this way?

3. Paragraph 3 tells of Mrs. Mallard's reaction to her husband's death. Why do you think she "wept at once," rather than

being "paralyzed" by such news the way many women have been? What does this tell you about Mrs. Mallard?

4. In paragraph 5, the author describes a town square from Mrs. Mallard's point of view: "new spring life . . . ," ". . . the delicious breath of rain . . . ," birds "twittering." How does Mrs. Mallard feel at that moment?

5. In paragraph 9, as Mrs. Mallard sits thinking in a chair, she thinks "there [is] something come to her and she [is] waiting for it, fearfully." What is "it"?

6. In paragraphs 10 through 12, "this thing that was approaching to possess her" is described as a "monstrous joy." Why is Mrs. Mallard's feeling described as "monstrous" and joyful? What is this feeling?

7. In paragraph 13, Mrs. Mallard thinks she will "weep again when she [sees] the kind, tender hands folded in death; the face that [has] never looked save with love upon her." Who is she describing here?

8. In paragraph 14, Mrs. Mallard contemplates her life by thinking, "There would be no powerful will bending hers . . . " What does she mean?

9. Mrs. Mallard recounts her marriage to her husband in paragraph 15 by saying she had loved her husband, yet "What did it matter!" Reread this paragraph and explain why you think she felt this way.

10. In paragraph 19, Mrs. Mallard prays "that life might be long," whereas "it was only yesterday she had thought with a shudder that life might be long." Why does she change her prospect of the future?

11. When Brently Mallard opens the door, in paragraph 21, his friend Richards tries to "screen him [Mallard] from the view of his wife." Why?

12. In the final paragraph, the doctors believe Mrs. Mallard has died "of heart disease—of joy that kills." Explain what they think has killed her and why they feel this way. Do you agree?

✿Literary Concept: *Tone*

In literature, the tone or attitude of the writer can be reflected in the choice of words and the events and details included in the story. For example, if a writer wants to evoke a depressing tone, he or she might describe a city with words like "drab" or "hopeless" as Jack Finney did in "Of Missing Persons." On the other hand, if Finney had wanted to create a story with a cheerful tone, he would have described the city using pleasant words and details.

In "The Story of an Hour," the tone changes because the story contains both happy and unhappy elements. Reread the paragraphs below. Then, in one sentence, tell briefly what happens in each paragraph, and identify the tone of each passage. Tone in literature is identified using descriptive adjectives such as bitter, sad, optimistic, joyful, matter-of-fact, etc.

1. In Paragraph 3, Mrs. Mallard _____

   _____.

   The tone of this paragraph can be described as _____

   because _____.

   The words in this paragraph that reflect the writer's tone are

   _____.

2. Paragraph 5 describes _____. Because

   the writer includes details such as _____

   _____, and uses words such as _____

   _____,

   the tone of this part of the story can be described as _____

   _____.

❧Literary Concept: *Theme*

Like other serious writers, Chopin intended her short story to be more than simply a tale about one woman's marriage and sudden death. As with other texts, "The Story of an Hour" contains different levels of meaning, and on these levels, themes, or main ideas, emerge.

With a partner, review the diagram below, which was presented in Chapter Three. Discuss themes that may be found in "The Story of an Hour," especially on the symbolic and universal levels. Below the diagram, write down your ideas about the major themes you detect.

LITERAL (concrete themes)

LEVELS OF
MEANING IN
LITERATURE

SYMBOLIC (historical, social or cultural themes)

UNIVERSAL (psychological themes)

"The Story of an Hour":

Symbolic Themes (social, historical, cultural): _____

_____

_____

Universal Themes (psychological): _____

_____

_____

❧Looking at Language: *Verb Tenses*

"The Story of an Hour," like most of the stories you have read, is written primarily in the simple past tense, as a narrative. However, other verb tenses are also used. Read the sentences below with a partner and identify the tense of each verb. Be prepared to explain why the writer uses each particular verb tense.

1. "Her husband's friend Richards was there, too, near her. It was he who had been in the newspaper office when intelligence of the railroad disaster was received . . . " (paragraph 2)

2. "In the street below a peddler was crying his wares. The notes of a distant song which some one was singing reached her faintly, and countless sparrows were twittering in the eaves." (paragraph 5)

3. "She knew that she would weep again when she saw the kind, tender hands folded in death; the face that had never looked save with love upon her, fixed and gray and dead." (paragraph 13)

4. "There would be no one to live for during those coming years; she would live for herself." (paragraph 14)

Looking at Language: *Guessing Vocabulary in Context/Restatement*

A. With a partner, use the context of the sentences to guess the meanings of the vocabulary items in italics. Define the words with a synonym or explanation. Then, use a dictionary to check your guesses.

B. After you have defined the italicized items, discuss the meanings of other unfamiliar words in the sentences with your partner. Together, write a brief restatement of each sentence. Try to use simple words other than those in the original sentence to state the main idea of the sentence. You may eliminate some details. The first restatement has been done for you.

1. veiled = _____

"It was her sister Josephine who told her, in broken sentences; *veiled* hints that revealed in half concealing." (paragraph 2)
Restatement: Josephine told her sister the news by hinting about it, not saying it directly.

2. sob = _____

"She sat with her head thrown back upon the cushion of the chair, quite motionless, except when a *sob* came up into her throat and shook her, as a child who had cried itself to sleep continues to *sob* in its dreams." (paragraph 7)

Restatement: _____

_____

3. elusive = _____

"What was it? She did not know; it was too subtle and *elusive* to name." (paragraph 9)

Restatement: _____

_____

4. persistence = _____

impose = _____

"There would be no powerful will bending hers in that blind *persistence* with which men and women believe they have a right to *impose* a private will upon a fellow-creature. A kind intention or a cruel intention made the act seem no less a crime as she looked upon it in that brief moment of illumination." (paragraph 14)

Restatement: _____

_____

_____

5. impulse = _____

"What could love, the unsolved mystery, count for in face of this possession of self-assertion which she suddenly recognized as the strongest *impulse* of her being!" (paragraph 15)

Restatement: _____

_____

Culture Point: *Women's Liberation*

Kate Chopin's stories have been considered controversial because they deal with the dreams of "freedom" of married women in the turn-of-the-twentieth-century United States. In fact, this theme is not outdated. Many women throughout the world still seek "freedom" from men, or the "freedom" to do what they wish.

Discuss in groups the themes of women and marriage as they relate to "The Story of an Hour" and life today. Consider these questions to start your discussion:

1. In "The Story of an Hour," Chopin presents Mrs. Mallard as an unhappy woman who has suffered years of repression in her marriage. Do you think she deserved to be dissatisfied with her life? Or do you think she should have been happy?

2. Are American marriages today the same as the Mallards' marriage? (Use the scant information you have from the story, or project what you think the Mallard marriage was like.)

3. How are the husband-wife relationships changing in marriages in your culture? Are the changes positive or negative?

READING JOURNAL

In your reading journal, share your opinions about Mrs. Mallard, the wife in "The Story of an Hour," by answering the questions below in a few paragraphs.

In paragraph 13, Mrs. Mallard thinks that she will weep when she sees her husband's body, "gray and dead." But instead of being sad, she thinks of her future without her husband optimistically. ". . . she saw beyond that bitter moment a long procession of years to come that would belong to her absolutely."

Do you think Mrs. Mallard is a bad person to have this reaction to her husband's death? Is she justified in feeling victorious and free?

VIDEO

To familiarize yourself with the historical period during which Chopin wrote, you may want to view the film versions of her two other stories, which deal with similar themes: women-men relationships. *The Awakening* is Chopin's most famous novel, and "The Storm" is her highly controversial short story. Both have been the basis for films that have aired on public television stations and may be available from your local public library.

If you cannot find one of these films, view *Kramer vs. Kramer* (1979), starring Dustin Hoffman and Meryl Streep. This film deals with a wife who is silently unhappy in marriage. Compare the situation of the wife in this film with Mrs. Mallard in "The Story of an Hour."

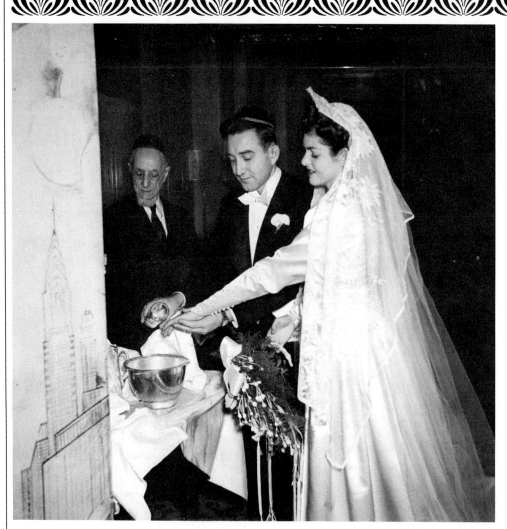

"It seemed to Leo that his whole life stood starkly revealed and he saw himself for the first time as he truly was—unloved and loveless . . ."

CHAPTER TEN

The Magic Barrel

by Bernard Malamud

About the Author

Bernard Malamud (1914–1986) grew up and lived in
New York City, so he knew well the urban life he wrote
about in his novels and short stories. His mother and
father were Russian immigrants who ran a mom-and-
pop grocery store in Brooklyn, New York. Having been
a high school teacher in New York, he began writing
late in life. His novels, including *The Assistant* (1957),
The Natural (1952), and *The Fixer* (1966), describe
urban Jewish life, as does his most popular short story,
"The Magic Barrel." Malamud's stories captured the

speech and manners of working-class American Jews, many recently immigrated, and also related the conflicts between Jews and gentiles in the United States.

At First Glance

1. The title of this story seems mysterious because a barrel that is used for storing things is described as magical. Why do you think the barrel is called "magic"?

2. Imagine that you had such a barrel. You could reach down into this barrel and retrieve one, only one, precious thing or person. What would you want to find? Compare the "contents" of your barrel with classmates.

The Writer's Perspective

1. Read the first paragraph of the story. What other stories have you read that begin "Long ago . . . " or "Once upon a time . . . "? What kind of story do you think this will be?

2. The first paragraph tells us this will be a story of a man who is looking for a wife. In your group, jot down several ways to find a husband or wife. Discuss the advantages and disadvantages of each method. Which does your group think is the best way to find a mate?

3. The man who is seeking a wife is studying to be a rabbi. What is a rabbi? Can you tell anything you know about the lives of people who study religion? What kind of people are they, generally?

The Magic Barrel

by Bernard Malamud

1   $\mathcal{N}$ot long ago there lived in uptown New York, in a small, almost meager[1] room, though crowded with books, Leo Finkle, a rabbinical student in the Yeshiva University.[2] Finkle, after six years of study, was to be ordained[3] in June and had been advised by an acquaintance that he might find it easier to win himself a congregation if he were married. Since he had no present prospects of marriage, after two tormented[4] days of turning it over in his mind, he called in Pinye Salzman, a marriage broker[5] whose two-line advertisement he had read in the *Forward*.

2   The matchmaker appeared one night out of the dark fourth-floor hallway of the graystone rooming house where Finkle lived, grasping a black, strapped portfolio that had been worn thin with use. Salzman, who had been long in the business, was of slight but dignified build, wearing an old hat, and an overcoat too short and tight for him. He smelled frankly of fish, which he loved to eat, and although he was missing a few teeth, his presence was not displeasing, because of an amiable[6] manner curiously contrasted with mournful eyes. His voice, his lips, his wisp of beard, his bony fingers were animated, but give him a moment of repose[7] and his mild blue eyes revealed a depth of sadness, a characteristic that put Leo a little at ease although the situation, for him, was inherently[8] tense.

3   He at once informed Salzman why he had asked him to come, explaining that his home was in Cleveland, and that but for his parents, who had married comparatively late in life, he was alone in the world. He had for six years devoted himself almost entirely to his studies, as a result of which, understandably, he had found himself without time for a social life and the company of young women. Therefore he thought it the better part of trial and error—of embarrassing fumbling—to call in an experienced person to advise him on these matters. He remarked in passing that the function of the marriage broker was ancient and honorable, highly approved in the Jewish community, because it made practical the

---

1. *poor,* 2. *a Jewish theological university in New York City,* 3. *authorized to be a rabbi,* 4. *painful,* 5. *arranger,* 6. *friendly,* 7. *rest,* 8. *by nature*

necessary without hindering⁹ joy. Moreover, his own parents had been brought together by a matchmaker. They had made, if not a financially profitable marriage—since neither had possessed any worldly goods to speak of—at least a successful one in the sense of their everlasting devotion to each other. Salzman listened in embarrassed surprise, sensing a sort of apology. Later, however, he experienced a glow of pride in his work, an emotion that had left him years ago, and he heartily approved of Finkle.

4   The two went to their business. Leo had led Salzman to the only clear place in the room, a table near a window that overlooked the lamp-lit city. He seated himself at the matchmaker's side but facing him, attempting by an act of will to suppress¹⁰ the unpleasant tickle in his throat. Salzman eagerly unstrapped his portfolio and removed a loose rubber band from a thin packet of much-handled cards. As he flipped through them, a gesture and sound that physically hurt Leo, the student pretended not to see and gazed steadfastly¹¹ out the window. Although it was still February, winter was on its last legs, signs of which he had for the first time in years begun to notice. He now observed the round white moon, moving high in the sky through a cloud menagerie,¹² and watched with half-open mouth as it penetrated a huge hen, and dropped out of her like an egg laying itself. Salzman, though pretending through eyeglasses he had just slipped on, to be engaged in scanning the writing on the cards, stole occasional glances at the young man's distinguished face, noting with pleasure the long, severe scholar's nose, brown eyes heavy with learning, sensitive yet ascetic¹³ lips, and a certain, almost hollow quality of the dark cheeks. He gazed around at shelves upon shelves of books and let out a soft, contented sigh.

5   When Leo's eyes fell upon the cards, he counted six spread out in Salzman's hand.

6   "So few?" he asked in disappointment.

7   "You wouldn't believe me how much cards I got in my office," Salzman replied. "The drawers are already filled to the top, so I keep them now in a barrel, but is every girl good for a new rabbi?"

8   Leo blushed at this, regretting all he had revealed of himself in a curriculum vitae¹⁴ he had sent to Salzman. He had thought it best to acquaint him with his strict standards and specifications, but in having done so, he felt he had told the marriage broker more than was absolutely necessary.

9   He hesitantly inquired, "Do you keep photographs of your clients on file?"

9. *preventing,* 10. *hold back,* 11. *continuously,* 12. *collection,* 13. *thin,* 14. *life history; résumé*

10   "First comes family, amount of dowry,[15] also what kind promises," Salzman replied, unbuttoning his tight coat and settling himself in the chair. "After comes pictures, rabbi."

11   "Call me Mr. Finkle. I'm not yet a rabbi."

12   Salzman said he would, but instead called him doctor, which he changed to rabbi when Leo was not listening too attentively.

13   Salzman adjusted his horn-rimmed[16] spectacles, gently cleared his throat and read in an eager voice the contents of the top card:

14   "Sophie P. Twenty four years. Widow one year. No children. Educated high school and two years college. Father promises eight thousand dollars. Has wonderful wholesale business. Also real estate. On the mother's side comes teachers, also one actor. Well known on Second Avenue."

15   Leo gazed up in surprise. "Did you say a widow?"

16   "A widow don't mean spoiled, rabbi. She lived with her husband maybe four months. He was a sick boy she made a mistake to marry him."

17   "Marrying a widow has never entered my mind."

18   "This is because you have no experience. A widow, especially if she is young and healthy like this girl, is a wonderful person to marry. She will be thankful to you the rest of her life. Believe me, if I was looking now for a bride, I would marry a widow."

19   Leo reflected, then shook his head.

20   Salzman hunched[17] his shoulders in an almost imperceptible gesture of disappointment. He placed the card down on the wooden table and began to read another.

21   "Lily H. High school teacher. Regular. Not a substitute. Has savings and new Dodge car. Lived in Paris one year. Father is successful dentist thirty-five years. Interested in professional man. Well Americanized family. Wonderful opportunity."

22   "I knew her personally," said Salzman. "I wish you could see this girl. She is a doll. Also very intelligent. All day you could talk to her about books and theater and what not. She also knows current events."

23   "I don't believe you mentioned her age?"

24   "Her age?" Salzman said, raising his brows. "Her age is thirty-two years."

25   Leo said after a while. "I'm afraid that seems a little too old."

26   Salzman let out a laugh. "So how old are you, rabbi?"

27   "Twenty-seven."

28   "So what is the difference, tell me, between twenty-seven and

---

15. *payment made to bride and groom by bride's parents,* 16. *wire-framed,*
17. *drew up*

thirty-two? My own wife is seven years older than me. So what did I suffer?—Nothing. If Rothschild's[18] daughter wants to marry you, would you say on account her age, no?''

29   "Yes," Leo said dryly.

30   Salzman shook off the no in the yes. "Five years don't mean a thing. I give you my word that when you will live with her for one week you will forget her age. What does it mean five years—that she lived more and knows more than somebody who is younger? On this girl, God bless her, years are not wasted. Each one that it comes makes better the bargain.''

31   "What subject does she teach in high school?''

32   "Languages. If you heard the way she speaks French, you will think it is music. I am in the business twenty-five years, and I recommend her with my whole heart. Believe me, I know what I'm talking, rabbi.''

33   "What's on the next card?'' Leo said abruptly.

34   Salzman reluctantly turned up the third card:

35   "Ruth K. Nineteen years. Honor student. Father offers thirteen thousand cash to the right bridegroom. He is a medical doctor. Stomach specialist with marvelous practice. Brother in law owns own garment business. Particular people.''

36   Salzman looked as if he had read his trump card.

37   "Did you say nineteen?'' Leo asked with interest.

38   "On the dot.''

39   "Is she attractive?'' He blushed. "Pretty?''

40   Salzman kissed his finger tips. "A little doll. On this I give you my word. Let me call the father tonight and you will see what means pretty.''

41   But Leo was troubled. "You're sure she's that young?''

42   "This I am positive. The father will show you the birth certificate.''

43   "Are you positive there isn't something wrong with her?'' Leo insisted.

44   "Who says there is wrong?''

45   "I don't understand why an American girl her age should go to a marriage broker.''

46   A smile spread over Salzman's face.

47   "So for the same reason you went, she comes.''

48   Leo flushed. "I am pressed for time.[19]''

49   Salzman, realizing he had been tactless, quickly explained. "The father came, not her. He wants she should have the best, so he looks around himself. When we will locate the right boy he will introduce him and encourage. This makes a better marriage than if a young girl without experience takes for herself. I don't have to tell you this.''

---

18. *prominent family of European Jewish financiers,* 19. *lacking time*

50   "But don't you think this young girl believes in love?" Leo spoke uneasily.

51   Salzman was about to guffaw[20] but caught himself and said soberly,[21] "Love comes with the right person, not before."

52   Leo parted dry lips but did not speak. Noticing that Salzman had snatched a glance at the next card, he cleverly asked, "How is her health?"

53   "Perfect," Salzman said, breathing with difficulty. "Of course, she is a little lame on her right foot from an auto accident that it happened to her when she was twelve years, but nobody notices on account she is so brilliant and also beautiful."

54   Leo got up heavily and went to the window. He felt curiously bitter and upbraided[22] himself for having called in the marriage broker. Finally, he shook his head.

55   "Why not?" Salzman persisted, the pitch of his voice rising.

56   "Because I detest stomach specialists."

57   "So what do you care what is his business? After you marry her do you need him? Who says he must come every Friday night in your house?"

58   Ashamed of the way the talk was going, Leo dismissed Salzman, who went home with heavy, melancholy[23] eyes.

59   Though he had felt only relief at the marriage broker's departure, Leo was in low spirits the next day. He explained it as arising from Salzman's failure to produce a suitable bride for him. He did not care for his type of clientele. But when Leo found himself hesitating whether to seek out another matchmaker, one more polished than Pinye, he wondered if it could be—his protestations to the contrary, and although he honored his father and mother—that he did not, in essence, care for the match-making institution? This thought he quickly put out of mind yet found himself still upset. All day he ran around in the woods—missed an important appointment, forgot to give out his laundry, walked out of a Broadway cafeteria without paying and had to run back with the ticket in his hand; had not even recognized his landlady in the street when she passed with a friend and courteously called out, "A good evening to you, Doctor Finkle." By nightfall, however, he had regained sufficient calm to sink his nose into a book and there found peace from his thoughts.

60   Almost at once there came a knock on the door. Before Leo could say enter, Salzman, commercial cupid,[24] was standing in the room. His face was gray and meager, his expression hungry, and he looked as if he would expire on his feet. Yet the marriage broker managed, by some trick of the muscles, to display a broad smile.

---

20. *laugh coarsely*, 21. *seriously*, 22. *blamed*, 23. *sad*, 24. *god of love*

61   "So good evening. I am invited?"

62   Leo nodded, disturbed to see him again, yet unwilling to ask the man to leave.

63   Beaming[25] still, Salzman laid his portfolio on the table. "Rabbi, I got for you tonight good news."

64   "I've asked you not to call me rabbi. I'm still a student."

65   "Your worries are finished. I have for you a first-class bride."

66   "Leave me in peace concerning this subject." Leo pretended lack of interest.

67   "The world will dance at your wedding."

68   "Please, Mr. Salzman, no more."

69   "But first must come back my strength," Salzman said weakly. He fumbled with the portfolio straps and took out of the leather case an oily paper bag, from which he extracted a hard, seeded roll and a small, smoked white fish. With a quick motion of his hand he stripped the fish out of its skin and began ravenously[26] to chew. "All day in a rush," he muttered.

70   Leo watched him eat.

71   "A sliced tomato you have maybe?" Salzman hesitantly inquired.

72   "No."

73   The marriage broker shut his eyes and ate. When he had finished he carefully cleaned up the crumbs and rolled up the remains of the fish, in the paper bag. His spectacled eyes roamed the room until he discovered, amid some piles of books, a one-burner gas stove. Lifting his hat he humbly asked, "A glass tea you got, rabbi?"

74   Conscience-stricken,[27] Leo rose and brewed the tea. He served it with a chunk of lemon and two cubes of lump sugar, delighting Salzman.

75   After he had drunk his tea, Salzman's strength and good spirits were restored.

76   "So tell me, rabbi," he said amiably, "you considered some more the three clients I mentioned yesterday?"

77   "There was no need to consider."

78   "Why not?"

79   "None of them suits me."

80   "What then suits you?"

81   Leo let it pass because he could give only a confused answer.

82   Without waiting for a reply, Salzman asked, "You remember this girl I talked to you—the high school teacher?"

83   "Age thirty-two?"

84   But, surprisingly, Salzman's face lit in a smile. "Age twenty-nine."

---

25. *smiling,* 26. *hungrily,* 27. *feeling bad*

85   Leo shot him a look. "Reduced from thirty-two?"

86   "A mistake," Salzman avowed.[28] "I talked today with the dentist. He took me to his safety deposit box[29] and showed me the birth certificate. She was twenty-nine last August. They made her a party in the mountains where she went for her vacation. When her father spoke to me the first time I forgot to write the age and I told you thirty-two, but now I remember this was a different client, a widow."

87   "The same one you told me about? I thought she was twenty-four?"

88   "A different. Am I responsible that the world is filled with widows?"

89   "No, but I'm not interested in them, nor for that matter, in school teachers."

90   Salzman pulled his clasped hands to his breast. Looking at the ceiling he devoutly exclaimed, "Yiddishe kinder,[30] what can I say to somebody that he is not interested in high school teachers? So what then you are interested?"

91   Leo flushed but controlled himself.

92   "In what else will you be interested," Salzman went on, "if you not interested in this fine girl that she speaks four languages and has personally in the bank ten thousand dollars? Also her father guarantees further twelve thousand. Also she has a new car, wonderful clothes, talks on all subjects, and she will give you a first-class home and children. How near do we come in our life to paradise?"

93   "If she's so wonderful, why wasn't she married ten years ago?"

94   "Why?" said Salzman with a heavy laugh. "—Why? Because she is partikiler.[31] This is why. She wants the best."

95   Leo was silent, amused at how he had entangled himself. But Salzman had aroused his interest in Lily H., and he began seriously to consider calling on her. When the marriage broker observed how intently Leo's mind was at work on the facts he had supplied, he felt certain they would soon come to an agreement.

96   Late Saturday afternoon, conscious of Salzman, Leo Finkle walked with Lily Hirschorn along Riverside Drive. He walked briskly[32] and erectly,[33] wearing with distinction the black fedora[34] he had that morning taken with trepidation[35] out of the dusty hat box on his closet shelf, and the heavy black Saturday coat he had thoroughly whisked clean. Leo also owned a walking stick, a present from a distant relative, but quickly put temptation aside

---

28. *promised*, 29. *locked box in a bank*, 30. *German for "Yiddish children"*;
Yiddish is a German dialect spoken by European Jews worldwide,
31. *particular*, 32. *fast*, 33. *stiffly*, 34. *felt hat*, 35. *fear*

and did not use it. Lily, petite and not unpretty, had on something signifying the approach of spring. She was au courant,[36] animatedly, with all sorts of subjects, and he weighed her words and found her surprisingly sound—score another for Salzman, whom he uneasily sensed to be somewhere around, hiding perhaps high in a tree along the street, flashing the lady signals with a pocket mirror; or perhaps a cloven-hoofed Pan,[37] piping nuptial[38] ditties[39] as he danced his invisible way before them, strewing[40] wild buds on the walk and purple grapes in their path, symbolizing fruit of a union, though there was of course still none.

97   Lily startled Leo by remarking, "I was thinking of Mr. Salzman, a curious figure, wouldn't you say?"

98   Not certain what to answer, he nodded.

99   She bravely went on, blushing, "I for one am grateful for his introducing us. Aren't you?"

100   He courteously replied, "I am."

101   "I mean," she said with a little laugh—and it was all in good taste, or at least gave the effect of being not in bad—"do you mind that we came together so?"

102   He was not displeased with her honesty, recognizing that she meant to set the relationship aright, and understanding that it took a certain amount of experience in life, and courage, to want to do it quite that way. One had to have some sort of past to make that kind of beginning.

103   He said that he did not mind. Salzman's function was traditional and honorable—valuable for what it might achieve, which, he pointed out, was frequently nothing.

104   Lily agreed with a sigh. They talked on for a while and she said after a long silence, again with a nervous laugh, "Would you mind if I asked you something a little bit personal? Frankly, I find the subject fascinating." Although Leo shrugged, she went on half embarrassedly, "How was it that you came to your calling[41]? I mean was it a sudden passionate inspiration?"

105   Leo, after a time, slowly replied, "I was always interested in the Law."

106   "You saw revealed in it the presence of the Highest?"

107   He nodded and changed the subject. "I understand that you spent a little time in Paris, Miss Hirschorn?"

---

36. *French for "informed,"* 37. *the god of woods, who has the torso and head of a man and body and feet, or hooves, of a horse,* 38. *wedding,* 39. *songs,* 40. *throwing,* 41. *urge to enter a profession*

108   "Oh, did Mr. Salzman tell you, Rabbi Finkle?" Leo winced[42] but she went on, "It was ages ago and almost forgotten. I remember I had to return for my sister's wedding."

109   And Lily would not be put off. "When," she asked in a trembly voice, "did you become enamored of[43] God?"

110   He stared at her. Then it came to him that she was talking not about Leo Finkle, but of a total stranger, some mystical[44] figure, perhaps even passionate prophet[45] that Salzman had dreamed up for her—no relation to the living or dead. Leo trembled with rage[46] and weakness. The trickster had obviously sold her a bill of goods,[47] just as he had him, who'd expected to become acquainted with a young lady of twenty-nine, only to behold, the moment he laid eyes upon her strained and anxious face, a woman past thirty-five and aging rapidly. Only his self control had kept him this long in her presence.

111   "I am not," he said gravely, "a talented religious person," and in seeking words to go on, found himself possessed by shame and fear. "I think," he said in a strained manner, "that I came to God not because I loved him, but because I did not."

112   This confession he spoke harshly because its unexpectedness shook him.

113   Lily wilted.[48] Leo saw a profusion[49] of loaves of bread go flying like ducks high over his head, not unlike the winged loaves by which he had counted himself to sleep last night. Mercifully, then, it snowed, which he would not put past Salzman's machinations.

114   He was infuriated[50] with the marriage broker and swore he would throw him out of the room the minute he reappeared. But Salzman did not come that night, and when Leo's anger had subsided,[51] an unaccountable despair[52] grew in its place. At first he thought this was caused by his disappointment in Lily, but before long it became evident that he had involved himself with Salzman without a true knowledge of his own intent. He gradually realized—with an emptiness that seized him with six hands—that he had called in the broker to find him a bride because he was incapable of doing it himself. This terrifying insight he had derived as a result of his meeting and conversation with Lily Hirschorn. Her probing questions had somehow irritated him into revealing—to himself more than her—the true nature of his relationship to God, and from that it had come upon him, with shocking force, that apart from his parents, he

---

42. *flinched,* 43. *inspired with love of,* 44. *relating to direct experience with God,* 45. *religious spokesman,* 46. *anger,* 47. *lied to her, slang,*
48. *became limp,* 49. *mass,* 50. *angry,* 51. *stopped,* 52. *sadness*

had never loved anyone. Or perhaps it went the other way, that he did not love God so well as he might, because he had not loved man. It seemed to Leo that his whole life stood starkly[53] revealed and he saw himself for the first time as he truly was—unloved and loveless. This bitter but somehow not fully unexpected revelation[54] brought him to a point of panic controlled only by extraordinary effort. He covered his face with his hands and cried.

115   The week that followed was the worst of his life. He did not eat and lost weight. His beard darkened and grew ragged. He stopped attending seminars and almost never opened a book. He seriously considered leaving the Yeshiva, although he was deeply troubled at the thought of the loss of all his years of study—saw them like pages torn from a book, strewn over the city—and at the devastating[55] effect of this decision upon his parents. But he had lived with knowledge of himself, and never in the Five Books and all the Commentaries—mea culpa[56]—had the truth been revealed to him. He did not know where to turn, and in all this desolating[57] loneliness there was no *to whom*, although he often thought of Lily but not once could bring himself to go downstairs and make the call. He became touchy and irritable, especially with his landlady, who asked him all manner of personal questions; on the other hand, sensing his own disagreeableness, he waylaid[58] her on the stairs and apologized abjectly,[59] until mortified, she ran from him. Out of this, however, he drew the consolation[60] that he was a Jew and that a Jew suffered. But gradually, as the long and terrible week drew to a close, he regained his composure[61] and some idea of purpose in life: to go on as planned. Although he was imperfect, the ideal was not. As for his quest of a bride, the thought of continuing afflicted him with anxiety and heartburn, yet perhaps with this new knowledge of himself he would be more successful than in the past. Perhaps love would now come to him and a bride to that love. And for this sanctified[62] seeking who needed a Salzman?

116   The marriage broker, a skeleton with haunted eyes, returned that very night. He looked, withal,[63] the picture of frustrated expectancy—as if he had steadfastly waited the week at Miss Lily Hirschorn's side for a telephone call that never came.

117   Casually coughing, Salzman came immediately to the point: "So how did you like her?"

---

53. *honestly,* 54. *realization,* 55. *overwhelming,* 56. *Latin for "through my fault,"* 57. *creating misery,* 58. *blocked,* 59. *sorrowfully,* 60. *comfort,* 61. *calm,* 62. *holy,* 63. *in addition, archaic*

118   Leo's anger rose and he could not refrain[64] from chiding[65] the matchmaker: "Why did you lie to me, Salzman?"

119   Salzman's pale face went dead white, the world had snowed on him.

120   "Did you not state that she was twenty-nine?" Leo insisted.

121   "I gave you my word—"

122   "She was thirty-five, if a day. At least thirty-five."

123   "Of this don't be too sure. Her father told me—"

124   "Never mind. The worst of it was that you lied to her."

125   How did I lie to her, tell me?"

126   "You told her things about me that weren't true. You made me out to be more, consequently less than I am. She had in mind a totally different person, a sort of semimystical Wonder Rabbi."

127   "All I said, you was a religious man."

128   "I can imagine."

129   Salzman sighed. "This is my weakness that I have," he confessed. "My wife says to me I shouldn't be a salesman, but when I have two fine people that they would be wonderful to be married, I am so happy that I talk too much." He smiled wanly.[66] "This is why Salzman is a poor man."

130   Leo's anger left him. "Well, Salzman, I'm afraid that's all."

131   The marriage broker fastened hungry eyes on him.

132   "You don't want any more a bride?"

133   "I do," said Leo, "but I have decided to seek her in a different way. I am no longer interested in an arranged marriage. To be frank, I now admit the necessity of premarital love. That is, I want to be in love with the one I marry."

134   "Love?" said Salzman, astounded. After a moment he remarked "For us, our love is our life, not for the ladies. In the ghetto they—"

135   "I know, I know," said Leo. "I've thought of it often. Love, I have said to myself, should be a by-product of living and worship rather than its own end. Yet for myself I find it necessary to establish the level of my need and fulfill it."

136   Salzman shrugged but answered, "Listen, rabbi, if you want love, this I can find for you also. I have such beautiful clients that you will love them the minute your eyes will see them."

137   Leo smiled unhappily. "I'm afraid you don't understand."

138   But Salzman hastily unstrapped his portfolio and withdrew a manila packet from it.

139   "Pictures," he said, quickly laying the envelope on the table.

140   Leo called after him to take the pictures away, but as if on the wings of the wind, Salzman had disappeared.

---

64. *stop,*   65. *scolding,*   66. *unnaturally*

141   March came. Leo had returned to his regular routine. Although he felt not quite himself yet—lacked energy—he was making plans for a more active social life. Of course it would cost something, but he was an expert at cutting corners[67]; and when there were no corners left he would make circles rounder. All the while Salzman's pictures had laid on the table, gathering dust. Occasionally as Leo sat studying, or enjoying a cup of tea, his eyes fell on the manila envelope, but he never opened it.

142   The days went by and no social life to speak of developed with a member of the opposite sex—it was difficult, given the circumstances of his situation. One morning Leo toiled up the stairs to his room and stared out the window at the city. Although the day was bright his view of it was dark. For some time he watched people in the street below hurrying along and then turned with a heavy heart to his little room. On the table was the packet. With a sudden relentless[68] gesture he tore it open. For a half-hour he stood by the table in a state of excitement, examining the photographs of the ladies Salzman had included. Finally, with a deep sigh he put them down. There were six, of varying degrees of attractiveness, but look at them long enough and they all became Lily Hirschorn; all past their prime, all starved behind bright smiles, not a true personality in the lot. Life, despite their frantic yoohooings, had passed them by; they were pictures in a brief case that stunk of fish. After a while, however, as Leo attempted to return the photographs into the envelope, he found in it another, a snapshot of the type taken by a machine for a quarter. He gazed at it a moment and let out a cry.

143   Her face deeply moved him. Why, he could at first not say. It gave him the impression of youth—spring flowers, yet age—a sense of having been used to the bone, wasted; this came from the eyes, which were hauntingly familiar, yet absolutely strange. He had a vivid impression that he had met her before, but try as he might he could not place her although he could almost recall her name, as if he had read it in her own handwriting. No, this couldn't be; he would have remembered her. It was not, he affirmed, that she had an extraordinary beauty—no, though her face was attractive enough; it was that *something* about her moved him. Feature for feature, even some of the ladies of the photographs could do better; but she leaped forth to his heart—had *lived*, or wanted to—more than just wanted, perhaps regretted how she had lived—had somehow deeply suffered: it could be seen in the depths of those reluctant eyes, and from the way the light

---

67. *living economically, slang,* 68. *persistent*

enclosed and shone from her, and within her, opening realms of
possibility: this was her own. Her he desired. His head ached and
eyes narrowed with the intensity of his gazing, then as if an obscure
fog had blown up in the mind, he experienced fear of her and was
aware that he had received an impression, somehow, of evil. He
shuddered, saying softly, it is thus with us all. Leo brewed some tea
in a small pot and sat sipping it without sugar, to calm himself. But
before he had finished drinking, again with excitement he examined the face and found it good: good for Leo Finkle. Only such a
one could understand him and help him seek whatever he was
seeking. She might, perhaps, love him. How she had happened
to be among the discards[69] in Salzman's barrel he could never
guess, but he knew he must urgently go find her.

144   Leo rushed downstairs, grabbed up the Bronx telephone book,
and searched for Salzman's home address. He was not listed, nor
was his office. Neither was he in the Manhattan book. But Leo
remembered having written down the address on a slip of paper
after he had read Salzman's advertisement in the "personals"
column of the *Forward*. He ran up to his room and tore through
his papers, without luck. It was exasperating.[70] Just when he
needed the matchmaker he was nowhere to be found. Fortunately
Leo remembered to look in his wallet. There on a card he found
his name written and a Bronx address. No phone number was
listed, the reason—Leo now recalled—he had originally communicated with Salzman by letter. He got on his coat, put a hat on over
his skull cap and hurried to the subway station. All the way to the
far end of the Bronx he sat on the edge of his seat. He was more
than once tempted to take out the picture and see if the girl's face
was as he remembered it, but he refrained, allowing the snapshot
to remain in his coat pocket, content to have her so close. When
the train pulled into the station he was waiting at the door and
bolted out. He quickly located the street Salzman had advertised.

145   The building he sought was less than a block from the subway,
but it was not an office building, nor even a loft, nor a store in
which one could rent office space. It was a very old tenement
house. Leo found Salzman's name in pencil on a soiled tag under
the bell and climbed three dark flights to his apartment. When
he knocked, the door was opened by a thin, asthmatic, gray-
haired woman, in felt slippers.

146   "Yes?" she said, expecting nothing. She listened without
listening. He could have sworn he had seen her, too, before you
knew it was an illusion.

---

69. *leftovers,* 70. *frustrating*

147   "Salzman—does he live here? Pinye Salzman," he said, "the matchmaker?"

148   She stared at him a long minute. "Of course."

149   He felt embarrassed. "Is he in?"

150   "No." Her mouth, though left open, offered nothing more.

151   "The matter is urgent. Can you tell me where his office is?"

152   "In the air." She pointed upward.

153   "You mean he has no office?" Leo asked.

154   "In his socks."

155   He peered into the apartment. It was sunless and dingy,[71] one large room divided by a half-open curtain, beyond which he could see a sagging metal bed. The near side of a room was crowded with rickety chairs, old bureaus, a three-legged table, racks of cooking utensils, and all the apparatus of a kitchen. But there was no sign of Salzman or his magic barrel, probably also a figment[72] of the imagination. An odor of frying fish made Leo weak to the knees.

156   "Where is he?" he insisted. "I've got to see your husband."

157   At length she answered, "So who knows where he is? Every time he thinks a new thought he runs to a different place. Go home, he will find you."

158   "Tell him Leo Finkle."

159   She gave no sign she had heard.

160   He walked downstairs, depressed.

161   But Salzman, breathless, stood waiting at his door.

162   Leo was astounded and overjoyed. "How did you get here before me?"

163   "I rushed."

164   "Come inside."

165   They entered. Leo fixed tea, and a sardine sandwich for Salzman. As they were drinking he reached behind him for the packet of pictures and handed them to the marriage broker.

166   Salzman put down his glass and said expectantly, "You found somebody you like?"

167   "Not among these."

168   The marriage broker turned away.

169   "Here is the one I want." Leo held forth the snapshot.

170   Salzman slipped on his glasses and took the picture into his trembling hand. He turned ghastly[73] and let out a groan.

171   "What's the matter?" cried Leo.

172   "Excuse me. Was an accident this picture. She isn't for you."

173   Salzman frantically[74] shoved the manila packet into his portfolio. He thrust the snapshot into his pocket and fled down the stairs.

---

71. *dirty,* 72. *illusion,* 73. *very serious,* 74. *nervously*

174   Leo, after momentary paralysis, gave chase and cornered the marriage broker in the vestibule.[75] The landlady made hysterical outcries but neither of them listened.

175   "Give me back the picture, Salzman."

176   "No." The pain in his eyes was terrible.

177   "Tell me who she is then."

178   "This I can't tell you. Excuse me."

179   He made to depart, but Leo, forgetting himself, seized the matchmaker by his tight coat and shook him frenziedly.[76]

180   "Please," sighed Salzman. "Please."

181   Leo ashamedly let him go. "Tell me who she is," he begged. "It's very important for me to know."

182   "She is not for you. She is a wild one—wild, without shame. This is not a bride for a rabbi."

183   "What do you mean wild?"

184   "Like an animal. Like a dog. For her to be poor was a sin. This is why to me she is dead now."

185   "In God's name, what do you mean?"

186   "Her I can't introduce to you," Salzman said.

187   "Why are you so excited?"

188   "Why, he asks," Salzman said, bursting into tears. "This is my baby, my Stella, she should burn in hell."

189   Leo hurried up to bed and hid under the covers. Under the covers he thought his life through. Although he soon fell asleep he could not sleep her out of his mind. He woke, beating his breast. Though he prayed to be rid of her, his prayers went unanswered. Through days of torment he endlessly struggled not to love her; fearing success, he escaped it. He then concluded to convert her to goodness, himself to God. The idea alternately nauseated[77] and exalted him.[78]

190   He perhaps did not know that he had come to a final decision until he encountered Salzman in a Broadway cafeteria. He was sitting alone at a rear table, sucking the bony remains of a fish. The marriage broker appeared haggard,[79] and transparent to the point of vanishing.

191   Salzman looked up at first without recognizing him. Leo had grown a pointed beard and his eyes were weighted with wisdom.

192   "Salzman," he said, "love has at last come to my heart."

193   "Who can love from a picture?" mocked the marriage broker.

194   "It is not impossible."

---

75. *hallway,*   76. *wildly,*   77. *sickened,*   78. *filled him with joy,*   79. *worn-out*

195   "If you can love her, then you can love anybody. Let me show you some new clients that they just sent me their photographs. One is a little doll."

196   "Just her I want," Leo murmured.

197   "Don't be a fool, doctor. Don't bother with her."

198   "Put me in touch with her, Salzman," Leo said humbly. "Perhaps I can be of service."

199   Salzman had stopped eating and Leo understood with emotion that it was now arranged.

200   Leaving the cafeteria, he was, however, afflicted by a tormenting suspicion that Salzman had planned it all to happen this way.

201   Leo was informed by letter that she would meet him on a certain corner, and she was there one spring night, waiting under a street lamp. He appeared, carrying a small bouquet of violets and rosebuds. Stella stood by the lamp post, smoking. She wore white with red shoes, which fitted his expectations, although in a troubled moment he had imagined the dress red, and only the shoes white. She waited uneasily and shyly. From afar he saw that her eyes— clearly her father's—were filled with desperate innocence. He pictured, in her, his own redemption. Violins and lit candles[80] revolved in the sky. Leo ran forward with flowers outthrust.

202   Around the corner, Salzman, leaning against a wall, chanted[81] prayers for the dead.

---

80. *items used in Jewish marriage ceremonies,* 81. *recited*

Understanding the Text: *Retelling the Story*

After you have read the story carefully, answer the questions below briefly in your own words.

1. In their first meeting, what reasons does Leo Finkle give to Pinye Salzman to explain why he has decided to consult a marriage broker?

2. Leo reacts unfavorably to the three marriage prospects Pinye suggests. Give the objections that Leo has for the three prospects below:

   a. Sophie P. _____

   _____

b. Lily H. _____

_____

c. Ruth K. _____

_____

3. After Leo meets Lily Hirschorn, he discovers two important truths about himself. What does he realize is the real reason that he has called in a marriage broker? What does he realize about himself and love? Try to find the exact words that Malamud uses to sum up how Leo sees himself.

4. Now, why does Leo not want to use the services of a marriage broker?

5. When Salzman leaves his portfolio of prospective brides' photos at Leo's apartment, what does Leo do at first? What does he later do?

6. What does Leo conclude about the small photograph he finds in the portfolio?

7. How does Salzman explain how the photo of his daughter was put in the portfolio?

8. How does Salzman describe his daughter to Leo?

Looking at Language: *Descriptive Vocabulary*

In the chart below, find the descriptive words and phrases used in paragraphs 2 and 4 to physically describe the matchmaker and the student, respectively.

Salzman

build: _____

clothes: _____

smell: _____

eyes: _____

voice: _____

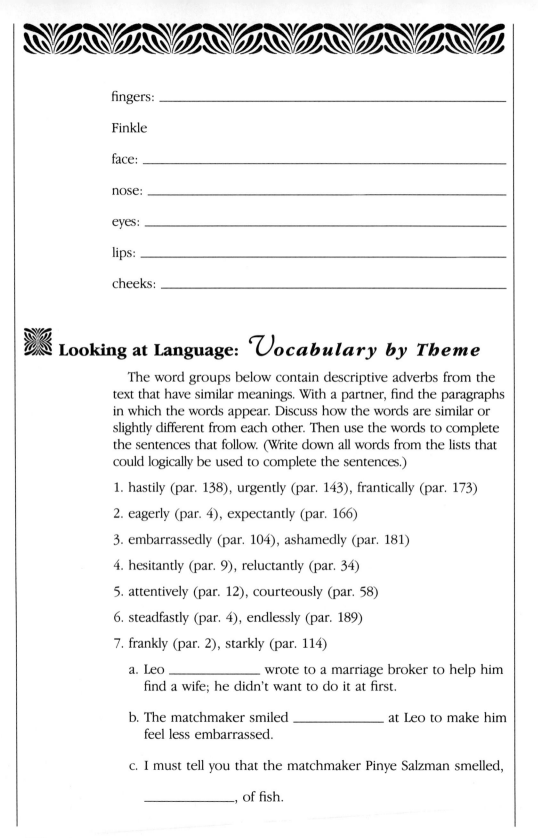

fingers: _____

Finkle

face: _____

nose: _____

eyes: _____

lips: _____

cheeks: _____

Looking at Language: *Vocabulary by Theme*

The word groups below contain descriptive adverbs from the text that have similar meanings. With a partner, find the paragraphs in which the words appear. Discuss how the words are similar or slightly different from each other. Then use the words to complete the sentences that follow. (Write down all words from the lists that could logically be used to complete the sentences.)

1. hastily (par. 138), urgently (par. 143), frantically (par. 173)

2. eagerly (par. 4), expectantly (par. 166)

3. embarrassedly (par. 104), ashamedly (par. 181)

4. hesitantly (par. 9), reluctantly (par. 34)

5. attentively (par. 12), courteously (par. 58)

6. steadfastly (par. 4), endlessly (par. 189)

7. frankly (par. 2), starkly (par. 114)

    a. Leo _____ wrote to a marriage broker to help him find a wife; he didn't want to do it at first.

    b. The matchmaker smiled _____ at Leo to make him feel less embarrassed.

    c. I must tell you that the matchmaker Pinye Salzman smelled,

    _____, of fish.

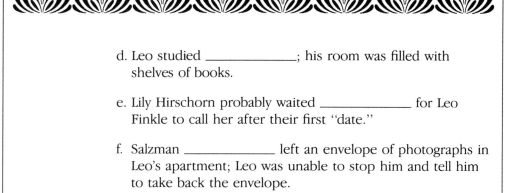

d. Leo studied _____; his room was filled with shelves of books.

e. Lily Hirschorn probably waited _____ for Leo Finkle to call her after their first "date."

f. Salzman _____ left an envelope of photographs in Leo's apartment; Leo was unable to stop him and tell him to take back the envelope.

g. After Leo found the photograph of the girl he wanted, he

_____ sought the matchmaker.

Looking at Language: *Participles as Adjectives*

"The Magic Barrel" is a story rich in vocabulary. As the list in the previous exercise proves, Bernard Malamud toiled endlessly to vary his vocabulary, to find new ways of expressing simple actions such as hurrying, running, or eating.

The many adjectives that Malamud uses in his story include present and past participles used as adjectives, before nouns or as predicate adjectives. Recall how participles occurred in phrases in Ursula K. Le Guin's story, "The Rule of Names," Chapter Eight.

In Malamud's story, we find the same participles functioning as adjectives. Look at how the words "troubled" and "devastating" are used in the passage below:

> "He [Leo] seriously considered leaving the Yeshiva, although he was deeply troubled at the thought of the loss of all his years of study . . . and at the devastating[1] effect of this decision upon his parents." (par. 115)

To explore this text further for participles as adjectives, with a partner, find the present and past participles listed below in the paragraphs in which they appear. Discuss the meanings and look up unfamiliar words. Then, use words from this list to complete the sentences that follow.

a. tormented (par. 1), tormenting (par. 200)
b. infuriated (par. 114)
c. desolating (par. 115)
d. arranged (par. 133)
e. astounded (par. 134, 162)
f. exasperating (par. 144)
g. depressed (par. 160)

1. *overwhelming*

1. Leo was _____ for two days, trying to decide whether to call a marriage broker, when he finally called Pinye Salzman.

2. The _____ loneliness of Leo's life, plus a practical need for a bride, caused him to seek a matchmaker's services.

3. Leo believed that _____ marriages were honorable and traditional.

4. When Pinye offered only six names of eligible girls, Leo was visibly _____. "So few?" he asked.

5. After Leo found the picture of his "dream girl," he could not find the telephone number nor the address of Salzman. "It was _____ [to Leo]. Just when he needed the matchmaker he was nowhere to be found."

Literary Concepts: *Foreshadowing*

"Fore" means before, and a "shadow" is a glimpse of a person or an idea. In literature, foreshadowing is used to give hints about what actions will occur in a story. Often you can find information (such as the qualities of a character, the situation, the setting) that predicts later events in a story.

In "The Magic Barrel," did you expect Finkle to choose the photo of Salzman's daughter as his prospective bride? Can you find clues in the story that suggest that Salzman purposefully left the photo of his daughter in the portfolio he gave to Finkle?

Literary Concept: *Characterization*

The two main characters in this story, Leo Finkle and Pinye Salzman, are pictured as very different men, both in their appearance and in their behavior. With a partner, think of one word that you would use to characterize each character, and find support in the form of examples of their behavior, that will support your assessment of their characters.

✿Culture Point: *Finding a Mate*

Read the personal advertisements below, which are becoming a popular means for American singles to find companions. Advertisements like these can be found in many newspapers and magazines. Samples:

TALL, HANDSOME BLONDE, DWM, 30s, over-educated professional, non-smoker. Seeks single white female for jogging/sailing companion, best friend. Prefer someone who's trim, health-conscious, free-spirited, adventurous, intellectually stimulating, professional, in 30s. Box #2013.

IS THERE A MAN who enjoys outdoors, long walks and quiet romantic evenings? Enthusiastic, eclectic, attractive 29-year-old SWF is stalking, I mean seeking, a mature, SWM, affectionate, humorous, financially secure man for adventure, sports, drama, romance. Sincere, reasonably hip gentlemen only, please. Must correctly answer skills-testing questions. Box #2459.

DESERTED WITHOUT A GOODBYE. Attractive SBM, 34, sense of humor, well-educated, honest, loyal, dependable, romantic, sensitive, caring, many interests. Loves tennis, flying, dining out, good movies, reading, the beach, etc. Not your Average Joe. Seeking Miss Magic. Box #1994.

Answer the following questions about the ads:

1. Find the abbreviations in one sample ad. What do you think the abbreviations mean?

2. Do such personal ads exist in your country?

3. What do you think of this method of finding a companion? a husband or wife?

READING JOURNAL

For your Reading Journal assignment, write on one of the two topics below.

1. Imagine that because you wish to meet a suitable companion, you have decided to write a personal advertisement for yourself. To attract the person of your desires, you must present your best attributes. Write briefly about your interests and characteristics and include any personal information you wish.

2. If you feel that personal advertisements are an unsuitable method of meeting companions, explain why.

VIDEO/READING JOURNAL

Crossing Delancey (1989), starring Amy Irving and Peter Riegert, is the story of a grandmother who hires a marriage broker for her modern, unmarried granddaughter. The prospective groom is the owner of a streetside pickle stand whose traditional life-style contrasts with the modern life of the granddaughter.

View this film and answer the following question in your Reading Journal:

What happens to the two couples (the couple in "A Magic Barrel" and the couple in *Crossing Delancey*) at the end of the story and film, respectively? What will be their futures?

A Dream within a Dream

by Edgar Allan Poe

About the Author

Edgar Allan Poe (1809–1849), an American poet, story writer, and literary critic, is well-known for writing mysterious tales and poems about death and other morbid subjects. His poems also have romantic themes. "The Gold Bug," "The Tell-Tale Heart," "The Pit and the Pendulum," and "The Murders in the Rue Morgue" are among his best-loved short stories. "The Raven," "Annabel Lee," and the poem in this chapter, "A Dream within a Dream," show his power as a poet. Poe was born in Boston, Massachusetts, grew up in

Virginia, and lived as a writer-journalist in New York City and Philadelphia. Physically and mentally devastated by the death of his wife, Poe died in Baltimore, Maryland, two years after his wife's death.

At First Glance

1. What do you think the title, "A Dream within a Dream," means?

2. How does a person feel when he or she thinks life is like a dream within a dream?

3. Read the first two lines of the poem: "Take this kiss upon the brow! And, in parting from you now . . . " Who do you think the narrator of the poem may be offering to kiss on the "brow"? What is the occasion for his offering a kiss?

Prereading Vocabulary

With a partner, find the lines below in the poem. Read the lines above and below it, and then use the context to guess the meanings of the italicized words. Afterward, check your guesses in the dictionary.

1. ". . . let me *avow*—" (verse 1)

2. ". . . who *deem* . . . " (verse 1)

3. ". . . a *surf-tormented* shore . . . " (verse 2)

4. ". . . with a tighter *clasp* . . . " (verse 2)

5. ". . . from the *pitiless* wave . . . " (verse 2)

A Dream within a Dream

by Edgar Allan Poe

Take this kiss upon the brow!
And, in parting from you now,
Thus much let me avow—
You are not wrong, who deem
That my days have been a dream;
Yet if hope has flown away
In a night, or in a day,
In a vision, or in none,
Is it therefore the less gone?
All that we see or seem
Is but a dream within a dream.

I stand amid the roar
Of a surf-tormented shore,
And I hold within my hand
Grains of the golden sand—
How few! yet how they creep
Through my fingers to the deep,
While I weep—while I weep!
O God! can I not grasp
Them with a tighter clasp?
O God! can I not save
One from the pitiless wave?
Is all that we see or seem
But a dream within a dream?

✿Understanding the Text: *Analysis*

Read the poem again carefully and answer these questions.

1. In the first five lines of verse 1, the narrator tells someone that he is "not wrong, who deem that my days have been a dream . . . " What does it mean when a person's days are a dream? What you think the unnamed person has said to the narrator of the poem?

2. In the second part of verse 1, the narrator asks, "if hope has flown away . . . is it therefore the less gone?" What does he mean here?

3. What do you think has happened to the narrator of this poem? What could he mean when he says, "all that we see . . . is but a dream within a dream"?

4. In verse 2, the narrator stands "amid the roar of a surf-tormented shore." Where is he?

5. He tells us that he is holding grains of sand in his hand. Why do you think he weeps when the grains fall through his fingers?

6. Why do you think the narrator asks God if one grain of sand can be saved from the "pitiless wave"?

7. Could the narrator be comparing himself to a grain of sand?

8. What do you think the narrator wants?

READING JOURNAL

1. Do you like this poem?

2. Do you understand the feeling the narrator has? Do you share his/her feeling?

Projects: UNIT FOUR

Project I: Original Story/Poetry Writing

Thus far in the course, we have read a variety of stories set in cities, small towns, and wild frontiers. We have met many characters who speak in different ways and display diverse values and behavior. One thread that ties together all of these stories is the fact that the writers who created them felt the need to put the stories down on paper. Many of the characters and settings we read here reflect the real-life experiences and people the writers have met. By giving us these texts, the writers have shared their unique views of the world and hopefully, taught us some valuable life lessons.

To accomplish this, the writers we have explored have written about times and places they knew well. Jack London wrote of the Yukon region of northwest Canada in "The White Silence" after having lived there himself. Likewise, Damon Runyon described in careful detail the lives of characters in 1920s and 1930s New York City where he spent years of his life.

Your project assignment for this unit will be to emulate the writers we have met thus far by writing a short story or poem about a subject and characters you know well.

This may seem a formidable task, but you can make it a fun and challenging piece of work if you write about something, someone or some place you know well, and really want to write about.

You may write a short story of any type—such as a narrative, a fantasy, or a mystery, or you may write a poem.

Do not attempt to copy the ideas of the writers we have read and discussed, because they wrote about their own unique worlds, not yours. Of course, you can certainly learn from the way these artists develop a story.

In general, do not worry about the length or form of your writing. Don't worry if your poem doesn't rhyme. Concentrate instead on telling an interesting story. Also, give your text an intriguing title.

You will be reading your classmates' stories and poems and discussing them in groups, so write your story legibly on standard notebook paper, skipping lines, or type it double-spaced on a typewriter or computer. Do not put your name on your story. When you turn it in, your instructor will record your name and the title of the story. The stories will be collected in a folder. Your instructor will assign the class dates for having read each text so that each may be discussed in class.

Project II: Dramatization

As in Unit Three, the second project in this unit will be to dramatize or act out a part of a story. In this case, you and a partner will act out the ending of "The Magic Barrel," which is not told at the close of the story.

To begin, reread the last paragraph of "The Magic Barrel." With a partner, imagine that you two are portraying Leo Finkle and Stella Salzman. What happens during your first meeting? What do you say to each other?

Will you see each other again? Is it possible you may marry, or are you two ill-suited for each other?

Discuss what might take place during this encounter. Write a short dialogue between you that suggests whether or not you will continue your relationship. Use the information you have about the backgrounds of Leo and Stella to create the conversation.

Practice the dialogue together and then present it to the class.

UNIT FIVE

*H*eart to *H*eart

The readings in Unit Five are presented last because
they are the most abstract of all the stories in this
text. By now, readers will have encountered the
strange and unexpected world of literature in many
forms, and should be well-prepared to handle plots
that do not follow the order of time, and passages
that contain emotionally powered inner monologues
and dialogues by the characters and narrators. In this
unit, readers will encounter "Snow," "I Stand Here
Ironing," and "The Letter," two stories and a poem
that depict the complex nature of heart-to-heart
relations. The emotions of these texts will be carried
out even further as students read chosen stories and
poems orally in a dramatic closure to the exploration
of *Life, Language, and Literature*.

"Who expects small things to survive when even the largest get lost? People forget years and remember moments."

CHAPTER ELEVEN

Snow

by Ann Beattie

About the Author

Ann Beattie was born in 1947 in Washington, D.C.
Among her works are the novels *Chilly Scenes of
Winter* (which was made into a commercial movie),
Love, Always, and several collections of stories,
including *Jacklighting*, *The Burning House*, and *Where
You'll Find Me*. The theme of female-male relationships
recurs in many of her stories. Beattie wrote of her
story, "Snow," "I do believe that 'seconds and symbols
are left to sum things up,' and I found when writing
this story that it could be very brief indeed."

At First Glance

1. Consider the title of this short story. What feeling does snow give you? What could the story be about?

2. Read the first two sentences of the text. Concentrate on the "content" words of the sentence: "the cold night," "the pile of logs," "a chipmunk," etc. What picture do you see in your mind of what is taking place in this story? Does this sentence make you feel the story will be happy or sad?

The Writer's Perspective

1. In "Snow," Ann Beattie begins her story with "I" and talks about "you" from the onset. Who do you think the narrator, or the "I," of the story is? Who could "you" be?

2. Beattie is a contemporary American writer who is still writing today. How do you think contemporary American women writers would portray male/female relationships?

3. If any of your group members have read any modern stories written by American women, what did the stories deal with?

Snow

by Ann Beattie

1 *I* remember the cold night you brought in a pile of logs and a chipmunk¹ jumped off as you lowered your arms. "What do you think *you're* doing in here?" you said, as it ran through the living room. It went through the library and stopped at the front door as though it knew the house well. This would be difficult for anyone to believe, except perhaps as the subject of a poem. Our first week in the house was spent scraping, finding some of the house's secrets, like wallpaper underneath wallpaper. In the kitchen, a pattern of white-gold trellises² supported purple grapes as big and round as Ping-Pong balls. When we painted the walls yellow, I thought of the bits of grape that remained underneath and imagined the vine popping through, the way some plants can tenaciously push through anything. The day of the big snow, when you had to shovel the walk and couldn't find your cap and asked me how to wind a towel so that it would stay on your head—you, in the white towel turban,³ like a crazy king of snow. People liked the idea of our being together, leaving the city for the country. So many people visited, and the fireplace made all of them want to tell amazing stories: the child who happened to be standing on the right corner when the door of the ice-cream truck came open and hundreds of Popsicles crashed out; the man standing on the beach, sand sparkling in the sun, one bit glinting more than the rest, stooping to find a diamond ring. Did they talk about amazing things because they thought we'd turn into one of them? Now I think they probably guessed it wouldn't work. It was as hopeless as giving a child a matched cup and saucer. Remember the night, out on the lawn, knee-deep in snow, chins pointed at the sky as the wind whirled down all that whiteness? It seemed that the world had been turned upside down, and we were looking into an enormous

---

1. *a small rodent resembling a squirrel,* 2. *wooden frames for supporting vines,* 3. *a headdress made of a scarf wound around the head*

field of Queen Anne's lace.[4] Later, headlights off, our car was the first to ride through the newly fallen snow. The world outside the car looked solarized.

2   You remember it differently. You remember that the cold settled in stages, that a small curve of light was shaved from the moon night after night, until you were no longer surprised the sky was black, that the chipmunk ran to hide in the dark, not simply to a door that led to its escape. Our visitors told the same stories people always tell. One night, giving me a lesson in storytelling, you said, "Any life will seem dramatic if you omit mention of most of it."

3   This, then, for drama: I drove back to that house not long ago. It was April, and Allen had died. In spite of all the visitors, Allen, next door, had been the good friend in bad times. I sat with his wife in their living room, looking out the glass doors to the backyard, and there was Allen's pool, still covered with black plastic that had been stretched across it for winter. It had rained, and as the rain fell, the cover collected more and more water until it finally spilled onto the concrete. When I left that day, I drove past what had been our house. Three or four crocuses[5] were blooming in the front—just a few dots of white, no field of snow. I felt embarrassed for them. They couldn't compete.

4   This is a story, told the way you say stories should be told: Somebody grew up, fell in love, and spent a winter with her lover in the country. This, of course, is the barest outline, and futile to discuss. It's as pointless as throwing birdseed on the ground while snow still falls fast. Who expects small things to survive when even the largest get lost? People forget years and remember moments. Seconds and symbols are left to sum things up: the black shroud over the pool. Love, in its shortest form, becomes a word. What I remember about all that time is one winter. The snow. Even now, saying "snow," my lips move so that they kiss the air.

5   No mention has been made of the snowplow[6] that seemed always to be there, scraping snow off our narrow road—an artery cleared, though neither of us could have said where the heart was.

---

4. *a plant with small white flowers,* 5. *plants with variously colored flowers,*
6. *a device for removing snow from paths*

✾Understanding the Text: *Analysis*

Answer these questions in your group:

1. In the first paragraph of the story, the writer says that the incident in which a chipmunk jumped into a country house "would be difficult for anyone to believe." Why do you think the writer begins with this unusual story of the chipmunk?

2. Paragraph 1 also recounts the work that two people did to an old house. When you read this paragraph, what feeling do you get about the relationship between these two people?

3. This first paragraph also contains another story—the story about what happened when one of the people lost his cap. How does this short anecdote make you feel about the couple?

4. What effect does the couple's living in the country have on their friends?

5. The narrator recalls: "Now I think they probably guessed it wouldn't work. It was as hopeless as giving a child a matched cup and saucer." Who are "they"? What is "it"? What do you think the writer meant by the analogy with a child and a cup and saucer?

6. When the writer describes the snow, she tells of a night "out on the lawn, knee-deep in snow." What do you think the couple was doing on that night?

7. Why does the author describe the world as looking "upside down"?

8. Again, recounting a past story, why do you think the couple drove "headlights off" "through the newly fallen snow"?

9. Paragraph 2 begins: "You remember it differently." This paragraph is telling the story from whose point of view? How do you think this person's viewpoint differs from the narrator's viewpoint?

10. The narrator remembers a "lesson in storytelling," which her partner gave her: "Any life will seem dramatic if you omit mention of most of it." What does this quotation tell you about the partner?

11. In paragraph 3, the writer tells of her return to the house. What does this tell you about the relationship between the couple?

12. Who do you think the narrator is talking to in this story?

13. Skim paragraph 4. What message is the narrator trying to relate about love and life?

14. The story ends with a final paragraph about a snowplow. Why do you think the writer calls the road "an artery" and ends the story by stating that "neither of us could have said where the heart was"?

Looking at Language: *Verb Tenses/Plot*

In "Snow," Beattie does not provide readers with a precise history of when events in the story took place or what has happened to the characters. However, by examining the tense of verbs, we can gain clues to the order and outcome of events in the story. Examine the passages below and use the verb tenses to help you better understand what has happened in this story.

1. Paragraph 1: "I remember the cold night you brought in a pile of logs . . . "
   When did the story take place?
   Why does the author write "remember" in the present?

2. Paragraph 2: "You remember it differently. You remember that the cold settled in stages . . . "
   Who is "you"?
   What is the status of this character? Is he or she alive or dead?

3. Paragraph 3: "I drove back to that house not long ago. It was April, and Allen had died. In spite of all the visitors, Allen, next door, had been the good friend in bad times. I sat with his wife in their living room."
   When did the author drive back to the house?
   When did Allen die?
   When was Allen a good friend?
   When did the author sit with his wife?

4. Paragraph 5: "No mention has been made of the snowplow that seemed always to be there, scraping snow off our narrow road—an artery cleared, though neither of us could have said where the heart was."
   Why does the author use the verb tense "has been made" in the last paragraph rather than "was made"?

Why does the author use the verb tense "could have said" in the last sentence? What is the meaning of this past tense modal verb?

Looking at Language: *Guessing Vocabulary from Context*

With a partner, guess the meanings of the italicized vocabulary words below by using the surrounding context.

1. Paragraph 1: "some plants can *tenaciously* push through anything . . . "

2. Paragraph 4: "*futile* to discuss"

3. Paragraph 4: "the black *shroud* over the pool"

4. Paragraph 5: "an *artery* cleared"

Looking at Language: *Vocabulary by Theme*

"Snow," by virtue of its title, contains vocabulary items that relate to cold weather. Examine the group of words below with a partner, defining the familiar items together or consulting a dictionary or the text glossary. Then, use the words to appropriately complete the sentences that follow.

shovel (par. 1)
solarized (par. 1)
whirl ("whirled," par. 1)
scraping (par. 5)
newly fallen (par. 1)

1. The old man was exhausted after _____ the snow from the sidewalk.

2. The reflection of the white snow made everything outside

    appear _____.

3. With a _____, the child piled the snow into large heaps to make a snowman.

4. When I walked in the _____ snow, I heard the sound of the snow crackle beneath my feet.

5. The wind blew fiercely, making the snow _____ in the air.

Literary Concept: *Narrator*

As we have discussed in previous stories, the narrator, or teller, of the story may be an observer or a character in a story.

1. In "Snow," is the narrator the main character, a secondary character, or an observer?

2. What biographical information can you guess about the narrator? (i.e., age, occupation)

3. Why do you think the narrator never gives his or her name, nor the name of the other main character in the story?

Literary Concept: *Theme*

As we have discussed, the themes, or central ideas, of a literary work can be found by examining a text on different levels.

With a partner, discuss the themes in "Snow" on the levels listed below and complete the sentences to identify the themes.

1. Concrete or literal level: On this level, the theme of "Snow" is

_____.

2. Metaphorical or symbolic level: On this level, the theme(s) of

"Snow" is/are _____.

3. Universal or psychological level: On this level, the theme(s) of

"Snow" is/are _____.

✾Literary Concept: *Tone*

We have also studied the tone of a literary text—the feeling, or mood that the writer creates through his or her emotional attitude.

Examine these sentences taken from "Snow." Consider carefully the way the writer describes the action and characters of the story. With your group members, write down adjectives of emotion that express how the sentences make you feel.

1. "The day of the big snow, when you had to shovel the walk and couldn't find your cap and asked me how to wind a towel so that it would stay on your head—you, in the white towel turban, like a crazy king of snow."

   Feelings: _____

2. "So many people visited, and the fireplace made all of them want to tell amazing stories . . . "

   Feelings: _____

3. "I drove back to that house not long ago. It was April, and Allen had died . . . I sat with his wife in their living room, looking out the glass doors to the backyard, and there was Allen's pool, still covered with black plastic that had been stretched across it for winter."

   Feelings: _____

4. "What I remember about all that time is one winter. The snow. Even now, saying 'snow,' my lips move so that they kiss the air."

   Feelings: _____

5. After examining these sentences, what overall tone does this story have? What is the general emotional attitude of the writer? Does the story have more than one tone?

✾Literary Concept: *Setting*

The setting refers to the place (country; region, state, city or town; and particular location) in which the story's action takes place, as well as the historical time, i.e., present-day, future, or

past of a story. As we have found in other stories, sometimes, the exact place or time of a story is not defined, but you can approximate the time (for example, early twentieth century) by using information from the story.

a. "Snow" is set in

place: ______________________________

particular location: ______________________________

b. The time is probably ______________________________

because ______________________________.

Culture Point: *The Temporary Nature of Love*

Through one woman's experience of lost love, "Snow" brings up one of the dominant features of modern culture: the temporary nature of love relationships. As societies become increasingly complex, the notion of a lifelong love relationship has become less and less prevalent. Divorce rates soar in countries like the United States, where both natives and outsiders to the culture begin to question whether long-term love is destined for failure. Consider questions related to this topic with members of your group.

1. In "Snow," how do you think the narrator of the story feels about the failure of this relationship? Sad? Relieved? Desperate? Or does she show very little emotion in telling the tale?

2. Do you get a feeling about whether the narrator has tried hard enough to sustain her love relationship?

3. You may read this story and feel the narrator has written it to her former lover. If you had to write a letter to a former lover about the reasons for your lost relationship, what would be the tone of your letter? Would you ever write such a letter?

READING JOURNAL: FREEWRITING

A. Think about a special place that holds good or bad memories for you. Write for three minutes about a particular incident

that occurred at that place. Describe how you felt in this place at the time the incident took place.

Now, read over your writing. Think about how you feel about this incident now. Write for three minutes about this experience in retrospect.

B. Think over the story you have just read. For homework, write in your Reading Journal in response to the questions below:

1. What do you think happened between the couple in the story? (You may create your own details.)

2. How does the narrator feel about what happened?

3. Answer question 3 in the Culture Point exercise by writing a letter to someone you formerly had a relationship with. Explain why you think the relationship failed.

VIDEO

To visualize the theme and tone of Beattie's "Snow," you may wish to view scenes from the film version of her novel *Chilly Scenes of Winter* (1979), starring John Heard and Mary Beth Hurt, and discuss these questions with classmates.

1. As you view the first scene, think about the similarity in theme between "Snow" and *Chilly Scenes of Winter*. What is the common theme?

2. Watching the opening scenes of the city in *Chilly Scenes of Winter* and the mental state of the main character, a young man named Charles Richardson, how are the tone of "Snow" and the film similar?

3. What kind of people are the characters in "Snow" and *Chilly Scenes of Winter*?

"And when is there time to remember, to sift, to weigh, to estimate, to total? I will start and there will be an interruption and I will have to gather it all together again."

CHAPTER TWELVE

I Stand Here Ironing

by Tillie Olsen

About the Author

Tillie Olsen was born in 1913 in Omaha, Nebraska, the daughter of Russian political refugees. She quit high school at age 15 to help support her family during the Depression. Like the mother in "I Stand Here Ironing," Olsen worked to support herself and a baby after her husband left them in the 1930s. Active in political causes throughout her life, during the Depression Olsen was a member of the Young Communist League and was involved in labor disputes. Her short story

collection, *Tell Me a Riddle* (1956) helped establish her reputation as a feminist writer.

At First Glance

1. Read the title of the story. What kind of work is ironing? Who generally performs this work?

2. People and events in literature are sometimes symbols for larger ideas that the writers wants to express. Imagine a person ironing. What do you think the action of ironing might symbolize?

3. Now read the first sentence of the story:
   "I stand here ironing, and what you asked me moves tormented back and forth with the iron."
   What does "tormented" mean? What picture do you have in your mind of the narrator? Guess who he or she is.

4. The second paragraph appears in quotation marks:
   "I wish you would manage the time to come in and talk with me about your daughter. I'm sure you can help me understand her. She's a youngster who needs help and whom I'm deeply interested in helping."
   Why do you think this paragraph has quotation marks? Who do you think is the speaker or writer of the words?

5. How did you feel when you got a note from school? How did your parents feel?

6. Reread the first paragraph. Why do you think the narrator feels "tormented"?

7. Finally, before you read, you often read the first and last parts of a story, especially if you want to know the ending. With your group, or as your instructor reads aloud, read carefully the next to the last paragraph of the story, paragraph 55. What does this tell you about the story?

The Writer's Perspective

1. Tillie Olsen's story takes place in "the prerelief, pre-WPA [Work Projects Administration] world of the Depression," that is, in

1930s America before the government instigated federal aid programs in which unemployed Americans were given public works jobs such as building highways.
What is meant by an economic depression?
What do you know about this "Great Depression," which affected not only the United States, but the entire world?

2. Olsen's story also deals with family relations. Do you think your parents have done a good job in raising you? Have they always given you and your siblings equal treatment?

3. If you are or plan to become a parent, how do you plan to raise your children differently than your parents did? In raising children, do you think the parents' good intentions are enough?

I Stand Here Ironing

by Tillie Olsen

1   *I* stand here ironing, and what you asked me moves tormented back and forth with the iron.

2   "I wish you would manage the time to come in and talk with me about your daughter. I'm sure you can help me understand her. She's a youngster who needs help and whom I'm deeply interested in helping."

3   "Who needs help?" Even if I came, what good would it do? You think because I am her mother I have a key, or that in some way you could use me as a key? She has lived for nineteen years. There is all that life that has happened outside of me, beyond me.

4   And when is there time to remember, to sift, to weigh, to estimate, to total? I will start and there will be an interruption and I will have to gather it all together again. Or I will become engulfed[1] with all I did or did not do, with what should have been and what cannot be helped.

5   She was a beautiful baby. The first and only one of our five that was beautiful at birth. You do not guess how new and uneasy her tenancy[2] in her now-loveliness. You did not know her all those years she was thought homely,[3] or see her poring[4] over her baby pictures, making me tell her over and over how beautiful she had been—and would be, I would tell her—and was now, to the seeing eye. But the seeing eyes were few or non-existent. Including mine.

6   I nursed[5] her. They feel that's important nowadays. I nursed all the children, but with her, with all the fierce rigidity of first motherhood, I did like the books then said. Though her cries battered[6] me to trembling and my breasts ached with swollenness, I waited till the clock decreed.[7]

7   Why do I put that first? I do not even know if it matters, or if it explains anything.

8   She was a beautiful baby. She blew shining bubbles of sound.

---

1. *surrounded,* 2. *occupation,* 3. *unattractive,* 4. *looking,* 5. *breast-fed,* 6. *beat,* 7. *ordered*

She loved motion, loved light, loved color and music and textures. She would lie on the floor in her blue overalls[8] patting the surface so hard in ecstasy[9] her hands and feet would blur.[10] She was a miracle to me, but when she was eight months old I had to leave her daytimes with the woman downstairs to whom she was no miracle at all, for I worked or looked for work and for Emily's father, who "could no longer endure" (he wrote in his good-bye note) "sharing want with us."

9   I was nineteen. It was the pre-relief, pre-WPA[11] world of the Depression. I would start running as soon as I got off the streetcar, running up the stairs, the place smelling sour, and awake or asleep to startle awake, when she saw me she would break into a clogged[12] weeping that could not be comforted, a weeping I can yet hear.

10   After a while I found a job hashing[13] at night so I could be with her days, and it was better. But it came to where I had to bring her to his family and leave her.

11   It took a long time to raise the money for her fare back. Then she got chicken pox[14] and I had to wait longer. When she finally came, I hardly knew her, walking quick and nervous like her father, looking like her father, thin, and dressed in a shoddy red that yellowed her skin and glared at the pock marks.[15] All the baby loveliness gone.

12   She was two. Old enough for nursery school they said, and I did not know then what I know now—the fatigue of the long day, the lacerations[16] of group life in nurseries that are only parking places for children.

13   Except that it would have made no difference if I had known. It was the only place there was. It was the only way we could be together, the only way I could hold a job.

14   And even without knowing, I knew. I knew that the teacher was evil because all these years it has curdled[17] into my memory, the little boy hunched in the corner, her rasp,[18] "Why aren't you outside, because Alvin hits you? That's no reason, go out, scaredy." I knew Emily hated it even if she did not clutch[19] and implore, "Don't go, Mommy" like the other children, mornings.

15   She always had a reason why we should stay home. Momma,

---

8. *blue jeans with a bib and straps,* 9. *joy,* 10. *become hard to distinguish,* 11. *Work Projects Administration,* 12. *choked,* 13. *cooking in a cheap restaurant such food as ground meat-and-potato hash,* 14. *contagious virus which causes red sores,* 15. *remaining permanent marks from chicken pox,* 16. *wounds,* 17. *melted,* 18. *harsh voice,* 19. *hold on*

you look sick, Momma. I feel sick. Momma, the teachers aren't there today, they're sick. Momma, we can't go, there was a fire there last night. Momma, it's a holiday today, no school, they told me.

16 But never a direct protest, never rebellion. I think of our others in their three-, four-year-oldness—the explosions, the tempers, the denunciations,[20] the demands—and I feel suddenly ill. I put the iron down. What in me demanded that goodness in her? And what was the cost, the cost to her of such goodness?

17 The old man living in the back once said in his gentle way: "You should smile at Emily more when you look at her." What *was* in my face when I looked at her? I loved her. There were all the acts of love.

18 It was only with the others I remembered what he said, and it was the face of joy, and not of care or tightness or worry I turned to them—too late for Emily. She does not smile easily, let alone almost always as her brothers and sisters do. Her face is closed and somber,[21] but when she wants, how fluid. You must have seen it in her pantomimes,[22] you spoke of her rare gift for comedy on the stage that rouses[23] a laughter out of the audience so dear they applaud and applaud and do not want to let her go.

19 Where does it come from, that comedy? There was none of it in her when she came back to me that second time, after I had had to send her away again. She had a new daddy now to learn to love, and I think perhaps it was a better time. Except when we left her alone nights, telling ourselves she was old enough.

20 "Can't you go some other time, Mommy, like tomorrow?" she would ask. "Will it be just a little while you'll be gone? Do you promise?"

21 The time we came back, the front door open, the clock on the floor in the hall. She rigid awake. "It wasn't just a little while. I didn't cry. Three times I called you, just three times, and then I ran downstairs to open the door so you could come faster. The clock talked loud. I threw it away, it scared me what it talked."

22 She said the clock talked loud again that night I went to the hospital to have Susan. She was delirious[24] with the fever that comes before red measles,[25] but she was fully conscious all the week I was gone and the week after we were home when she could not come near the new baby or me.

23 She did not get well. She stayed skeleton thin, not wanting to eat, and night after night, she had nightmares. She would call for

---

20. *condemnations*, 21. *serious*, 22. *acting out scenes without speaking*,
23. *causes*, 24. *mentally confused*, 25. *contagious childhood illness*

me, and I would rouse from exhaustion to sleepily call back: "You're all right, darling, go to sleep, it's just a dream," and if she still called, in a sterner voice, "Now go to sleep, Emily, there's nothing to hurt you." Twice, only twice, when I had to get up for Susan anyhow, I went in to sit with her.

24   Now when it is too late (as if she would let me hold and comfort her like I do the others) I get up and go to her at once at her moan or restless stirring. "Are you awake, Emily? Can I get you something, dear?" And the answer is always the same: "No, I'm all right, go back to sleep, Mother."

25   They persuaded me at the clinic to send her away to a convalescent home[26] in the country where "she can have the kind of food and care you can't manage for her, and you'll be free to concentrate on the new baby." They still send children to that place. I see pictures on the society pages of sleek young women planning affairs to raise money for it, or dancing at the affairs, or decorating Easter eggs or filling Christmas stockings for the children.

26   They never have a picture of the children so I do not know if the girls still wear those gigantic red bows and the ravaged[27] looks on the every other Sunday when parents can come to visit "unless otherwise notified"—as we were notified the first six weeks.

27   Oh, it is a handsome place, green lawns and tall trees and fluted[28] flower beds. High up on the balconies of each cottage the children stand, the girls in their red bows and white dresses, the boys in white suits and giant red ties. The parents stand below shrieking up to be heard and the children shriek down to be heard, and between them the invisible wall "Not To Be Contaminated by Parental Germs or Physical Affection."

28   There was a tiny girl who always stood hand in hand with Emily. Her parents never came. One visit she was gone. "They moved her to Rose Cottage,"[29] Emily shouted in explanation. "They don't like you to love anybody here."

29   She wrote once a week, the labored writing of a seven-year-old. "I am fine. How is the baby. If I write my leter nicly I will have a star. Love." There never was a star. We wrote every other day, letters she could never hold or keep but only hear read— once. "We simply do not have room for children to keep any personal possessions," they patiently explained when we pieced

---

26. *nursing home,* 27. *devastated,* 28. *pointed,* 29. *small house*

one Sunday's shrieking together to plead how much it would mean to Emily, who loved so to keep things, to be allowed to keep her letters and cards.

30   Each visit she looked frailer. "She isn't eating," they told us. (They had runny eggs for breakfast or mush[30] with lumps, Emily said later. I'd hold it in my mouth and not swallow. Nothing ever tasted good, just when they had chicken.)

31   It took us eight months to get her released home, and only the fact that she gained back so little of her seven lost pounds convinced the social worker.

32   I used to try to hold and love her after she came back, but her body would stay stiff, and after a while she'd push away. She ate little. Food sickened her, I think much of life too. Oh, she had physical lightness and brightness, twinkling by on skates, bouncing like a ball up and down up and down over the jump rope, skimming over the hill, but these were momentary.

33   She fretted[31] about her appearance, thin and dark and foreign-looking at a time when every little girl was supposed to look or thought she should look like a chubby blond replica of Shirley Temple.[32] The doorbell sometimes rang for her, but no one seemed to come and play in the house or be a best friend. Maybe because we moved so much.

34   There was a boy she loved painfully through two school semesters. Months later she told me how she had taken pennies from my purse to buy him candy. "Licorice[33] was his favorite and I brought him some every day, but he still liked Jennifer better'n[34] me. Why, Mommy?" The kind of question for which there is no answer.

35   School was a worry to her. She was not glib[35] or quick in a world where glibness and quickness were easily confused with ability to learn. To her overworked and exasperated teachers she was an overconscientious "slow learner" who kept trying to catch up and was absent entirely too often.

36   I let her be absent, though sometimes the illness was imaginary. How different from my now-strictness about attendance with the others. I wasn't working. We had a new baby, I was home anyhow. Sometimes, after Susan grew old enough, I would keep her home from school, too, to have them all together.

37   Mostly Emily had asthma,[36] and her breathing, harsh and labored, would fill the house with a curiously tranquil sound. I would bring the two old dresser mirrors and her boxes of

---

30. *hot cereal,* 31. *worried,* 32. *a famous child movie star,* 33. *a type of candy,* 34. *better than,* 35. *verbally clever,* 36. *breathing disorder*

collections to her bed. She would select beads and single earrings, bottle tops and shells, dried flowers and pebbles, old postcards and scraps, all sorts of oddments; then she and Susan would play Kingdom, setting up landscapes and furniture, peopling them with action.

38   Those were the only times of peaceful companionship between her and Susan. I have edged away from it, that poisonous feeling between them, that terrible balancing of hurts and needs I had to do between the two, and did so badly, those earlier years.

39   Oh, there are conflicts between the others too, each one human, needing, demanding, hurting, taking—but only between Emily and Susan, no, Emily toward Susan, that corroding[37] resentment. It seems so obvious on the surface, yet it is not obvious. Susan, the second child, Susan, golden- and curly haired and chubby, quick and articulate and assured, everything in appearance and manner Emily was not; Susan, not able to resist Emily's precious things, losing or sometimes clumsily breaking them; Susan telling jokes and riddles[38] to company for applause while Emily sat silent (to say to me later: That was *my* riddle, Mother, I told it to Susan); Susan, who for all the five years' difference in age was just a year behind Emily in developing physically.

40   I am glad for that slow physical development that widened the difference between her and her contemporaries, though she suffered over it. She was too vulnerable[39] for that terrible world of youthful competition, of preening[40] and parading, of constant measuring of yourself against every other, of envy, "If I had that copper hair," or "If I had that skin . . . ." She tormented herself enough about not looking like the others, there was enough of the unsureness, the having to be conscious of words before you speak, the constant caring—what are they thinking of me? What kind of an impression am I making?—there was enough without having it all magnified by the merciless physical drives.

41   Ronnie is calling. He is wet and I change him. It is rare there is such a cry now. That time of motherhood is almost behind me when the ear is not one's own but must always be racked[41] and listening for the child cry, the child call. We sit for a while and I hold him, looking out over the city spread in charcoal with its

37. *causing gradual deterioration*, 38. *word play*, 39. *open to attack*,
40. *self-grooming*, 41. *strained*

soft aisles of light. *"Shoogily,"* he breathes and curls closer. I carry him back to bed, asleep. *Shoogily.* A funny word, a family word, inherited from Emily, invented by her to say: *comfort.*

42   In this and other ways she leaves her seal, I say aloud. And startle at my saying it. What do I mean? What did I start to gather together, to try and make coherent? I was at the terrible, growing years. War years. I do not remember them well. I was working, there were four smaller ones now, there was not time for her. She had to help be a mother, and housekeeper, and shopper. She had to set her seal. Mornings of crisis and near hysteria[42] trying to get lunches packed, hair combed, coats and shoes found, everyone to school or Child Care on time, the baby ready for transportation. And always the paper scribbled on by a smaller one, the book looked at by Susan then mislaid, the homework not done. Running out to that huge school where she was one, she was lost, she was a drop; suffering over the unpreparedness, stammering[43] and unsure in her classes.

43   There was so little time left at night after the kids were bedded down. She would struggle over books, always eating (it was in those years she developed her enormous appetite that is legendary in our family) and I would be ironing, or preparing food for the next day, or writing V-mail[44] to Bill, or tending the baby. Sometimes, to make me laugh, or out of her despair, she would imitate happenings or types at school.

44   I think I said once: "Why don't you do something like this in the school amateur show?" One morning she phoned me at work, hardly understandable through the weeping: "Mother, I did it. I won, I won; they gave me first prize; they clapped and clapped and wouldn't let me go."

45   Now suddenly she was Somebody, and as imprisoned in her difference as she had been in anonymity.

46   She began to be asked to perform at other high schools, even in colleges, then at city and state-wide affairs. The first one we went to, I only recognized her that first moment when thin, shy, she almost drowned herself into the curtains. Then: Was this Emily? The control, the command, the convulsing[45] and deadpan[46] clowning, the spell: then the roaring, stamping audience, unwilling to let this rare and precious laughter out of their lives.

47   Afterwards: You ought to do something about her with a gift

---

42. *uncontrollable emotion,* 43. *speaking hesitantly,* 44. *"Victory" mail: mail sent overseas to American soldiers in World War II,* 45. *laughing,* 46. *straight-faced*

like that—but without money or knowing how, what does one do? We have left it all to her, and the gift has as often eddied[47] inside, clogged and clotted as been used and growing.

48 She is coming. She runs up the stairs two at a time with her light graceful step, and I know she is happy tonight. Whatever it was that occasioned[48] your call did not happen today.

49 "Aren't you every going to finish the ironing, Mother? Whistler painted his mother in a rocker. I'd have to paint mine standing over an ironing-board." This is one of her communicative nights and she tells me everything and nothing as she fixes herself a plate of food out of the icebox.[49]

50 She is so lovely. Why did you want me to come in at all? Why were you concerned? She will find her way.

51 She starts up the stairs to bed. "Don't get me up with the rest in the morning." "But I thought you were having midterms." "Oh, those," she comes back in, kisses me, and says quite lightly, "in a couple of years when we'll all be atom-dead they won't matter a bit."

52 She has said it before. She *believes* it. But because I have been dredging the past, and all that compounds a human being is so heavy and meaningful in me, I cannot endure it tonight.

53 I will never total it all. I will never come in to say: She was a child seldom smiled at. Her father left me before she was a year old. I had to work her first six years when there was work, or I sent her home and to his relatives. There were years she had care she hated. She was dark and thin and foreign-looking in a world where the prestige went to blondness and curly hair and dimples, she was slow where glibness was prized. She was a child of anxious, not proud, love. We were poor and could not afford for her the soil of easy growth. I was a young mother, I was a distracted mother. There were the other children pushing up, demanding. Her younger sister seemed all that she was not. There were years she did not want me to touch her. She kept too much in herself, her life was such she had to keep too much in herself. My wisdom came too late. She has much to her and probably nothing will come of it. She is a child of her age, of depression, of war, of fear.

54 Let her be. So all that is in her will not bloom—but in how many does it? There is still enough left to live by. Only help her to know—help make it so there is cause for her to know that she is more than this dress on the ironing-board, helpless before the iron.

---

47. *moved against the current,* 48. *caused,* 49. *slang, refrigerator*

✺Understanding the Text: *Retelling the Story*

The events in "I Stand Here Ironing" may seem difficult to follow because they are told emotionally and not always chronologically by Emily's mother.

To help you reconstruct the major events of this story, discuss in a group what you think are the turning points in Emily's life. Then, complete the chart below by telling briefly the key events that happened to Emily at certain ages. (You may also want to refer back to paragraph 55 for a summary of these events.)

MAJOR EVENTS IN EMILY'S LIFE:

Infancy	Emily was beautiful. Her father left her and her mother before she was one year old.
1–2 years old	_____
2 years old	Emily returned to live with her mother. She began going to nursery school while her mother worked_____
2–3 years old	Emily got "a new daddy."
6–7 years old	Emily's sister Susan was born.

Now continue the chart of major events in Emily's life. Guess her age at the time of events based on information in the text.

✻Understanding the Text: *Analysis*

After you have read "I Stand Here Ironing," answer the questions below (either on your own or in a group), which deal with the story's main points.

1. The narrator of the story tells you in paragraph 3 in answer to her daughter's teacher's request for a parent-teacher conference: "Even if I came, what good would it do?" How does the mother feel about her ability to help her daughter?

2. Reread paragraph 4. What do you think takes up this mother's time? What does she mean by what "cannot be helped"?

3. Paragraph 8 tells you that Emily's father wrote in his good-bye note he "could no longer endure sharing want with us." What does this mean?

4. Reread paragraphs 12 and 13. Where does the mother leave Emily while she works? What does the mother think of these places?

5. In paragraph 14, how does Emily feel about school? Why?

6. You learned in paragraph 16 that as a four-year-old, Emily never rebelled. Read this section again and describe in your words what kind of young girl Emily must have been.

7. In paragraph 17, an old man tells Emily's mother that she "should smile at Emily more." Why doesn't the mother smile at her daughter?

8. In paragraph 19, you find that Emily "had a new daddy." What has happened?

9. Paragraphs 23 through 26 inform you that Emily became ill and was sent to a "convalescent home" in the country. Why was she sent away? How do you think Emily felt?

10. At this "home," Emily is not permitted to keep letters and cards from her family. How is this place characterized by Olsen in paragraph 30?

11. Emily returns home, but in paragraph 32 the mother tells you that Emily would push away if her mother tried to hold her. Why do you think Emily does this?

12. Skim paragraphs 35 and 36. Why does Emily's mother "let her be absent" from school? What do you think of this?

13. How does Emily feel about her sister?

14. Skim paragraphs 42 and 43. How does Emily's mother explain her treatment of Emily? How would you describe the relationship between mother and daughter?

15. After Emily has a success at performing in a school play, her mother comments in paragraph 47 about Emily's future. Does the mother think her daughter has a future? What is your reaction to her prediction?

16. Furthermore, Emily's mother tells you in paragraph 50, "She [Emily] is so lovely. Why did you want me to come in at all? Why were you concerned?" Who is the "you"? In other words, who is Emily's mother talking to? What is your opinion of Emily's mother's attitude here?

17. In paragraph 51, Emily responds to her mother's question about midterm examinations by saying that "in a couple of years when we'll all be atom-dead they won't matter a bit." Is Emily optimistic or pessimistic? Why do you think she feels like this?

18. In the last paragraph, the mother's final wish is that Emily know "she is more than this dress on the ironing board, helpless before the iron." What does the mother want?

Understanding the Text: *Drawing Inferences*

After you have read the story once quickly, and again with a dictionary, answer the following questions:

1. From the beginning paragraphs of the story, we can infer that the daughter

   a. is a model student
   b. is a troubled girl
   c. is a perfect child.

2. When the mother recalls her daughter Emily's infancy and childhood, the mother remembers

   a. the mistakes she had made as a mother

b. how well she had raised Emily

c. how terrible a child Emily had been.

3. Emily's father apparently left the family because

a. he couldn't live with Emily's mother
b. he found another woman
c. the family was very poor.

4. Emily resented her sister Susan mostly because

a. Susan was more confident and beautiful
b. Susan broke Emily's toys
c. Susan was younger than her.

5. Many of Emily's childhood problems stemmed from

a. her lack of confidence
b. her ugliness
c. her being the eldest in the family.

6. Emily's mother believes in the future her daughter will

a. live her life to its fullest
b. be a very happy person
c. probably not fulfill her potential.

Looking at Language: *Verb Tenses*

As you examined the first paragraphs of the story, you found that the narrator, Emily's mother, is "talking" to one of Emily's teachers who has written her a note. This teacher is the "you" whom Emily's mother addresses in the story.

Especially at the beginning and the end of the story, you can find further examples of Emily's mother "talking" to this teacher by using "you," asking questions and using command verbs to tell teacher what to do.

Below are examples of the narrator addressing the teacher.

"Even if I came, what good would it do?" (paragraph 3)
"You did not know her all those years . . . " (paragraph 5)
"Let her be." (command) (paragraph 55)

Scan the beginning and end of the story and find at least five more examples. Cite the paragraphs in which they appear.

❋Looking at Language: *Descriptive Vocabulary*

With a partner or on your own, scan the story to find the words or phrases used to describe the main characters.

1. Find at least five descriptive adjectives that contrast the physical qualities of Emily and her sister Susan. Cite the paragraph in which you find each word.

	Emily	Susan
1.		
2.		
3.		
4.		
5.		

2. The mother is never described physically. Use five of your own adjectives to describe her emotionally.

1. _____
2. _____
3. _____
4. _____
5. _____

❋Looking at Language: *Vocabulary by Theme*

With a partner, compare the words you located in the previous exercise with the two lists below, which present emotions and behavior of Emily and her mother. Define all the words listed with your partner, using a dictionary or text glossary if necessary. Then, discuss the differences and similarities between the feelings/behavior of Emily and her mother.

Emily's mother

tormented (par. 1) _____

engulfed (par. 4) _____

racked (par. 41) _____

hysteria (par. 42) _____

distracted (par. 53) _____

Emily

fretted (par. 33) _____

suffered (par. 40) _____

tormented (par. 40) _____

vulnerable (par. 40) _____

stammering (par. 42) _____

imprisoned (par. 45) _____

Looking at Language: *More Vocabulary by Theme*

In "I Stand Here Ironing," we also find a great number of vocabulary items dealing with illness, since Emily was often sick as a child. Read over the words below from the text. Define them with a partner and look up unfamiliar words in the dictionary and the text glossary. Then, use the words to complete the sentences that follow.

lacerations (par. 12)
delirious (par. 22)
conscious (par. 22)
convalescent home (par. 25)
contaminated (par. 27)
frailer (par. 30)

1. Emily's mother felt bad about having to send Emily to child

   care. The mother felt Emily suffered emotional _____ by spending all day in a day-care center.

2. The fever that Emily had with red measles, a contagious,

   flu-like illness, made her _____; she wasn't completely aware of what was happening around her.

3. Afterward, Emily became fully _____ again and recovered from her illness.

4. Later she became so sick that city social workers urged her

   mother to send Emily to a _____ so that the child could recover.

5. Instead of getting better, however, Emily looked

   _____ each time her mother went to visit her.

6. Parents and patients at the convalescent home could not physically touch each other. The officials believed the patients

   would become _____ by their parents' germs.

Literary Concepts: *Theme — Symbolism*

To explore the symbols in Olsen's story, answer these questions in a group, making sure to explain your interpretations by recalling events in the story that "prove" your ideas. You may find that your ideas differ from your classmates'.

1. You discussed the action of "ironing" and the symbol it might represent before you read the story. Having read the story, can you add information about what the ironing might represent? What might the iron symbolize?

2. How is ironing characteristic of Emily's mother's life?

3. Is Emily's life like ironing, too?

4. Could ironing symbolize conditions in other people's lives? What people? What conditions?

5. In the last paragraph, Emily's mother says she hopes Emily will be more than the dress "helpless before the iron." Why does the mother compare her daughter to a dress? How does this show how the mother feels about her own ability to control Emily's life?

Culture Point: *Working Mothers*

Child care is a subject of controversy in many homes today, as more mothers work and face decisions about the care of their children. Think about this issue and answer these questions:

1. In the story, in what different places does Emily receive child care?

2. How does Emily's mother feel about having to send Emily outside the home for child care?

3. Do you feel mothers should work and send their children to nursery schools or other child care facilities?

4. How are children of working mothers cared for in your culture?

5. What is the best way to handle this situation?

READING JOURNAL

Consider the feelings that the mother telling this story has about how she has raised her eldest child, Emily.

Imagine that in your journal, you have the opportunity to tell Emily's mother how well or poorly you think she has raised her daughter Emily. You can be as honest as you like. Tell her what she should have done, if you feel she failed. Or try to console her if you think she did the best she could. Give her advice about her future relationship with Emily.

Freewrite for ten minutes. Begin . . .

Dear Emily's mother,

_____

_____

_____

_____

_____

_____

_____

Sincerely,
(Your name)

VIDEO

Many other literary texts, as well as films, relate the delicate relationships between mothers and daughters. Two examples of this theme in films are *Stella* (1990), starring Bette Midler and Trini Alvarado, and *Mermaids* (1990), starring Cher and Wynona Ryder. In both films, the mothers and daughters have difficulty relating to each other. You may wish to view either of these films outside of class or with classmates and compare the mother-daughter relationships with that of "I Stand Here Ironing."

The Letter

by Emily Dickinson

About the Author

Emily Dickinson, one of America's best known poets, wrote about her inner feelings of love and loss. She was born in Amherst, Massachusetts, in 1830, lived there all her life, and died there in 1886. In that small town, she appeared to be a devoted family member, thoughtful neighbor and spinster; however, her poems reveal her private bitterness at having once been disappointed in love. Dickinson was considered an

unconventional poet because her feelings burst out of the usual pattern of rhyme and meter in Western poetry.

At First Glance

1. Dickinson's poem entitled "The Letter" uses command verbs throughout, such as in the first verse:

   "Going to him! Happy letter! Tell him—
   Tell him the page I didn't write;
   Tell him I only said the syntax,
   And left the verb and pronoun out."

   Who do you think Dickinson is "commanding" with the command verbs?
   Who is "him"? Who is "I"?

2. Imagine that the female writer of the poem is writing an important letter to a man. What might the letter contain?

Prereading Vocabulary

Find the italicized words below in the poem and guess their meanings from the context. Check your guesses with a classmate and then a dictionary.

1. ". . . they *waded* slow, slow, slow;" (verse 1)

2. ". . . you could see what *moved* them so." (verse 1)

3. ". . . from the way the sentence *toiled*;" (verse 2)

4. ". . . you may *quibble* there," (verse 2)

5. ". . . the old clock kept *neighing* 'day!' " (verse 3)

6. "What could *hinder* it so, to say?" (verse 3)

The Letter

by Emily Dickinson

1   "Going to him! Happy letter! Tell him—
    Tell him the page I didn't write;
    Tell him I only said the syntax,
    And left the verb and the pronoun out.
    Tell him just how the fingers hurried,
    Then how they waded, slow, slow, slow;
    And then you wished you had eyes in your pages,
    So you could see what moved them so.

2   "Tell him it wasn't a practised writer,
    You guessed, from the way the sentence toiled;
    You could hear the bodice tug, behind you,
    As if it held but the might of a child;
    You almost pitied it, you, it worked so.
    Tell him—No, you may quibble there,
    For it would split his heart to know it,
    And then you and I were silenter.

3   "Tell him night finished before we finished,
    And the old clock kept neighing 'day!'
    And you got sleepy and begged to be ended—
    What could it hinder so, to say?
    Tell him just how she sealed you, cautious,
    But if he ask where you are hid
    Until to-morrow,—happy letter!
    Gesture, coquette, and shake your head!"

Understanding the Text: *Analysis*

Read the poem and answer the questions below about each verse.

1. In verse 1, the narrator instructs "the poem" to "tell him the page I didn't write." Why do you think the narrator wants the

poem to tell its recipient another page she did not write? What does the narrator mean?

2. In verse 1, the narrator continues by writing that "you [the poem] wished you [the poem] had eyes in your pages, so you [the poem] could see what moved them so." If the poem did have "eyes," what would the poem tell the recipient about what moved (emotionally affected) the writer of the poem?

3. The narrator says in verse 2 that the poem "could hear the bodice (corset, or tight shoulder-to-waist undergarment)" of the narrator pulling, "as if it [the bodice] held but the might of a child." Why do you think the narrator compares her might to that of a child?

4. Later in verse 2, the narrator also says the poem "almost pitied" the narrator. But then the narrator suggests the poem be silent about this, "for it would split his heart to know it." What does this mean? Why do you think the recipient of the poem would feel this way?

5. In the last verse, the narrator uses different pronouns. She describes herself and the poem as "we" and herself as "she." Read this last verse and think about why the narrator switches from "you" and "I" to these pronouns.

6. Finally, in the last lines, the narrator commands the letter: "if he asks where you are hid . . . " "gesture, coquette, and shake your head!" What do these lines mean? Why would the narrator say this?

Culture Point: *Changing American Women*

The type of woman that you envision in your mind as the writer of this poem is probably different from the modern American woman. Here, the writer worries that her letter will not impress its male recipient, who is likely her lover. In the end, the writer even asks the letter to "gesture, coquette, and shake your head," so that the letter can "tease" its recipient with "feminine" appeals. Think about the ways that women and men impress and attract each other in modern times. Begin your discussion with the questions that follow.

1. Are women nowadays "coquettish," like the writer of this poem? (If you are unsure of the meaning of this word, look it up in a dictionary or discuss it with your instructor.)

2. Does the idea of a woman acting this way appeal to you or offend you? Why?

3. Imagine that a modern American woman were writing a poem sending her lover a letter. What do you think the poem would say?

4. Does this poem characterize the behavior of women toward men in your culture today? How?

READING JOURNAL

Read Dickinson's poem again and think about how the narrator feels about the recipient of the letter, and how the recipient must feel about her.

Use your imagination to compose a letter that she might write to him that would reflect their feelings. Address the letter to someone you know (or an imaginary person) for whom you have similar feelings and sign your name.

Projects: UNIT FIVE

Project I. Written Theme Analysis

For the third writing assignment, your task will be to write about the main theme of one story or poem you have read. As you have discussed earlier, the themes, or central ideas, of a story generally relate to the values, behavior, or conditions of a historical, social, or cultural group, or human-kind in general.

Your assignment will be to write a paragraph, then expand the paragraph into an essay about the theme in a story or poem you have read.

A. GETTING IDEAS

First, work with a partner to brainstorm which story or poem and which theme you will focus on. It is probably best to begin with the stories or poems that you liked the most. Then, focus on one idea, one character, one event, or one object in the text. Discuss with your partner what themes may exist in the work. (Also, refer back to exercises you have completed in previous chapters that relate to Theme.)

Once you have chosen a literary text and a theme, remember that just as you did when you identified qualities of a character for your written charac-ter analysis, you will have to "prove" the presence of the theme you have identified in the text. To do so, you will again need to draw sentences or passages from the story to show that they represent a certain theme.

In a small group, discuss the stories in the list below and the suggested themes that you find next to them. Consider whether these words and phrases represent the central ideas of these stories.

1. "The Luck of Roaring Camp"   luck
2. "The White Silence"   fierceness of nature
3. "The Corduroy Pants"   greed
4. "The Standard of Living"   superiority
5. "Butch Minds the Baby"   honor among thieves
6. "The Cop and the Anthem"   stupidity of police
7. "Of Missing Persons"   self-dissatisfaction
8. "The Rule of Names"   monsters in literature
9. "The Story of an Hour"   women's domination by men
10. "The Magic Barrel"   self-regeneration
11. "Snow"   lost love
12. "I Stand Here Ironing"   regret

B. ANALYZING A SAMPLE PARAGRAPH

Keeping your story or poem and theme in mind, analyze the sample paragraph below, which identifies and supports the presence of a theme in a story. Then, answer the questions that follow.

Self-Examination in "The Magic Barrel"

In Bernard Malamud's short story "The Magic Barrel," the theme of self-examination is illustrated through the main character, rabbinical student Leo Finkle. Finkle hires a matchmaker to find him a bride. In the process, he meets a prospective bride who questions him about religion. When the girl reveals that she thinks Finkle is deeply religious and "enamored of God," the student begins to examine himself, admitting to himself that he does not love God. He makes an even more startling self-realization: ". . . he saw himself for the first time as he truly was—unloved and loveless." Finkle realizes that he neither loves God nor anyone other than his parents. After a "long and terrible" week of contemplation and self-examination, Finkle decides that only through a marriage of love, rather than arrangement, can he find love and himself. Through this story, the reader can see the human need to examine one's self, that after harsh self-examination, a person can attain true "knowledge of himself," as Malamud's character does.

Sample Paragraph Analysis:

1. What is the Topic Sentence of this paragraph?
2. How does the paragraph "prove" the existence of the theme identified here?
3. In what order are the supporting proofs given in the paragraph?
4. Are quotations used? Paraphrase?
5. What does the concluding sentence do?

C. WRITING THE PARAGRAPH

Choose a story/poem and theme (or an alternative of your choice) as a topic for a paragraph on theme. Then, write a short paragraph in which you use features of the story/poem to show how the text relates this central theme. Follow standard paragraph format, including a Topic Sentence, Supporting Proofs and Concluding Sentence. Also, consider the techniques used in the sample paragraph. When you have finished your paragraph, exchange it with a partner, or partners, and discuss your ideas.

D. EXPANDING THE PARAGRAPH INTO AN ESSAY

Next, you will expand your paragraph into an essay that identifies the theme in the story or poem you have analyzed. Use your paragraph as one of the body paragraphs in your essay, considering any suggestions made by your instructor. You will need to expand your written analysis into an essay by adding two more body paragraphs. In each body paragraph, you will identify one part of the story/poem, one aspect of a character, or another feature of the text that shows the presence of the theme you have identified in your Thesis Statement.

Suggested way to organize your thematic essay:

I. Introduction

Thesis Statement: Identify story/poem, author, and major theme

II. Body Paragraph

Identify one part of the story/poem, one aspect of a character, or other feature in the story which exemplifies the theme.

III. Body Paragraph

Identify another part of the story/poem that illustrates the existence of the theme you have selected.

IV. Body Paragraph

Choose one more part of the story/poem to illustrate the theme.

V. Conclusion

Restate the Thesis Statement and give your opinion of the story/poem or its use of the theme.

Project II: Oral Reading

Writers often give oral readings of their works, which is a unique opportunity to hear the writer express his or her words orally and personally. This way the listener can actually *hear* what the writer *felt* when he or she wrote.

For your final project, you will have an opportunity to select a literary text that you like and "interpret" it orally through a formal reading. You will select a passage from a literary text, or a poem, to read aloud to the class. This passage or poem may be from any literary text in English.

To select a text, first go to the library and explore the literature section to find a sample of writing from a writer you admire, or ask the reference librarian for suggestions. If you are uncertain about choosing a text, find a collection of stories and poems in English. These anthologies will offer many choices. You may want to select a writer whose work you have studied in this textbook, and find another of his or her literary works in the library. In general, a short, simple text on a subject that you have some interest or knowledge in, or a writer whose art you admire, are also good criteria for text selection.

The text that you read orally should not exceed two or three minutes, so you will probably need to select a poem or a passage of several paragraphs from a story. If you choose a story, select several paragraphs that, read by themselves, are fairly complete and understandable as a unit. You may want to select two possible texts to allow you to practice delivering both the reading and timing.

As in reading poetry, read the passages you have selected slowly and repeatedly. Time your readings more than once. Select the one short reading that you feel you can present best to the class, a passage that will hold the class's interest, and that is not too difficult for you to pronounce. As you practice, underline words that carry emotion or importance; stress those words/phrases when you read. At points of greatest importance in your passage, read more slowly, with emphasis. Go over parts of the text that are difficult to pronounce with your instructor. Work with a classmate in reading your passages aloud.

In the presentation itself, you will organize your reading as a short speech. In the introduction, you will need to identify the work and its author, as well as tell briefly what happens in the text. Then, introduce the reading and deliver it. After you read the text, comment on why you like it.

SUGGESTED PLAN FOR ORGANIZING YOUR READING:

I. Introduction of Literary Text/Author

Identify the passage/poem you will read. Also, give background information about what occurs in the passage, and other parts of the story, if necessary.

II. Introduce and read the passage.

III. Conclusion

Give your opinion on the passage, or the writer.